PLAYING DAYS

Playing Days

Tony Lewis

Stanley Paul
London Melbourne Sydney Auckland Johannesburg

To Joanie, Joanna and Anabel

Stanley Paul & Co. Ltd
An imprint of Century Hutchinson Ltd
17–21 Conway Street, London W1P 6JD

Hutchinson Publishing Group (Australia) Pty Ltd
PO Box 496, Hawthorn, Melbourne, Victoria 3122

Hutchinson Group (NZ) Ltd
PO Box 40–086, Glenfield 10, Auckland

Hutchinson Group (SA) Pty Ltd
PO Box 337, Bergvlei, 2012 South Africa

First published 1985

Set in Baskerville by Tradespools Ltd, Frome, Somerset

Printed and bound in Great Britain by
Anchor Brendon Ltd, Tiptree, Essex

British Library Cataloguing in Publication Data
Lewis, Tony
  Playing days : an autobiography.
  1. Lewis, Tony   2. Cricket players—Wales—Biography
  3. Sportswriters—Wales—Biography
  I. Title
  796.35'8'0924   GV915.L4

ISBN 0 09 162280 8

Contents

Acknowledgements

For permission to reproduce copyright photographs, the author and publishers would like to thank Sport & General Press Agency, John Yates of Merthyr and All-Sport Photographic, R.H. Wright, Bill Smith and *Cambridge Daily News*.

1

Cricket Debut

I once took my cricket boots for re-spiking to 'Boss' Harris, the cobbler in the lane off the bottom of Harle Street in Neath, the town where I was brought up. They came back with aluminium rugby studs in them. That was South Wales! Life's focus from the cradle was a school cap filled with cotton wool and rags, folded over and sewn, a rugby ball for the street: young lives lost to the fantasy of scoring the winning try for Wales against England at Cardiff Arms Park. Dutifully, by the age of 19, I had bequeathed my front teeth to a rugby pitch in the Amman Valley with the help of an opponent's toe-cap. The schoolmaster put a duffle coat over me as I left the field.

'When you fall, boy, fall on top of the feet of the forwards, not two yards in front of them. Only two teeth this time. Be the bloody lot next time.' But I knew that I had paid at least some of the toll for the right of becoming a grown man in South Wales.

There was plenty of cricket in summer, but it was only a breather between scrummages, a four-month injury-free zone – except for the time I top-edged a hook shot into my eye and settled, without difficulty, on never hooking again in my life. You see, cricket had something against it, rather like tennis which few played. It was played better by the English.

However stylishly Gilbert Parkhouse was batting for Glamorgan, Denis Compton was doing it better in Middlesex. But rugby football was different. When Bleddyn Williams side-stepped an England centre, for that sweet moment Wales itself had given history the slip. The Anglo-Saxons were groping.

There was rugby and there was music. When I was young, to hear Trevor Anthony's resonant voice on stage at the Gwyn Hall in Neath, or a recording of the tenor Walter Glynne, or the rich cadences of the Pendyrus Male Voice Choir gave me shivers of Welshness. Rugby football and music were the starting points of Welsh identity. What do we do better than the English? Play rugby and sing hymns. Right then, everyone will kick with both feet and have his voice tested. Even if you failed at both, you could always sidestep your way through life saying that Cliff Morgan knew your father, or that your uncle used to play kick-the-tin in the Cilfynydd quarry with Geraint Evans.

At Cardiff Arms Park on international day, rugby and music of sorts come famously together. It is the day when we insist on telling the world who we are. It is unsubtle, jingoistic, but born of inferiority and absolutely essential.

Cricket was played in rugby's shadow, and so it will not surprise you to know that the winter playing headquarters of Glamorgan Cricket Club was secreted in one of the giant Cardiff Arms Park rugby stands: the tall, black, corrugated North Stand. Under its front hood were two tiers for sitting rugby spectators, for the great stand disdainfully turned its high, straight back on the cricketers the other side. Cricketers got changed for action in the Cardiff and Wales rugby dressing rooms, and could take the field on a fragrant June evening reeking of dubbin and wintergreen. You could never escape rugby football. Take a guard at any crease in Wales, look around and you saw rugby posts at the other end of the ground.

Inside the North Stand, the second-floor corridor was transformed into a cricket arena by a lot of tugging of net and white tarpaulin and the laying down of 22-yard strips of ship's lino. On Tuesday evenings in the winter, from the age of 13 to 18, I used to miss a double period of Spanish at Neath Grammar School and take an hour's trip to Cardiff to join the most promising young players in Wales. There was no heating and no hot water: it was a four-sweater event in deep December. Frost seeped through the old walls, a tempest hurtled along the corridor. Once I even saw snow lying on the lino. But I was proud to be there.

The coach was George Lavis: immaculate diction, properly dressed, a cricketing evangelist. For him, nothing was serious enough to stop play. One dark winter's afternoon I plodded from Cardiff Station in the snow, along Westgate Street and in through the Gwyn Nicholls Gates. There was no light on at the top of the North Stand steps. There always was. This time practice must be off. With the West Wales contingent I made my way through the innards of the big, black monster grandstand, eventually coming to a light and George Lavis's voice. 'Come.' We pulled back a tarpaulin sheet and saw the coach stoking away at a couple of charcoal braziers. On went the lights. Our breath turned to freezing fog just inches from our mouths. But we played.

'We never closed', at the Glamorgan Indoor School. At least, only at 9.30 p.m., after getting our expenses. We tried to make ninepence clear, so that we could buy a Lyon's fruit pie at the station on the way home.

On 20 August 1955, I walked the familiar path from Cardiff Station to the Arms Park, but it was in the morning. I stopped for a moment outside the General Post Office to put my *Western Mail* into the dustbin. I did not want the players in the dressing room to guess how many times I had opened and re-opened the paper in the train on the way up from Neath. I could remember the headline anyway – 'Schoolboy Star to play for Glamorgan'. The practice was over. The sub-heading was even more embarrassing – 'Youth Orchestra's Loss is County's Gain'.

True. My bags had been packed, my violin tenderly polished with Hydersol fluid, and I had been ready to go on the Welsh National Youth Orchestra's summer course. It was to be a glamorous year for the orchestra.

Tucked away in the ranks of the first violins I was about to perform concerts in Llangefni, Rhyl, the Royal National Eisteddfod in Pwllheli, Port Talbot, Newport and Cardiff, and ultimately at the Edinburgh International Festival. But the cricket fraternity got the whisper about my intended defection. I guess my father squealed. Quickly, little cogs in the Neath cricket club started bigger ones rolling in Cardiff and the letter which landed on my breakfast table, typed on note paper embossed with the yellow daffodil of Glamorgan County Cricket Club, was from the biggest cog of the lot – the man all Wales called The Skipper. A man not to be refused, Wilfred Wooller.

I had seen The Skipper once or twice, but never met him face to face. I could recall him barging into a Glamorgan second XI dressing room, issuing loud advice, and shouting a bit of coaching down a net. Wilfred Wooller was a colossus. He lived in no one's shadow and his 18 Welsh rugby caps were his passport to Welsh immortality. Rugby folk just nodded tolerantly at his cricket – just his summer eccentricity.

'Dear Tony,' he had written. 'I have been delighted to hear of your good form with the bat and would like you to play for Glamorgan in the last two County Championship matches of the season – Leicestershire at Cardiff and Warwickshire at Neath.'

Dear Mr Wooller, Yes, thank you. I next addressed a large envelope to Y Cyd-Bwyllgor Addysyg Cymreig – the Welsh Joint Education Board – sadly put the violin parts in it and said sorry. Out came the Gray-Nicholls bat.

20 August was a Saturday. I was slowly padding along that pavement to Cardiff Arms Park, a week or two after my 17th birthday. I wanted to turn and run home. Do dreams have to become real? Was it not better to be still batting in my bedroom mirror? In bed I tended to score more runs that Gilbert Parkhouse of Glamorgan and England. A ten-house cul-de-sac by night is cosy; Cardiff Arms Park in daylight made me sweat.

In through the Nicholls Gates, down the ramp, the giant North Stand, side-on, ahead of me. To the left the great rugby ground and echoes of roaring finishes to the great hymn tunes. To the right of the North Stand, through Cardiff Athletic Club's small car park, along a narrow alley around the back, the professional cricketers went to work.

Up the stairs, through the dark skittle alley and bar, along corridors so dark. There was a stench of stale beer. My eyes were firmly fixed to the floor. Each step was taking me nearer to an entry in the Births and Deaths pages of *Wisden* – Lewis, Mr A. R. (Glamorgan), b. 6 July 1938 – I would have settled for that and then have gone straight home.

I wished my cricket bag was leather like the ones the pros had, not thin canvas. Mine was long enough to get a whole bat inside, handle and all, but between the three straps bulged the home-knitted, cable stitch sweater. A novice arrives. Carefully guarded from rain were two pairs of white flannels into which my father, that morning, had ironed creases for eternity.

I slipped as unobtrusively as possible into the 'Home' dressing room. Between chair legs, where I was mainly looking, and under benches, I could see torn Cardiff rugby jerseys, the famous Cambridge blue and black hoops, touch flags and two rugby balls, out of shape but heavily dubbined to stretch another year.

I was shocked to discover my Glamorgan idols arguing. Haydn Davies, the wicket-keeper, was shouting at the Skipper. Surely not Haydn, the popular Panda as we spectators knew him! He used to pad to the wicket wide shoulders hunched forwards and then, at the crease, take huge swipes like a bear swiping flies with an angry paw. Six or out. Allan Watkins was supporting Haydn Davies in the argument. He was wearing an MCC touring sweater, the one with the yellow, red and navy trim. Watkins sounded to be winning at least on volume of words. And then, elegantly arguing from another corner, also against the Skipper, was Gilbert Parkhouse, but no

one seemed to be hearing him. How dare they? In every
match I had played on Bracken Road (and I had
appeared in over a thousand Tests), I had been Parkhouse. I lie. I was Denis Compton twice and Len Hutton
once, but as soon as I had found out their weaknesses I
went back to Parkhouse who played so very much better
than they did on Welsh roads. You see, Compton and
Hutton were no good against the tennis ball which had
been dunked in a pool of water, the one which throws
spray in the eyes of the batsman as it gets close to him,
and then skids swiftly off the hard surface. They were
beaten by sheer speed off the pitch. Not Parkhouse.

The shouting ended with a blast from the Skipper in
my direction. 'Hello Tony. Welcome to the madhouse. A
bunch of cloth-ears here. Hear you're in good form. Well
played. The boys will show you around.'

The seniors carried on shouting, the juniors I followed
down to the dining room for tea and biscuits. All food
was served in a dark area at ground level tucked away in
one of the brick recesses of the stand. 'Dining room'
would have been a flattering description. Next to it, the
ground staff kept their machines, stored the fertilizers
and dressings, returfing spades, forks, scarifiers and
barrows. What an unforgettable smell. When I took my
tea, two ladies, immortal in Glamorgan cricket catering
history, Elsie and Theresa, had already started the
process of softening up large potatoes in metal boilers
next to the big mowing machines. By lunchtime the
dining room would be full of steam and the potatoes still
no softer. Later in my career, I saw professional cricketers come in from the field looking ruddy and weather-
beaten and leave blanched by the mixed fumes of
overboiled potatoes and two-stroke engine fuel.

Back to the debut: back to the dressing room. Where
would I change? I was greeted by a 'Jim changes there',
or 'That's Shep's peg', until I found harmless lodgings
on the radiator between the shower room and the
lavatory: This unattractive thoroughfare between the
nervous pee and the main watering hole was available to

12

all temporary lodgers.

Skipper won the toss. We bat. The order was set. Parkhouse, Pressdee, Pleass, W.E. Jones, Watkins, Wooller, Ward, Lewis, H.G. Davies, Shepherd, and H.D. Davies. Number eight! I had never batted in the bottom half of an order in my life, but never mind. What was I doing here anyway with Parkhouse of the flowing strokes; Willie Jones, the small man with the eye to lie back and cut every ball for four; Watkins, the Test all-rounder, the magic short leg; Shepherd of the looping action and the loping run-up, and, of course, the Skipper and his long spells with the ball and massive crouch at silly mid-on. I had watched them all so closely on my junior member's ticket at St Helens in Swansea.

During the innings there was a lot of talk about the pitch. 'How can you expect us to get runs on that, skipper?' was the general drift. 'Like a bleedin' road,' said Watkins. 'How do you expect young players like Wardy there to play their shots? Made with roller and rake in that bleedin' order if you ask me.'

The Skipper stood up, grabbed a bat, and demons- trated, 'If you play there ... you see, with your bat there, and your pad there, they can't get you out. Impossible. I'll tell you, if I had five lives out there, I'd get more runs than the ten of you put together. I'll have Tony to push up the other end. You could do that couldn't you Tony?' I smiled pathetically.

Glamorgan's total was 179 for 6 when I gathered my belongings and set off down the dark corridor, down the steps and out through the dinky little member's enclo- sure onto Cardiff Arms Park. Jim Pressdee, the opener, passed me: out for a fighting 67. I was armed with Len Hutton autographed, brown, sausage-finger gloves, a Gray-Nicolls Walter Hammond autographed bat, and the only inconspicuous cap I had which was an England Secondary Schools cap, navy with the rose on the front.

To the right of me were the tall Westgate Street flats; a whole boundary length of high red brickwork and pretty verandahs. To the left, in a huge sweep around the top

13

end of the pitch, flowed the river Taff. It was amazingly quiet in a city centre. Ahead of me was a circle of Leicestershire green caps. I arrived, took guard in the middle of them. They did not spread out but tightened the noose. I paused, looked around the faces. There were two rather pale men in spectacles who had been pointed out to me as the amateurs, Charles Palmer, the captain, and an Oxford University cricketer called M.J.K. Smith.

The bowler's name was Walsh and he was supposed to carry many deceptions in his wrist spin, left arm over the wicket, but, strangely enough, the moment I settled in the stance I felt confident. The apprehension was going away. I knew I could bat and was just about to do what I could do well. Down came the first ball. Nerves already gone. It was wide, slanted way out to second slip. I moved across on the back foot and padded up. A sighter. The ball buzzed and pitched and then amazingly bit into the turf and leapt in towards me. Before I could move it struck me under the right knee.

'Owzat?'

A swarthy, short man named Jones was standing 22 yards away in a white coat with his finger up. Out first ball. I left. I felt sick again. I faintly heard sympathetic words from the crowd and I departed to a mini-ovation. Up the stairs, my spikes clanking along the dark corridor, into the dressing room. It was silent now. 'Bad luck, Tony. Len Hutton started that way too.' Gilbert Parkhouse spoke first.

As I unbuckled my pads Willie Jones moved to me and in a whisper said, 'Anyone tell you to play forward to Jack Walsh until you know what's going on?'

'No,' I mumbled. 'Is that what to do?'

'Ay.' Willie continued to whisper as if he would be in trouble if he was caught. 'Push out Tony bach; if it turns in, you're covered, if it doesn't, well you never know, God might be on your side.'

The Skipper said nothing. He gave me some time to recover. He then proclaimed, because he was not one for

14

whispers.

'Mark down every Leicestershire name out there, Tony. Catch up with the bastards one day and make them pay.'

At the end of my first day in County Cricket, I left sadly through the skittle alley bar. The players of both sides were having a pint. As I went my sleeve was tugged. I turned and faced Jack Walsh. His accent was broad Australian.

'None of this one-off-the-mark for me son. Did it once. Never again. Young man's been whacking me around England ever since. Fella called Peter May.'

On the bus back to Neath I read the *South Wales Echo* – late pink edition. 'This brought in Tony Lewis. Unhappily he got in front of a guileful delivery from the veteran Walsh and was out first ball in his first Championship match.'

Monday, 22nd at last. Late afternoon. Glamorgan's second innings. The strong sun was sliding down westward, across the Taff. 'Push out Tony bach. God might be on your side.' The whisperings of Willie Jones. God might be . . . I had sung a strong bass line in Gnoll Road Congregational Church choir, morning and evening on the rest day . . . but I do not think so. I was on my own, walking towards the same end of the pitch where I had gone for nought in the first innings, to face the same bowler Jack Walsh.

Again the green circle of caps tightened like a tourniquet. The big wicket-keeper Firth thumped a gloved fist into a palm, then someone spoke to me. He was tall, blonde, handsome like a filmstar, right in front of me at silly mid off. 'Hit it to me son and you'll be alright.' It was a man called Maurice Tomkin.

A plot. Trying to trick me. Here comes Walsh. His left hand twirls out of the sun. What is it? Googly, chinaman, God-knows-what. I lunge forwards. Clonk! A full toss. The ball strikes the bat a sour blow just under the splice. It goes to ground, and runs to the golden-haired Tomkin. Amazing! He lets it go through his legs. Shall I run?

15

Where is the ball? It is away to the covers ... there is no one fielding there. 'No,' I shout down the pitch. Now there's a chapel upbringing for you. 'Beware false prophets ...' Unfair on Maurice Tomkin who was honestly trying to save me from a 'pair' in my first-class debut.

After a long pause the ball is retrieved. Walsh is ready again. Second ball. Forward lunge. Smother the china-man. 'Over' is called: a pinnacle reached. I've seen off Jack Walsh.

'Stylish Lewis' sub-headlined the *Western Mail* next day, Wednesday 24th. '17-year-old Tony Lewis had got off the mark with a streaky single through the slips off Munden to avoid a 'pair of ducks' in his first county match. He played a few stylish scoring strokes and then, stretching forward, he was beaten by Munden's spin and gave a slip catch.' Lewis c. Lester b. Munden V. 9.

My six-day baptism was half over. Three more days to go against Warwickshire at Neath. However, I had already decided that I did not want to be a full-time cricketer. My father wanted me to be a solicitor. I guessed I would be a teacher.

Western Mail. 26 August 1955

'Tom Dollery, Warwickshire's popular professional captain who made his last appearance at the Gnoll yesterday, was presented with a copper and bronze coal scuttle by the Neath Cricket Club during the tea interval, in recognition of his services to Warwickshire and England cricket.

South Wales Evening Post. Same day.

In the Glamorgan innings nothing pleased the Neath crowd more than to see 17-year-old Tony Lewis help Wooller to put on 72 runs for the seventh wicket. During his stay of just under two hours, the Neath youngster played some elegant strokes which had all the marks of class batsmanship.

The total attendance for the two days was 6,500 and receipts £375, returns well below normal for the ground.

Not mind-blowing news, but it meant that both Tom Dollery and I were on our way in opposite directions. I had, as the pros loved to say, spent some time in the middle. Even now, 30 years later, I can smell the dryness of that August. There were patches of charred grass on the outfield, most unusual, because the Neath ground caught the full flow of moisture from the slope down from the Gnoll woods.

At home, at 10 Bracken Road, there had been a flurry of washing and ironing when I got back from the debut match at Cardiff. I had never played six days out of seven before; it put a strain on the home laundry system, with only one pair of flannels for batting and one for fielding. I soon discovered that the convenience of playing in my own home town ended when I got to the ground. Since that day I never enjoyed playing at home. Locals whom I knew only vaguely were lecturing me intimately. 'Hey. Cut out that nonsense outside the off stump now. Runs for you today. Okay?'

'What's that duck in Cardiff, then? Get yer'ead down this time. Great pitch out there; bags of runs. Can't let your 'ome town down.'

Of course, I stood for their own fears and ambitions. Two men penned me in around the back of the scorebox. 'We 'aven't 'ad an England batsman since Cyril Walters. Tell him, tell him,' one instructed the other 'Neath Grammar boy too, captained England, Cyril Walters. Lovely player. Beautiful leg glide. Remind him. Remind him.' He prodded his mate again.

I was dragged by another Neath cricket lover to the photograph of C.F. Walters in the clubhouse. From the frame on the wall a young man looked down on me, languid, relaxed, confident, everything I was not at that moment. Those who knew and cared, passed me by with a nod or just a word or two. 'Anything you need?' from Eddie Davies, and he meant it. 'Feeling good?' from Terry Shufflebotham. 'Get out there and enjoy yourself' from a man who had done it himself for Glamorgan, Stan

Trick. 'Nought or nothing Tony bach, I'll buy you a pint at the close of play,' from Cyril Michael, mentor and coach.

What else do I remember? Leaving 10 Bracken Road by the large double doors at the bottom of the back garden; 50 yards along the unmade lane, throwing my bag on Steven's garden shed, over the high spiked wall and climbing into the field. I forgot the gate would be open at our end of the ground for the County match. Glamorgan always changed in the dressing rooms of the indoor cricket school, leaving the club pavilion to the visitors. The indoor school looked like an emporium. The nets were pulled back to make way for the itinerant office staff who set up on trestle tables. Scorecards were squeezed out of an erratic duplicating machine by the violent turn of a handle. They were then tucked under the arm of Steve, the faithful whitecoated vendor.

Next to the office were the lunch tables, collapsible ... very. Come lunchtime I was led by the Skipper to a smaller table reserved for captains, amateurs and committeemen. Beset by the protocol, I had looked at the scorecard to check if Warwickshire had any amateurs. They did not. For Glamorgan it was just W. Wooller and A. Lewis. I shied past the players' table, separation did not feel natural.

The Skipper made my detour more conspicuous by bellowing 'C'mon Tony. You'd better get used to the committee table. You'll be dealing a lot with them when you are captain.' Just like that. My second game and I was lined up for captaincy! I suppose the words were half lost in the stumbling confusion of my start in county cricket, but they are clear now. There I was, at last in the company of my heroes, and someone dare suggest that I would one day be the captain.

Looking back, and knowing Wilfred Wooller as I did in the end, I realize that he was making no prophesy, no show of comfort as a young lad tripped along to the amateurs' table for the first time in his life. He knew I would be captain one day because he had decided. As

18

simple as that. It was not to be easy to be such an obvious pretender to the throne but it was the Wooller way. He was really saying, 'As captain you can never be one of the boys. Start now.'

I dare say this would have been easier for a young public schoolboy who owned a sports suit, brown brogue shoes, viyella checked shirt and who, when under threat, could boom an aggressive 'Hello' without a single movement of the lips. He would not have learned his cricket with professionals as I had. For a local grammar school boy with leatherpatches on his school blazer, who spoke rarely, except in short machine-gun bursts, the amateur act was unnatural. Nor was I bolstered by a family fortune. If I could have vaulted the tables and sunk myself in the professional corps, I would have done so there and then.

Warwickshire batted first and were out quickly. The pitch was slow and took spin. It was even more lethal when the ball was cut at medium pace by Allan Watkins, left arm over or around the wicket, and Don Shepherd, right arm off-cutters.

One innings stood above all others. The Skipper opened the batting, stuck a massive left foot down the pitch and stayed in the middle for seven hours and nine minutes. I recall going out to join him at number eight, aware that he was waiting to greet me, aware of favourite schoolmasters sitting on the benches behind the bowler's arm at the Llantwit end, aware of the attention of everyone willing and wishing. Someone less sensitive would have been less distracted. Dick Spooner crouched behind the stumps and a young fast bowler called Roly Thompson retreated to the canvas sightscreen. As I took guard from Jones, the umpire who had given me out first ball at Cardiff in the last match, Warwickshire crowded around. I had an attack of claustrophobia. I wanted to slog. I made my blockhole mark, looked up and saw Roly Thompson framed against a giant sign 'Fish and chips down lane first left' painted on the side of a house in Oakwood Road.

19

But no, a leg glance. I was off the mark first ball. This is a better game. I fixed my eye to the humming, in-drifting flight of a Hollies leg-break and shook with the thrill of actually picking his googly! But he got me out before too long – c. Spooner b. Hollies 19. However, I had had an embarrassing moment. The Skipper, after seven hours batting, got to 99 and turned a ball behind square on the leg side. 'Yes' I called. Off we went for his century. However, I had never seen the fielding skills of a man called Horner. Wearing light rubber shoes, Norman Horner whizzed silently over the ground from square leg. Disaster! The ball was in his hand before we had crossed. I would be out. But he looked at me as if to say, I shall not waste this great opportunity on you son, and took aim for the Skipper's end. The ball went like an arrow. The ground shook under the frantic tread of Wooller, the old Welsh centre three-quarter, 45 years old, stretching for his life in his size twelves for a rare first-class century. I turned. I saw the ball bounce in front of the wickets. He was a mile out. Then it skimmed over the top of the middle stump; there was no one there; the Skipper was home. He came plodding down the pitch towards me, bat raised high to acknowledge the applause. He was smiling to the crowd, but shouting to me at the same time. He was big, massive in the sunshine and he was smiling. 'Do that to me again and I'll wrap this bat right around you.' I was quite frightened.

Wooller's alright, decent sort, they were saying at Neath. Got a hundred but still got time to talk to our Tone. He had, but he had made his point.

2

Rugby Debut

At the age of six I tried to betray the Welsh nation by deciding never to play rugby football again. I made this monumental choice during a Swansea home match. I had been taken there by my uncle David. We were watching from the shallow enclosure in front of the grandstand. Swansea's full-back Phillips booted the ball up into the roof girders of the stand, and it cannoned back full toss onto my head. The All Whites went all green. I was told that I passed out. All I do know is that I sat on the steps for the rest of the match, staring at cigarette butts and trouser turn-ups seeing no play, hating rugby, and vowing never to leave my fort and lead soldiers ever again on a Saturday afternoon.

Two years later, in 1946, I was introduced to my father on platform 2 of the GWR railway station at Neath. I was supposed to remember him from his last army leave, but the face and the uniform meant nothing to me.

The moustached Captain W. L. Lewis had decided to move his wife, son and daughter from Swansea to Neath. He said that he longed to see Welsh rugby again. So affiliations changed from Swansea's All Whites to the Neath All Blacks. Also, when he took up residence at 10 Bracken Road, he had got himself a prime view of an endless flow of rugby – street rugby, night and day. Play was only ever interrupted by two horse-and-cart merchants, Hopkins the Milk and Arthur the Oil; by two lorries, the coalman and the Our Boys pop lorry; lastly, there was a major concession for the only car-owner in the street, Mr Stevens, who parked his Wolseley, smelling of real leather and engine oil, in the turning circle at the dead-end of the road.

Bracken Road was a cul-de-sac, shaped like a lollipop, the first 50 yards flanked by six-foot walls which more or less kept the ball in play, and then, when the ten semi-detached houses began, towards the circle, the walls were low and topped by hopeful privet hedges which sagged where wingers had been ditched through them into the gardens.

The ball was usually an old school cap stuffed with rags and sewn to an oval shape. However, on brilliant days, one of us could produce a Gilbert 'Match' leather ball which was supposed to be kept for the grass pitches or the Gnoll woods, but eventually got out onto the road when the owner fell for the line, 'Fetch it out on the road, mun. We'll only pass it.'

For big matches, say against Oakwood Road, Glen Road or Hazelwood, our front garden was the dressing room. Not that there was any dressing or undressing, but it gave us the chance to run out onto the pitch like the All Blacks did down at the Gnoll. We cheered ourselves as we flipped the ball to each other on the way out and someone would announce team changes. 'Number twelve Roy John is injured. He is replaced by Micky Williams. For Keith Maddocks substitute Tony Randall on the left wing. Coming in at number one for Viv Evans is Tony Lewis. When we played as Wales, national anthems were sung, and we stood stiffly to attention in our Fair Isle pullovers.

Bracken Road was usually awash with blood and bruises. It was the hard way to learn. To stay alive you had to learn to beat a man in a small space, side-step, dummy, get rid of the ball before being thumped into a wall, and above all drop a goal from any position with either foot because dropped goals counted four points and beat a try.

Being tackled into one of the low, sharp-edged walls was like having a leg amputated, especially as the final shove sent you through the privet hedge. The Micky

Williams hand-off was one to be avoided; he left it late before ramming the bony butt of his hand into your nose. Clive Harris was infamous for his secondary tackling. He preferred others to make the initial stop so that he could follow up with a vicious neckhold, dishing out twisting Chinese burns and shouting 'Drop it or else.'

Easily the worst death was the ankle tap from behind. Just when you thought you were away through the gap, the ankle flip would have you missing a stride, stumbling, half recovering, stumbling again, and then it was arms out for a belly flop, the skid along the tarmac and the torn hands and knees.

Bracken Road reeked of iodine and TCP. Tudor Thomas wore elastoplast strips like war medals: Peter Jenkins was the hardy hooker, unbeatable in a bunny scrum, one against one. My various skills thus honed on Bracken Road, I felt confident of doing well when I got to the grammar school. Rugby was compulsory. Soccer was forbidden. However, I took a long time to find a suitable position in a 15-man side.

I started at outside half. Unfortunately the ball never came my way because we never won a ball from line-out or scrum. One day, assuming instant leadership, I transferred myself to hooker, the modest little ruse being to win the scrummage ball and then, when the scrum had broken, dash around in a great loop behind the centres, take the pass outside the wing and score the try.

I threw my arms around my props. Suddenly all daylight disappeared. I was locked in the blackness of my first 16-man scrum, and seized immediately both by a crucifixion complex and by claustrophobia, the worst bout since they strapped on my Mickey Mouse gas mask during the war. The other front row was much bigger. Our vertebrae tinkled like xylophones in unison. I was now looking upside down at a tiny bit of blue sky at the end of the dark tunnel. 'Comin' in now,' shouted the inside half. To my horror the ball tumbled in straight for my head. I was locked. The only parts of my body which I could move were my eyes.

We lost that particular strike. The opposing hooker swung a violent leg, removing layers of skin from my scalp on the way with the nails sticking through his worn-down leather studs.

They were waiting for me to arrive at the next scrum when the master in charge, Mr Sam Evans, saved me.

'What are you doing at hooker boy?'

'Dunno, sir.'

He blasted on the whistle. 'Free kick against you. Dull play. You're an inside half, boy. Stay there from now on.'

It was four years later that I limped out of the scrum half position. My trouble was lack of speed. I had the skills honed on the road but performed them elegantly rather than quickly. Loiter in the scrum half war zone and it gets rough.

I particularly lost the taste for the job whenever I played against Terry Jenkins from Cadoxton school. Terry, I must admit, was perfectly fashioned for the job. He was short, well muscled, red-haired, aggressive, nippy, and able to cope with all the niggles which might follow a bad-tempered line-out and was not above performing his own thuggery too – everything I was not.

I was made for him. No sooner had I landed face down after my languid, though long and accurate, diving pass, than he was trampling heavily up my back. There was enough of me for him to take a substantial stroll if you included my head, which he usually did. Stoically, match after match, I offered him an elongated carpet of navy blue with thin gold stripes, and gingerly he ran up it.

Maybe as a reward for bravery in the field, I was made Terry Jenkin's reserve in the Neath Schoolboys side, under 15 years old. Yet the only game I got was on the wing. There had been a last-minute cry off. I took the field at Stradey Park, Llanelli, terrified that some swarthy little West Walian was going to side-step past me all afternoon. What I did not bargain for was a 12½-stone giant from Felinfoel, an anatomical freak for that part of the world.

Just before half time he got the ball tucked under his

armpit and ran towards me in front of the stand. By treading water and showing him space near the touch-line, I gave him the hint that I wanted him to try to get past me on the outside. Then I would narrow the angle ... if I could catch him. Precision stuff: the angles would be vital.

It was when he was five yards off that I first realized that subtleties were beyond him. He was simply taking the shortest route between two points, i.e. through me to the try line. I stopped him alright, by hitting him full on the knees with my nose. Blood spurted from both nostrils over the white maltese cross on my black jersey, yet I clung on. He took some time to fall. In the end I think he was weakened by the nausea of the carnage beneath him.

I was led from the field for smelling salts but within a minute was racing back, snorting through bloody cotton-wool plugs like Puff the Magic Dragon. The great game had again conveyed its message to me. Give up hooker, give up the wing. Give up scrum half. I never visited those positions again.

The problem with centre three-quarter, where I roamed for several seasons, was again lack of speed. I was operating two yards behind everyone else. This was camouflaged by the help and friendship of two outstand-ing players, both Secondary Schools internationals, Rhys Thomas and Clive Phillips. Rhys was an angelic-looking centre with tumbling fair hair and cherubic lips, but who had the feint, change of pace and swerve of the devil. Clive was the lean greyhound of a wing with sharp Neath Valley knees to knife through any tackles. Floating about between them was a pleasure. Perhaps centre would be the place after all.

A couple of seasons later, a current Aberavon rugby player named Roy Bish became the school first XV rugby master. 'You're a full-back,' he said. Roy Bish was a fine analyst of the game. After he retired he helped Cardiff to conspicuous achievements as coach. He was right about me, and by the end of my school days I had captained the school through an unbeaten season and had knocked very hard on the door for a Secondary School cap.

To give you an idea of the precedence which rugby took at Neath Grammar School, I must relate the story of Walter Thomas, the senior French master, a big man suffering usually from sinusitis, but with a love for literature and a strong way with words himself. His brother Gwyn Thomas, author, playwright and broadcaster, was a deal more famous, but Walter lacked nothing of his brother's sharp eye and shattering phrase.

One day he prepared to conduct a lesson with the Upper Sixth in Room 5 which overlooked the rugby field. '*Les Fleurs du Mal*', he announced, noisily cleaning his sinuses. 'Baudelaire.' He flipped open the text book. 'Turn to "La Charogne". It means the decaying carcass. Filthy stuff but compulsory.' Then, looking sideways out of the window, he saw one of the tiniest school sides taking the field against local opposition. Waller, as we called him, turned.

'Who are they, and who are they playing?'

'The Under-13s, playing the Tech, Sir.'

He raised his index finger. 'Come.' He got up from his desk and walked out. The dozen of us trailed after him. Along the corridor, amazingly down to the senior school lavatories. He went to the high window and took up his look-out post for the rugby match. 'Right!' he proclaimed. 'We will remain here in the bogs for two periods where you and that rotten sod Baudelaire will be far more at home, and where I can witness the uncoached delights of the Under-13s.'

Every small boy in Neath wanted to play for the town one day, wear the all-black shirt with the white maltese cross and respond to the partisans shouting for 'The Mourners' every Saturday. My favourite player was Viv Evans, the full back. He caught the ball beautifully, screw-kicked huge lengths with his left foot, was safe with his right, tackled when he had to, and made the odd run with the backs. Short with flaxen hair, he was called Snowball. He played an immaculate season for Wales quite late in his career.

The most celebrated opposition was Cardiff. They attracted all the star players from other clubs and had a constant flow of genius down the Rhondda valleys. I saw my first Cardiff player when I was ten years old in 1948. The biggest man I had ever seen. I had climbed over the wall in Oakwood Road to get into the Gnoll ground without paying, up over the spikes. Then, with the other boys, I raced for cover, down the terrace full of people on the open side, just near the 25-yard line. It was raining.

We had just got to our vantage point, squeezed in low, pressed right up against the black railings, when the whistle blew. Suddenly my whole vista turned black and blue, the famous Cardiff colours. A giant was backing up on me. It was the Cardiff player to take a penalty kick from the touch line. He blotted out everything: the two grandstands on the other side of the field, and the whole skyline of the Drummau Mountain beyond them. His legs glistened with wintergreen – one of them was as big as me – and there were large dollops of vaseline behind his ears; his boots were matt, not shiny like mine.

He blew out some air as he stood still to attention, a few paces behind the ball which was placed upright. I had not seen his face. He lumbered off like an elephant, squelching through the mud and then he sunk a boot into the back of the ball with a dull thud. The ball revolved only once on its path goalwards. It went like a sack of potatoes, and at only one point did it rise over the level of the cross bar – the important point. The tinny loud-speaker voice announced among the boos and faint applause, 'That penalty was kicked for Cardiff by W. E. Tamplin.' The giant trudged away.

Next day, in Gnoll Road Congregational Chapel, as the Reverend W.J. Samuel's sermon moved to its articulate crescendo, I was lost in dreams of standing upright in the aisle like Tamplin, expelling the air from my chest, and placing penalty goals over the spread of the organ pipes which made some sort of heavenly goal, upstairs behind the pulpit, high above the choir stalls. Unlike Tamplin's, my kicks revolved beautifully.

27

The finest rugby institution in Neath was and maybe still is the Neath Athletic Club. Quite detached from the Neath senior club, it did two splendid jobs – it scooped up anyone who wanted a decent game in one of their teams and it also reunited lots of boys who had been rather brusquely separated at the early age of 11 by the scholarship examination. Boys from college, university, public school or state school, the colliery or the Co-op, got stuck in together, most of them shepherded into it by Rees Stephens, Welsh international captain, later a selector, and forever a worker for the youth cause in his home town, Neath. The Athletic was a stepping stone to first-class rugby and I turned out whenever I was free of school matches or later when I was doing my National Service in 1957.

It was in the March of 1958 that the great moment came. A/C Lewis went home to Neath on a week-end pass from the Air Force. I was listening to some music at lunchtime on Saturday. It was a brilliantly sunny day. I recall that because our small front room suddenly went dark. A bus had pulled up outside on the road. The only buses that ever came down Bracken Road were for street outings to the Mumbles.

A very short man named Theo Davies appeared at the front door. This was the Neath first-team bus. They were a man short. Bill Young had cried off. Would I play full-back? Within minutes I was on the bus with jockstrap, boots and towel.

'Who are we playing?' I asked.

'Gloucester', they said. 'Away.'

Back whence I had come, but it did not matter. I ran out on Kingsholm in the black jersey with the white maltese cross under the captaincy of the Welsh and British Lions prop forward Courtenay Meredith. The *Sunday Times* writer L.J. Corbett recorded the event by observing that 'T. Lewis, making his first appearance at full back, came through a trying ordeal with credit.'

Back to Neath on Saturday night: back to Gloucester again on Sunday, now as a first-class rugby player.

28

3

Cricket or Music

At 12 years old, I was a mite which flitted into the golden web of Neville Cardus. I never tried to escape. Around me spun a language which bound music and cricket together. Suddenly, in cricket, I could see bravura passages, and in music deftness and control. Cardus read Dickens by lamplight on foggy Manchester streets. I read Cardus by gaslight too, but in the warmth of my bedroom which caught the dull yellow glow of the street gaslamp outside, late at night.

I knew his A. C. Maclaren, 'the noblest Roman of them all'. I could put myself into the mind and body of the young Cardus. I felt that I was the 14-year-old who one day got into the district train outside Old Trafford after a Lancashire and Yorkshire match and saw A. C. Maclaren and Walter Brearley enter his own compartment; and trembled in the presence of these two 'gods come down for a while to walk the earth'. And if Cardus had been my 'O' level set book, six years later, I could have recited what he wrote next, to a word. 'There was no other mortal being in the compartment except myself, and I held my breath. And Maclaren said to Brearley, "Well, Walter; you're a nice sort of bloody fast bowler." and Agamemnon answered Ulysses thus: "And you're a bloody fine slip fielder aren't you, Archie?"'

But I was also inside the skin of young Neville in 1908 on 3 December standing at the back of the Free Trade Hall in Manchester and hearing the first performance of Elgar's A Flat Symphony – the broad long opening melody marching before me 'treading its way over a slow steady bass, broad as the broad back of Hans Richter', conductor of the Halle Orchestra.

There was a well-known musical strain on the Lewis side of the family. My father's great uncle had been a bard, Elfed Lewis, blind preacher, teacher, hymn-writer, and poet. However, the only living proof of talent was the singing of two aunts. Eirlys, small pretty and kind from Fairfach near Llandeilo, trilled gorgeously through the coloratura soprano repertoire. The Welsh language was her natural expression. Not a cup clinked against a saucer when she sang Clychau Aberdyfi at Sunday tea.

A more formidable lady, with a deeper contralto voice, was Aunt Kathleen. She always took up the same theatrical position at the piano side, legs firmly set apart, a steadying arm on the open top of our upright, directing powerful solos at the far wall. The ever so attentive audience never dared even to lift cup from saucer when she was in full flow.

My father did nothing to extend the Lewis music, but my mother did strike a note or two for her side of the family, the Flowers. She could tinkle many a popular tune by ear in safe key signatures. The family's finest musician was my sister Heather. From the time she was five to the moment she left home at 18 to read a B. Mus. and M. Mus. at the University College of Wales in Cardiff, our small semi-detached home shuddered with scales and arpeggios for pianoforte. If I were to take up an instrument, the possibilities were likely to be deafening. I did, and that was by the persuasion of the music master at Neath Grammar School. He was also the junior cricket master. When I first went to the school he grabbed me from a horde of heaving satchels and gym bags in the main corridor. 'Can you sing? Let me give you a voice test. A scale, boy, a scale. Ready? Pitch it. Doh, ray, mi. Gottit? Go.'

Nervously and almost silently I climbed the scale. 'You're in tune, boy. You're in tune. Come and see me at four o'clock.' By ten past four I was walking down Dwr-y-Felin Road carrying the soprano part of the Mozart

Gloria and a cello. His parting words had been 'Sing till your voice breaks, then play in the orchestra. I'll bring a book for you tomorrow. I want you to read a writer called Cardus. Neville Cardus.'

That was John Hopkin Jones, called Hoppy. He was of medium height, particularly thin, and often unwell. His weak chest attracted coughs and colds and he missed school for long periods. I always thought it a cheat that someone who needed stamina to conduct choirs as dramatically as he did, to play Chopin as he did, and to keep wicket as energetically as he did, should be so short of nature's help. Yet he always harboured and planned the grand design. His school choir, in four parts, and full orchestra were always rehearsing for a big concert in the Gwyn Hall. Rehearsals were called at lunchtimes. Boys would be told to make a swift retreat from the canteen to the school hall. More often than not they would arrive late sweating from swift games of touch-rugby.

Down in front of the stage, the orchestra, some 60 players, would spread out and tune. Half way up the hall, Hoppy would take to the rostrum – a chair. The loose leaves of his score would flap, pullovers, one after the other, would peel off as he approached the moment for the baton raising. Then, when this frail man took a deep intake of air and raised the baton, he truly believed he was Barbirolli. He admitted it. Barbirolli, you see, loved cricket ... and there was the Halle connection ... and Cardus.

Alas, the preparations for practice were hopelessly overelaborate for a school lunch-hour. Eventually Hoppy would set the orchestra going on the long preamble into the coronation anthem Zadok the Priest. After a stop and start or two, the time would come for the impatient choir to make its joyful pronouncement, Zadok the Priest and Nathan the Prophet annointed Solomon King. But every time, just as the four-part message soared, the bell rang for afternoon school. Boys would bustle and barge off stage; instrument cases were slammed shut, canvas double-bass covers buckled up and timps slackened off.

31

J. Hopkin Jones would be left alone among the debris, not understanding, frowning, disbelieving. Philistine timetable! The glory of music should transcend such things. Slowly he would have to gather up the pages of his loose-leafed score, tug on one pullover after another. For him it was always like taking guard to bat for England in a Lord's Test match and having everyone suddenly walk off for bad light. In all my time at Neath Grammar School we never made the Gwyn Hall for the big concert.

However, he did exchange my cello for a violin: school issue of course. Some years later, by sixth-form time, I was leading his orchestra and, when obscene school bells interrupted, I stayed on with him when possible. We played violin and piano to no one but ourselves. He decided it a fair swop for him to lead me to Bach through the violin concerto in E Major if I allowed him to keep wicket when I batted in the summer nets.

By that time I was set on becoming a professional violinist. I longed to play cricket for Glamorgan, but I never imagined cricket as a full-time job. What better life than to make music all day?

My sister and I had all-day music-making sessions. We would close the door of the front room and set up for a day of piano and violin sonatas, playing our way through books, front cover to back. My father bought me my own violin. It had belonged to a member of the Swansea Empire theatre orchestra. I felt the professional importance. I polished the fiddle, furnished it with chrome spun strings and a Menuhin chin-rest. When I put it into the case I covered it with a yellow duster. I had two bows! Now that was a genuine violinist.

Through my teenage I had violin lessons on Saturday nights, 7 o'clock until 8.30. At the same time I knew that the Good Companions Youth Club would be in full swing in Gnoll Road Congregational Church. I was therefore missing table tennis, snooker and girls; mostly girls, and mostly Joan Pritchard, who had the patience to wait a decade for me to attend to the business of marrying her.

The violin lessons were given by a young schoolmistress called Nest Saunders, the daughter of one of my father's work colleagues. As her lessons ended I was always edging to leave. I could race to the church in 15 minutes, fiddle case under arm. She preferred to prolong lessons into conversations about music.

One Saturday she insisted that I went through to the sitting room. We drank tea. She put on a gramophone record. 'Psh!' she said. 'Just listen.' We did not exchange a word, not even as one record side ended and another record dropped automatically on top. I was fifteen and I had never before heard the Beethoven Violin Concerto. Much more dramatically, I had never been so mesmerized by the sound of the violin. I can still hear the music race and swirl and float; noble tones, crisp and calm.

Nest Saunders sat, legs curled up on the sofa, like a guru. 'Did you like that?' she asked.

'I have never heard a violin like that before,' I confessed.

'Always remember, then, that it was Joseph Szigeti who first made the violin speak to you ... and Beethoven of course. Are you off to the Youth Club?'

'Too late,' I said. 'Perhaps we can play some more.'

Three times a year the Glamorgan Youth Orchestra, a hundred or so specially chosen young musicians, went off to Ogmore school camp on courses. Here I grew to wear the badge of serious musicianship on my neck, a permanent scar of hardened skin from the violin chinrest. Not that I fooled Alfredo Wang, the first-violins' tutor. He was always aware that I rushed to sectional rehearsals from the playing field. Once he pointed to my finger nails: 'Ah. Filthy. I have recommendation for zose who vant to play zee games not zee violin.' He stared at me without a smile. 'Getta zee fingurs cut.'

Every course led up to two or three concerts. My first, by chance, was at the Gwyn Hall in Neath. Unfortunately, the stage was so deep and flat and I was so short that the conductor, Mr Russell Sheppard, decided that I and one or two other shorties would have to play the whole concert standing up so that the audience could see us. Heartless! Could he not realize that we longed to sit at a violin desk, straight-backed just like proper musicians. I suspect I am one of the first orchestral players in the world to have played the Overture Leonore No. 3, the Peer Gynt Suite, Beethoven's Piano Concerto No. 4 and the fifth Brandenburg Concerto all standing up.

There are varied recollections. At Maesteg the French horns and orchestra failed to synchronize at the opening of Tchaikovsky's Valse des Fleurs. 'Stop!' shouted Sheppard in front of a full house. 'Stop! Start again and watch, you naughty people.'

At the Porthcawl Pavilion the acoustics were so treacherous that I could hear only myself play; no one else. It sounded as if I was performing the whole of Tchaikovsky's Fourth Symphony unaccompanied, and it did not go too well! Then again in the College of Further Education in Port Talbot, after a mid-afternoon rehearsal, an eminent alderman bid the orchestra leave the stage and take tea, which was spread on tables behind him in the hall. 'Come down by'yer gals and boys, tea is ready. But', he said, pointing to five double basses, 'mind the 'arps as yew go.'

So John Hopkin Jones, Heather Lewis, Nest Saunders, the Glamorgan Youth Orchestra, and the tolerance of the homestead, all took me to the point of painful decision, just after my 17th birthday, whether to accept the offer from Y Cyd-Bwyllgor Addysg Cymreig inviting me to play the violin with the National Youth Orchestra of Wales, or the one with the embossed daffodil letterhead saying come and play cricket for Glamorgan.

Music and cricket. It was a cruel showdown. Cricket won. There would be time to come back to music. There never was.

4

University Interview

I had no idea of the time when I woke up. I had no watch nor travelling alarm clock, so, in panic, I bumbled around the guest room on Q staircase imagining that I would be late for my interviews. I looked at the letter again. 10 a.m. – Dr C.L.G. Pratt, Senior Tutor. 10.30 a.m. – Dr J.H. Plumb. I wished I was back home in Neath Grammar School. I strained to hear the clang of the College clock, but when I went to the window I knew why it sounded like the faraway toll of a buoy at sea. Christ's College, Cambridge, was muffled in a heavy, gloomy mist. Of course, I could have left the room, walked through the courts and taken a closer look at the clock myself, but I had no courage.

I had seen the resident undergraduates when I arrived the previous afternoon. They sounded confident, loud, all with public school accents. It was agony for this Welsh, gownless grammar schoolboy, out of his depth, stumbling on the pronunciation of every word. I thought I heard the clock strike eight o'clock. I was already suited; charcoal grey, with Glamorgan players' tie, navy with tiny daffodils on it, tightly knotted on a starched, white, detachable collar.

The College porter had told me when I arrived that I could have dinner in Hall, but those pukka accents echoing through the courtyards had sent me running to hide. I had slunk away to the tiny guest room, starved and waited. The room was a prison even though there was no key. I could have gone to breakfast, but I did not.

As the first interview came closer, I took an unrealistic

35

dive at the writings of J. H. Plumb on eighteenth-century Britain so that I would be better prepared to meet the author himself. At last, when the third quarter of an hour struck after nine, I was on my way.

I had been all set to go to Manchester University, given good A levels, before the Skipper, Mr Wooller, had announced one day that he had written to his old college and that I should expect communication from a Dr Pratt.

It was Dr Pratt who shouted 'Come in!' He was smaller than the voice. He wore gown, glasses and had a purple birthmark on his face. I caught sight of an upside down daffodil on the note paper in front of him. I sat down. He followed my glance.

'Yes. We do have a letter from a certain Mr Wilfred Wooller, but I must tell you that it is not necessarily to your benefit. Mr Wooller, I recall, was a very destructive gentleman. D'you know he once cut and knotted the cables of a public telephone box in Cambridge? Also the last time he called in to my rooms, it was feet first through the half-timbered ceiling, from a party in the room above.'

Dr Pratt left a gap. I mumbled and risked a smile.

He went on. 'What do you hope to read?'

'History, Sir.'

'Any of your relatives been up at Cambridge?'

'My father's second cousin ... er, I think ... er ... Caius College ... er, I think.'

As I was mumbling he was turning to lift a large reference book from the shelves behind him. 'Find him in there.' He tossed the tome straight at me. I caught it.

'Good', smiled Dr Pratt. 'But don't forget – get behind it, tuck your elbows in and turn your shoulder into the advancing forwards.' Help. I wanted to go home.

Dr J. H. Plumb's rooms were in First Court. I responded to his 'Come in.' He was sitting in a winged armchair near the window. He did not look up from his book. He had a bald head and owl-like spectacles, a short man. I shifted my ground waiting for an invitation to sit.

At last he spoke, still not looking up.

'You are Lewis the cricketer, are you not?'

'Well ... er ... I suppose I am sir.'

Still not looking, he went on, 'Yes. My brother once umpired a match for Leicestershire second team.'

'I'm ... er ... sorry Sir, but I don't think I've ... er ... met him Sir.'

Then he looked. 'No I did not think you would have, but that is probably the only thing you and I will have in common for the next three years.'

Half an hour later, perspiring, mumbling worse than ever, I fled the awesome, academic dream-world of Christ's College, Cambridge. I raced by bus, by train, by London underground and by train again to the down-line platform of Neath General Station. Out I went past Mayer's the Fish, around to the market to talk to Micky Williams who ran a fruit, veg and gardening stall with old Billy Betts his uncle; Micky, the best bowler we ever had in Bracken Road. Then slowly I walked home. By the time I passed the Gnoll rugby and cricket ground, my small stage was firm under my feet again and I discovered I could talk out loud again.

Quite easily the most important letter of my life arrived a few days later.

Dear Lewis,
Subject to you obtaining three G.C.E. A level passes, and your National Service first, there will be a place for you at Christ's College to begin the Michaelmas Term in 1959.
Yours sincerely,
C.L.G. Pratt
Senior Tutor

5

Marking Time

The corporal at Bedford Station yelled an inch from my face. 'Get fell in round the back of that truck you bleedin' rabble. Move it; move it.' And then one long screech: 'Move!' I moved.

I was to become an inmate of Royal Air Force Cardington. School fields behind me, I was now, almost anonymously, 5051643 A.C. 2 Lewis A.R.

For a few days it was a joke. Cardington did not specialize in off-the-peg uniforms. The camp tailor chalked you up and then piece by piece, day by day, another item of working blue or best blue was ready. This meant that new recruits were marched about for several days half in blue and half in mufti.

'Atten. .shun,' screamed the corporal. 'T'th'right, right turn.' And off I would march in Air Force beret, shirt and tie, check sports coat, cavalry twill trousers, service socks and suede chukka boots. You could not laugh out loud because the corporal with thunder lungs was striding out alongside, 'Yift, yight, yift, yight. Stop posin' you 'orrible great strings of yuman race.'

I was lonely from the start: I was not one of the boys. This I suspect was because I walked in my sleep on the first night. I was woken up by someone yelling. The lights went on. What was I doing sitting on this fella's bed across on the other side of the hut?

'Hey! Geddoff to your own bed,' he said as he gathered the front of my pyjama jacket with a clenched fist.

'What've we got 'ere then, a right little Taffy pansy.'

I was viewed with suspicion and a giggle, and I finally

38

wrote off my claim to be a macho member of the billet a couple of days later when I applied to join the band! I had not worked out how one performed a military march-past on a violin but I was prepared to remuster to clarinet. The officer selecting our trades shook his head. 'Three years minimum. Sign here.'

'Well, a commission?' I asked.

'Same form,' he said. 'Regulars only, unless you've got a degree or something.'

I shook my head. 725 days to go. I was irretrievably in the mob. I soon moved house – nice little place in the country – Hut 252, RAF West Kirby, Larton, Wirral. I did share this desirable address with the rest of Churchill Squadron, but for three months it was home. I was there to square-bash. I was guided through this tricky little stage of my life by a Corporal Bellingham and a Sergeant O'Grady. Bellingham was almost civilized, a young man obviously misemployed as a drill instructor. O'Grady, with the flushed complexion, Irish accent and broken nose, was older, distinctly persuasive and obviously in the right job. His voice was like a rampant chainsaw as he threatened to ram the rifle so far up my rear that I would be using the foresight as a collar stud. We drilled and drilled and slept and slept.

I put on a stone in weight and got extremely fit. This was the only advance in my games playing. I did turn out for the camp rugby team on Wednesdays and for one of Birkenhead Park's lower tribes, usually at Rhyl or Bangor in pouring rain, on a Saturday.

Otherwise this was a period of forced experiment in non-ball sports. Orienteering turned out not to be my strength. I lost the way in the Welsh mountains on the first day of a week's camping there, so was instantly made cook for our tent of ten. Next day, when the others went off on their 15-mile reconnaisance with compass and maps, I was at work with the two primus stoves, skilfully timing the heating of the soup, beans, sausages, bacon, pom, eggs and fried bread to coincide with their return.

However, I did have to take part in the exercise which had the whole squadron wading through marshes, up to the knees in freezing water in icy, slanting rain. A flash went up from the nearby hillside. Our instructions had been clear – the flash is an atomic bomb; you have exactly one second in which to decide, whether to fall flat on your face or dig a six foot trench.

No one obeyed. Not one face went down into the bog, everyone crouched and looked around. Suddenly a figure strode onto the skyline; the Irish NCO raged.

'Cowardice in the field. The bloody firing squad for you lot.' He appeared to be loading his gun. 'The split second for your survival starts now.' He took aim at us; there were deep sploshes as airmen disappeared under water, staying there long enough for the atomic bomb to have time to wipe out the whole of Merseyside, let alone the Wirral.

I joined in. I do not think this taught me much about war, but there was certainly a lesson there about individual commitment to team effort.

National Servicemen were mostly concerned about their permanent postings. I wanted St Athan in Glamorgan because it was close to family, friends and the County Cricket Club. After training to be a clerk at Hereford I was given two train warrants, three bus warrants and told to proceed with full kit to RAF Upwood, in East Anglia. It was what they called 'operational'. The only aeroplane I had seen to date was chained to the guard room at West Kirby!

I was the leave clerk in the Upwood orderly room, until on the third day I was handed a telegram. It was from the RAF Record Office in Gloucester saying that A.C. Lewis had been posted in error, that he was to proceed to RAF Innsworth in Gloucester. The two men behind this sudden shift from the East of the country to the West turned out to be Group Captain Fred Roberts, Pontardawe-born, an occasional amateur cricketer for Glamorgan in the mid-thirties and Wing-Commander Maurice Jones, rugby fanatic. They were both based in

Gloucester.

From then on for 18 months, I spent the winters in rugby teams – the unit, home command, often reserve to the full-backs in the Air Force team, Bernard Wright of Wasps and Don Rutherford of Percy Park. I did get the odd game for the Air Force, but not in the inter-services matches. In the summer it was cricket for unit, command, Air Force and Combined Services. Only once did I get three days off to play for Glamorgan. I had sport in quantity but not quality.

My only games-playing advance in National Service was in rugby football because I joined the Gloucester club and won a regular place at full-back. On Tuesdays and Thursdays I trained at Kingsholm. This meant nothing more strenuous than running up and down the field a few times passing the ball among the backs and perhaps doing a gentle lap or two around the touch-lines. The serious training began in the Spread Eagle Hotel where we heaved down pints of beer.

Gloucester were a good, hard side, because their players were recruited from a most competitive local league. Micky Booth was a mischievous scrum half chivying his forwards and looking around for his faithful outside-half Dave Phelps. 'Wur yer goin' now then Phelpuur?' There were forwards like Vic Leadbetter, Brian Green, Roy Long, Brian Hudson and the gentleman prop George Hastings. International centre Bill Patterson joined just before I left. The captain was Cyril Thomas, the hooker, a hard but kindly man from the Forest of Dean.

Kingsholm was smooth and firm, fine for running. Not that we ran the ball too much. The home crowd hated frivolous play. In the grandstand there were plaid rugs covering the legs of ladies wearing silk headscarves. Under the shed on the opposite side the mixed crowd could rave or riot. They shouted in the first half against the opposition, then, if the match was not going too well for us, against the referee, and in the last quarter, if we were still losing, against us. No mercy.

41

My lowest moment at Kingsholm was on a Boxing Day. After the seasonal celebrations I took the field in festive mood with feeble body. Out of a maul came a prop forward. He sold me a giant dummy and scored a try right under the posts. Head down, I waited with the others for the conversion to be taken. Over it went, then ooch! Something big, hard and sharp struck me between the shoulder blades. My back arched and I fell forwards. It was a missile from one of the disapproving crowd at the city end – half a household brick!

Gloucester were a splendidly durable side. We needed to be, in local derbies. Matches against Stroud, Lydney and the local Gordon League were much more war exercises than anything I ever did in Her Majesty's Services. Bristol were different. They had a side of brilliant runners with Bill Redwood and John Blake the most original thinkers, incisive players, a delight to watch if not to oppose. However even the most dazzling runners in the land could be pinned down by two most destructive wing forwards, Peter Ford and Derek Ibbotson, and when that happened Gloucester performed the simple exercise of going forwards as well as anyone in the land.

We did come heavily adrift at Swansea in one match. There was a Gloucestershire county match and a flu epidemic. We went to St Helens with two-thirds of the first team missing but were only 6–3 down at half time. Thereafter the Swansea outside-half got loose, a brilliant player who also happened to be a hero of mine at Neath Grammar School, Bryan Richards. Bryan got a Blue at Cambridge and a Welsh cap. He was an outstanding cricketer and an athlete too. His style of outside-half play was unorthodox but quite devastating on its day.

Swansea's effort was firmly based on the formidable front row of W. O. Williams, Norman Gale, and Gwyn Lewis, and early in the second half I began to see much more than was healthy of the back-row men Clem Thomas and John Faull, international players flying off the scrums. Then came Dewi Bebb, the multi-capped left wing. I recall diving at Dewi's iron thighs, bouncing off and seeing him swerve out and around the back of the posts to score. They put twenty points on us.

In a generous write-up in the *South Wales Evening Post* which my father sent up to Innsworth during the next week, rugby writer Ron Griffiths had reported: 'For hard-pressed Gloucester, Tony Lewis was a courageous though sadly overworked full back.'

Hard pressed! How true. Norman Gale, a hefty and hard international hooker, led a foot rush along the touch-line down towards the Mumbles end, in front of the grandstand. I scooped the ball from his hacking feet. Norman grabbed my shirt one-handed and began to twirl around like a discus-thrower. The whistle went, but Norman had started, so he finished. He released me into the railings. Hard pressed? He grilled me. I slumped. To calm the referee, he pretended to be interested in my welfare.

'Alright wuss?' he said.

I staggered back into play.

In the clubhouse afterwards, Bryan Richards told me, 'Good job you were Welsh. If you got an "alright wuss" from Norman, that was a major apology.'

Unfortunately, in cricket there were no signs of obvious improvement in my play during the two years of National Service. Indeed my Service cricket began with a mild embarrassment. Before going off to join the RAF side for the first time, I had to attend a two-day trial match with Home Command at White Waltham. An officer came out with a pep talk. 'Now Lewis, the RAF selectors may think you are a good player but we've seen no evidence of that, so it is jolly important that we see what you can do over these next two days.' It was a hot, humid, glorious mid-summer climate; dragon-flies hovered and the green grass was being drained white with every day's sunshine.

My head dropped a little at first slip: a small reverie. There was a snick, a flash of leather and pow! I had been wounded by a direct hit to the jockstrap. I doubled up.

Half an hour later I was in bed in sick quarters with my private and most painful parts encased in a medical pouch. I did return to the game on the next day, but bruised and swollen. The officer in charge decided I should bat. Instantly I was bowled out, but was told to stay on. Next I was caught and was told to have one more chance. A few balls later I was bowled. When the Home Command side was chosen, I was not selected.

Happily, a couple of days later, I got runs against the RAF for Col. Stevens X1 at Eastbourne and won a place in the Air Force side. It was full of good players, many of them attached to county clubs – Peter Parfitt, Middlesex, Graham Atkinson, Somerset, Derek Semmence, Sussex, Malcolm Scott, Northants, Barry Knight, Essex, Ian Buxton, Derbyshire, and Rodney Pratt, Leicestershire. The skipper was the former Kent amateur Squadron Leader Maurice Fenner, a popular man, always understanding the aspirations of we National Servicemen in his side. He was supported by Flight Lieutenant Rufus Leggett, one of the great characters of Air Force cricket, as well as Squadron Leaders Eric Senior and Ian Dunn.

In such company the life was good. We played three-day matches against counties, about six of them before the inter-services games at Lord's. Travel was not easy. There was a lot of waiting around at bus stops and railway stations with kit bag and holdall. Expenses often read: bus, Innsworth to Gloucester 2/-; train to Andover 9/3; meal 5/-; Andover to Euston 10/-; Euston to Manchester £1.2.0; taxi 1/6: laundry 5/6; meal on train 10/-; rail, Manchester to Gloucester 19/7; taxi to camp 12/-. Expenses for five days on the road playing cricket, £5.2.0.

Overnight stays were at Air Force camps or, notoriously, in London, for the non-commissioned, at the Union Jack Club in Waterloo. Here you did your best to sleep in a cubicle, separated from grunting, snoring, farting, early-rising or late-home neighbours by a thin partition with wire netting top. Whole regiments appeared to be marching along the linoleumed corridors all night. In the early hours of the morning soldiers, sailors and airmen would thunder out in their studded boots to catch a boat train past those singing their way in, drunk and disorderly.

In fact, rather than stay at the Union Jack Club, Graham Atkinson and I once decided to travel overnight from the West on the milk train, and to sleep on a bench at Paddington until the London underground started. We were playing against the Royal Navy at Lord's.

There was excitement in touring. The Air Force did a trip to Gibraltar. The Combined Services went to Holland. It was in Amsterdam that I waited in a taxi for an unnamed warrior to emerge from a red-light bed-room. I got the taxi driver to blast the horn after 15 minutes, as was the arrangement. The first-floor window was flung open, and my friend leaned out.

'It's alright, mate. You can go home. I'm claiming the extra half hour.'

As my second cricket season in the Air Force passed I became more and more afraid that I had lost the academic strain. The Education Officers at Innsworth, both friends, Mervyn Goldstein and Colin Evans, excel-lent rugby players both, saw to it that my bedside cupboard was crammed with text books of the required reading for historical tripos at Christ's College in Cam-bridge, but I had to conclude that two years of aimless cricket and rugby had been nothing more than a pleasant irrelevance.

6

Rugby Blue

On Thursday I was a Senior Aircraftman saluting everything that moved in the RAF. Five days later I went up to Cambridge passing for a gentleman.

The First Court of Christ's College, which had once looked so unfriendly – grey stone, with unyielding staircases, eminently private – now rather smiled at me. I was one of them. In fear, three years before, when I was up for interview, I had not noticed the beauty of this little courtyard; how colourful it was with its circular lawn of manicured green and its vines twisting autumn foliage around the windows. I had not sensed the peace transmitted by the corner chapel. Now I was not afraid for them to touch me.

So this time I went confidently through the screens into the Second Court which led either straight on to the ornate iron gates set in a handsome building, or, by a pathway inclining to the left, to the Third Court. To the left, then, into the courtyard and along to the right on the ground floor to the room called W7. I quickly met my bedder, Mrs Tompkins, a plumpish lady, who said: 'I don't mind who I find you in bed with in the mornings Sir, as long as it's not another fella. I've 'ad enough of that in my time.'

In this room I made a hefty decision about games. I would not play any rugby football at Cambridge. No Freshman's Trial. My rugby career was over; a game for Neath, a season with Gloucester. That was it. It had to be the books. I knew before I arrived that I would do just that, so I had taken the precaution of leaving my rugger boots at home, just in case I weakened. Eight weeks later I was standing under high up-and-unders at Twickenham kicked by the Oxford freshman Richard Sharp in the University match.

At the start of term, I was afraid I would not be able to manage the historical tripos. The learning process had been suffocated by the good fun of the Air Force; the mind had staggered to a standstill. I expected to win a cricket blue in the summer term, and imagined that a first-class fixture list would leave no time for study.

So the winter was for dark libraries, obscure books illuminated by hooded lights, coffee, the pursuit of thoroughbred learning.

A week later, knee-deep in historical tomes, I looked up to a knock on the window of W7. I lifted it. Clive Snowdon said he was the secretary of the college rugby club and would I fill in at full back for the college trials? Someone had said I could play. I explained that I was suffering academic flushes, educational yips, and all the symptons of those who feel they are about to scale the academic glacier without map, rope or pick axe. I thought I had triumphantly clinched it by saying that I had no boots. Snowdon was not put off. He slipped into the sermon which third-year students are entitled to give juniors, of how Christ's maybe a small college, but we all pull together. Letting the side down and all that.

It had been an exceptionally sunny, dry autumn. It was a bright and warm day. I sniffed the light breeze off the trees which wavered in the Master's garden, and I wavered too and fell. But I said I would have to play in basketball boots. 'Anything to make up the numbers,' he said.

Up Huntingdon Road on my newly purchased old bicycle, the number painted on the rear mudguard and a new lock in the saddle bag. In the dressing rooms nervous freshmen, with great aspirations in university rugby, threaded new white laces into shiny black boots. Mr and Mrs Bentley, curators of the college sports pavilion and grounds, searched out shorts, socks and jersey for me. The game went well. The college first XV captain was there. Who had I played for? Why hadn't I put my name down? Neath? Gloucester? So you are a first-class player!

That evening I was sipping a half of bitter at the bar of the tiny college buttery when Dr Pratt, the senior tutor, walked in. He sipped sherry for a while and called to me.

'Who are you?'

I went over to him, and he repeated. 'Who on earth are you? I didn't accept anyone looking like you into Christ's.'

'I'm Lewis, Sir.'

'School?'

'Neath Grammar School, Sir.'

'I never forget a face ... don't know yours. Anyway. I hear you played a good game of rugby, but you don't have any boots.'

'No Sir.'

'Why?'

'I left them at home so I could concentrate on my work, Sir.'

He paused, sipped more sherry. No trace of a smile. Then he leaned across the bar and prodded my chest. 'Look here my boy. You come to Christ's College to give not to take. Write to your Mummy. Ask her to send your rugby boots straightaway.'

'Yes Sir,' and I turned away.

'And Lewis,' came another bellow and now a delayed smiled. 'Have you brought that violin?'

'No Sir.'

'Then tell her to send that as well.' And a warmer smile. 'Give us all you've got. You come to Christ's to give, not to take.'

By half-way through this first Michaelmas term I was the University's second XV full back, but I turned down the offer to be a fiddler in the C.U.M.S. second orchestra. The first team full back was also a Christ's freshman called Ian Balding who had played for Bath and county rugby for Dorset and Wilts. He spent some of

48

his time going off to National Hunt meetings to ride
horses for his brother Toby Balding, the trainer.

After the match between the Varsity and the Seconds,
who were called the Sixty Club, Ian and I were swopped.
So, now in the first team, the last month of this first term
was an agony of waiting for team selections. No studying
could be done. I was trapped. The mind kept wandering
to Twickenham. Learning of your selection or non-
selection was a ritual torture. Matches were played on
Wednesdays and Saturdays and the team was posted in
the window of Ryder and Amies, gentleman's outfitter in
Kings' Parade. No other notice was given. Therefore, the
hopefuls had to spend Monday and Thursday mornings
pretending not to be patrolling the pavements outside
Ryder and Amies or occasionally stopping to admire a
Panama hat or a double-breasted blazer. Sometimes I
feigned the deepest interest in King's College chapel or
whistled slowly round and round the market square.
Once, on my third circuit, I opened a bank account with
the Midland just to fill in time before the team was
posted. You could bump into four or five expectant full-
backs all opening bank accounts.

There was an even greater agony – injury. In one
training session I was attempting to run the length of the
field with Kenny Scotland on my back, an ancient
custom, when my left hamstring overstretched. It was
Monday. Good grief! I had to be fit to play against
Leicester at Grange Road on Wednesday.

I spent hours in Jesus Lane in small rooms run by a
diminutive physio called Mr Pope. He linked my leg to
all manner of machines, but on Wednesday morning
gave me the thumbs down. Ian Balding would play. It
had been announced that Gordon Waddell was almost
certainly out of the University match. Ken Scotland
would play outside half. So the full back position was
officially up for grabs. I went to watch the Leicester
match from the terraces. I should have spared myself the
pain. Every time Ian got the ball he ran half the length of
the field. I cursed the lousy Leicester tackling. It had to

49

be Balding. I left, head down among the crowd.

By Thursday I was fit again. It was four games from the Varsity match. Ian and I looked at each other across the table at breakfast. He had read the morning papers too. It looked certain that one of us would get a blue. We decided that we should drink rather than stare and in the evening we met in the Red Lion in Petty Cury. We did not know it then, but we had sealed an unshakeable friendship.

It was an agony, walking around the well-worn paths at Ryder and Amies, but at last the notice came up for the next match. Full back – A.R. Lewis, Neath GS and Christ's.

Thereafter I stayed in the side. The first clue that I would make it was a request by Steve Smith, the captain, to host tea after training one day. I shared the cost of crumpets, chocolate cake and biscuits with an old blue, David Bird in Queens. The team to play Oxford would be announced after the game against Steele Bodger's XV. It was, but only 13 places were filled. Full back and right wing were ommitted. Uncertainty again. There was just one match left before the University match, against the Harlequins at Twickenham.

The Quins kicked seven shades of daylight out of us. They were stacked with old Oxford blues reliving their pasts. I went off just before half time to have five stitches in a gash above my eye. I returned and wandered around with double vision. Ken Scotland insisted I went off. That, I thought, was that.

The team returned to Cambridge, stopping as usual at the Clock Restaurant for a steak. By ten o'clock I was in bed, lights out, with a crashing headache. A little later there was a knock at the door. It was Steve Smith. He smiled. 'I know it's late and you've had a bump, but I thought you would like to receive this.' He handed me an envelope. I took out a card bearing the Emmanuel College crest. If I was not doing anything else a week on Tuesday, would I turn out for a match against Oxford at Twickenham.

Port and nuts at Pembroke College. Fifteen under-
graduates with their President, Dr Windsor Lewis, stand
to curse the enemy. The toast, gentlemen, is GDBO –
God Damn Bloody Oxford. The preparation was over.
No more staggering the length of Grange Road with
Kenny on my back; no more breathless sprints with
Mike Wade or Alan Godson. I was no longer on trial – I
had my card. I read it over and over to be sure. I sipped
the port and savoured the turn of events. 'You come to
Christ's to give not to take.'

On the night before the University match, I shared a
bedroom with another Christ's man, John Brash, a
Fettesian who lived in Yorkshire. We were both freshmen and drawn by our similar fates into friendship
strong enough to make a confession or two before lights
out.

'D'y know Johnny,' I felt compelled to tell him. 'My
ribs hurt. Those bloody Quins last week: five stitches in
my eye and a helluva boot in the ribs. Do you think I
should strap it up before the game, sort of admitting I've
had a bump or should I pretend I'm alright and then get.
strapped up after five minutes play?'

'Oh, God!' said John. 'I'm glad you told me that.' He
got up and walked to a space in the room and started to
bend to touch his toes. He stopped suddenly and in some
pain, his finger tips well above his knees. He reached for
his back. 'They got me too, the bastards, a big boot right
up the jacksie. Can't even tie my shoes up.'

'We'll just say nothing and get out there and get on
with it shall we?' I suggested.

'Yes,' he grimaced, trying to touch his toes again. 'The
bastards.'

On the bus which nosed through the crowds at
Twickenham, I was wrapped up in light blue regalia –
the blazer with the red lion rampant, the sweater
carrying the crest and the large letters C.U.R.U.F.C.

It was a dull Tuesday. I felt ill before the kick off. We
went out for a team photograph. There were not many in
the ground but I was white.

Before leaving the dressing room, David McSweeney, large Irish international, came across to me urgently, and tapped me on the bottom.

'Have a good one Tony.'

'Thanks,' I said.

'Cos if you don't, I'll stuff you,' he said.

We ran out again. This time 57,000 roared. In the actual match an American called Dawkins kept throwing the ball half-way across the field. Very annoying. Then this young man called Sharp kept booting the ball half-way to heaven. I dropped a few and caught a few but no one crossed our line. We lost. Three penalties to Wilcox, one to Bearne.

The noise never abated throughout the game. I was just beginning to enjoy myself, thought I would try a run or two, when I looked up and saw it was ten to four. All over. Back to the dressing room, now cold and quiet. Heads fell into hands. There was only the sound of the hot water creaking in the pipes. Can death be worse? Beaten by bloody Oxford.

7

Dr C. L. G. Pratt

The day after I was picked to play against Oxford at Twickenham, I happened to meet Dr Pratt outside the Kenya Coffee House, alongside the college.

'So a freshman rugger blue,' he said, but not smiling.

'Yes, I heard last night, Sir,' and I gave a wide show of teeth.

His thin mouth smirked. 'And just think. You are the third-best full back in Christ's.'

Pratt could throw you and seriously enjoyed doing it. He was the man we all wanted to please – the Senior Tutor, the man who had taken us into the college in the first place, but you never knew whether to trust the smile or believe the scowl. He was prodding you, trying to get some guts out of you, a scream, a laugh, a tear. He loved confidence; loathed conceit. He had his favourites. I never felt that I was one, despite his love of games. What I think went wrong on that occasion, December 1959, was that I had won the University full-back position ahead of the man he had earmarked for it – Ian Balding. I had upset his plans.

Lucan Pratt had a purple mark which covered part of his face. Some said it was a birthmark, others said more dramatically that it was the result of an underwater explosion sustained when he was a frogman during the war. The first theory was likely but we researched the second too. We discovered that Pratt had spent the years leading up to the Second World War lecturing in philosophy at Magdalen College, Oxford. Then, when in June 1939 the submarine *Thetis* sank and nearly a

53

hundred lives were lost, a Commons committee of enquiry suggested that the men in the submarine had been poisoned by carbon dioxide. Send for Dr C.L.G. Pratt. For six and a half years he worked in the experimental branch of the Royal Navy Physiological Laboratory at Gosport. He worked with all underwater craft; his overalls were a frogmans suit. He was a member of a record underwater trip from Gibraltar to England to test out the snorkel device which he had played a part in perfecting, and spent his time elaborating the equipment of midget submarines. He was an underwater OBE. We settled for the birthmark theory. In any case he would not discuss war games. Lucan Pratt, you see, was a debunker of posture, sometimes a rather sanguine cutter-down-to-size.

Pratt was quixotic and needed to be understood. I only learned this many years later. I was sipping a whisky soda on the second-floor balcony of Windsor Villa, off the old Warren Road in Bombay. I was at the home of Dr Yusef Hamied and wife Farida.

Yusef had been at Christ's before me and had stayed on as a research fellow after graduation. I never met him then, but a decade later, when I was playing cricket for the MCC in India. Yusef too felt that he owed Pratt as well as Alec Todd, now Lord Todd, almost everything. He never lost touch with them. Each summer now, he leaves his most successful chemical business, CIPLA, in Bombay and Bangalore, and flies to Cambridge for the annual Christ's College dinner.

Yusef smiled when I explained that Pratt could be so contrary. 'No, no, that's just Pratt,' he replied. 'I'll show you a letter.' Yusef went off to fetch it and told me his story. 'I wrote to Pratt, telling him how much Christ's meant to me, and how grateful I was and my father too ... you see, I had no 'A' levels when he accepted me, only 'O's. Anyway, after finishing my research and coming back to India I felt that I wanted to meet him again on my next visit. I wrote and this is what I got as a reply.' He gave me the letter.

From the Senior Tutor, Christ's College, Cambridge 25th May 1961
Dear Yusef,
Many thanks for your charming letter of 22nd May. By a great feat of memory, much prodding from my various secretaries, reference to old Tripos lists and the local police records, I am just able to recall you as a tall, dark, handsome man who contrived to augment the diameter of my apilus region by approximately two centimetres per annum during his period of residence – and little did you care how much I worried about you. If you will turn up here on June 5th there is nothing I can do to prevent it. If you do, I shall do my best to suppress my natural ill humour and exhibit all the olde world graciousness for which I am world famed. Till we meet.
Fr. The Senior Tutor, Christ's College, Cambridge.

Pratt was an academic who, by his modest upbringing first in Hackney then later in Liverpool, by his deep involvement in the affairs of war, understood life well beyond the confines of the college walls. That he could impart it in the bookworm environment was his strength.

It would be good to write a happy conclusion, but I cannot. The position of Pratt was undermined by those who argued that Cambridge should not be lumbered with what they saw was an excess of sporting types. The knives came out in the Christ's Senior Combination room as they had in the days of C.P. Snow in the fifties. The casualty in the seventies was Pratt.

Thereafter Christ's was inherited by all those Pratt had scorned most, not by the academics, but by a body of dons who had taken themselves and their pursuits too seriously. I believe in Pratt's law – intellectual excellence like sporting excellence is to be applauded; the pursuit of either for its own sake is to be debunked.

What became of our vintage of Pratt's people; all the rugger blues?

Ian Balding became a leading racing trainer, including among his owners Her Majesty the Queen, and Mike Lord the Conservative MP for East Suffolk; of the Welsh internationals, Brian Thomas, a metallurgist, is among the top management of the Steel Company of Wales in Felindre, near Swansea. Roger Michaelson was the first graduate taken into the London fruit market and Migrant Fruits is his own business. Then the England caps – scrum half Trevor Wintle is a doctor, prop forward Bev Dovey a housemaster at Millfield School, and David Wrench is a schoolmaster at Taunton. The Irish international David MacSweeney is a psychiatrist, John Brash the Scottish player is a highly inventive self-employed agent in the building world. The gymnast, Roger Dalzell, is a senior executive of Hobson's Press in Cambridge and if I need go on, it is only to say that Richard Hutton played for Yorkshire and England and became an accountant and businessman.

Probably none of us would be admitted to Christ's College, Cambridge, these days when admission is strictly linked to a high academic performance at 'A' level, neither A.R. Lewis nor Dr Yusef Hamied. Of course, I believe that Lucan Pratt was right and his successors wrong. He composed a community of wide interests based on formal academic pursuit with room in abundance for the pursuers of academic excellence. However, if you were to go down from Cambridge with a lower second- or a third-class degree then you had best have given your all to the Milton Society, the Rowing Club, the Chapel, the hockey side or whatever, or you had let him and yourselves down.

Nowadays, Cambridge University makes no commitment to excellence at games. A dimension of University experience has been firmly removed by the scalpels of the Admission tutors. It is probable that first-class cricket and rugby will soon end at Fenners and Grange Road and the Boat Race will be no more than a spring scuffle between overgrown schoolboys. Cambridge will only have impact on the narrow world of academic achievement, not on the wider world. It will shrink by its own myopia.

8

Cricket at Fenners

Cambridge life was quite different from anything I had known before, a new dimension of competition, manners, public school self-confidence, elegance, English language, independence.

Academically, I was no longer force-fed; socially, I eased into habits of drinking sherry before meals, port after, of patrolling cloisters in brown brogue shoes, cavalry twill trousers, sports coat and Hawks' Club tie. Formally I wore my gown after dusk and requested ladies to leave College by eleven in the evening: informally I pedalled my third-hand bike to lecture room or playing field, or slouched in easy chairs, developing the cult of drinking coffee through all-night conversations which bred friends for a lifetime.

I was privileged among games players. A double blue as a Freshman, I had the unwritten licence to gate-crash parties or select from the forest of invitation cards which spread on the mantelpiece and window sills of my rooms. Off to the St Caths Kittens, to the Emma Lions or the Woodpecker's Ball on the river in black tie and light blue blazer as if Gatsby lived. No longer did my mumbling and highly indistinct Welsh grammar schoolboy accent matter, and in any case I could see that the resonant intonations of the public schoolboy usually covered his own insecurities.

I was in my pomp in my third year, living in rooms at the top of T staircase in Third Court, a floor shared with another Welshman, Roger Michaelson. He was captain elect of the University rugby club. I was captain of cricket. T7 and T8 were like throne rooms to anyone joining the manic scrap for a Cambridge blue.

The cricketer's day in a summer term began with a rush to the books because it was the examination term too. Six o'clock alarm. My history supervisor, John P. Kenyon, was a delightful man, shy, unable to keep his eyes on anyone in conversation, but he understood my timetable problems. He would review my weekly essay and be prepared to discuss its immense deficiences at 8.30 in the morning so that I could be at Fenners by 10.30, one hour before the start.

I did catch him unprepared one day. His door opened, he looked less than ready to meet the doom of another Lewis treatise, and, was that coffee percolating and did I catch the very tiniest glimpse of a female peignoir? He hooded his eyes completely to announce, 'I think it is in your interest as well as mine, Lewis, indeed in the interest of history itself, if you retreat to the library and come back in half an hour.'

John Kenyon groaned at my struggles with the historical tripos but also encouraged my cricket. We enjoyed a most friendly dissonance. Quite opposite was a don called Dr Lewiter who supervised my final year's French studies. When I refused to comply with his instruction that I remove myself from Fenners altogether, he wagged his little French hat at me, repeating the words, 'lamentable and ludicrous Lewis'. To be fair to Lewiter, by the third year the signs of my academic mediocrity were plain.

So after that early-morning dash to the books, I would walk up Regent Street, cut in at the University Arms Hotel and across Parker's Piece, the wide acreage where all sorts of cricket matches could go on at the same time, to Fenners, the University ground. Fenners could be icy; Fenners could be generous and warm. Fenners was gorgeous in balmy days after tripos when lads drank pints of ale from the Tolly tent and picnicked with pretty girls on the boundary edge. Fenners was trim, firm, green and airy.

It was exhilarating to trust the turf and swing the bat into your smartest cover drive. Bowling, they say, was different. If the eastern winds had whipped the moisture from the pitch it could be the ultimate test of bowling skills, requiring faultless line and length; concentration and patience, even stoicism.

Of all the bowlers with whom I played at Fenners, the most accurate was Alan Hurd who sometimes played for Essex. He was an off-spinner who varied his flight, spun the odd ball, but always kept his accuracy. Unfortunately for Cambridge bowlers, the edges which came off the opponents' bats did not always stick in amateur hands. It makes Ossie Wheatley's record of 80 wickets in a Cambridge term all the more remarkable.

The Fenner's groundsman for more than 40 years was Cyril Coote. He was a father-confessor and adviser. He was blunt but never uncharitable. He knew his cricket and his cricketers too. He had a deformity of the leg which made him limp severely, but it had not stopped him being one of the best minor county cricketers. He watched us play and would help if asked.

When we were batting, he often held court in a chair at the end of the Long Room, the big clock by Munsey of Cambridge clicking away behind on the panelled wall above the large fireplace. Each panel bore the gold-leafed names of past sides. Cyril would turn and point. 'There he is, Sir, Mr May, Sir. He wouldn't have played a shot like that, Sir. He'd have had his head down, Sir, past 40. They'd know they'd have t'bowl at him all day then, sir. You chucked it away.'

Or yet another tale of Jehangir Khan from the thirties. 'If you'd been up then, Sir, you'd have seen an international cricketer ... bowl all day ... bat all day. There wasn't anything he couldn't do Sir, that Jehangir.' There was always Mr Doggart, Sir, or Mr Dexter, Sir, or Mr Sheppard Sir, but always it came back to Mr May, Sir. 'Y'see, Sir, with Mr May, Sir, county bowlers dreaded coming here.'

The pavilion was built in 1877 from money raised by

the Rev. A.R. Ward. He was a former Cambridge captain who became President and Treasurer in 1873. He raised money by personal appeal and among the contributors was Edward VII who had a special wicket reserved for him at Fenners while he was up at Trinity.

In my day the pavilion was happy and friendly inside, and on the outside, handsome Victorian – a couple of rows of white seats on the roof, and then, below, a wide canopy over the ground-floor verandah which was supported by delicate wrought iron filigree, this leading down a gentle incline of half a dozen steps through the small members' enclosure to the field. Alas, it is all gone. Now a functional pavilion stands at the other end of the field.

Out old dressing rooms were gloomy, tucked away in the back of the building, the University team on the ground floor, the opposition above. Our showers and baths were in the basement and it was a tough route to get there, over gnarled and splintered wooden floors and down the winding stairs into the icy blasts.

A shower was the best bet because the eight hip baths did not offer total immersion. It was just possible to lie back in one and place one's ankles and feet in the next one, but mainly one sat, cross-legged, guru-like, boiling beneath the groin and freezing above it. When I was a nervous freshman I wandered into a dressing room space next to an Indian, Santosh Nayini Reddy, a little man with small frame and thick spectacles. He spoke with an inconsistent lisp that was a delightful affectation not an impediment. He would greet me every day with an old colonial 'Hello Lulu, thmashing day.'

In the very first match I played, against Surrey led by Alec Bedser, Santosh tried to hit Tony Lock over Hugh's Hall at the far end of the ground but skied the ball many a mile, straight up in the air, and was caught three yards away by Micky Stewart. He returned to our corner, his lightweight Indian body snuggled into a giant towel, his Magoo spectacles lodged on the top. 'Dash it, Lulu! I couldn't thtay out there with that Micky Thtewart

thitting in my back pocket at short-thqware leg. It was
Locky or me Lulu. You do thee don't you?' Then he
looked up and fixed his eye on a colourful picture, a page
from a magazine pinned up at the side of the fireplace; a
full coal fire was glowing in the grate. 'That's Thusan
Dexter up there,' he said. 'Look at those legs Lulu. They
thay that Lord Edward used to thtand in front of that
picture for inspiration before going out to bat. God,
Lulu, I'd hit Locky out of sight if I had a thmashing
birdie like that.'

Chris Howland was the genial captain. He built up a
happy side. He would arrive of a freezing morning and
announce that he had fixed a coal supply for the fire and
asked Mrs Coote to make us really hot potatoes for
lunch. It was his way of saying that he had lost the toss.

However, week by week, through the term, Fenners
blossomed into the most beautiful ground, the tall trees
grew green and spread ancient branches; undergraduates sat on the grass pretending to study, and in the
pavilion the most loyal collection of members I have ever
known took their places. At Fenners there were always
lovely strokes, lots of runs and pleasant people. In cricket
matters, I believed in Cyril Coote. 'Throw me a few,
Cyril. Come and tell me what I am doing wrong.'

'Well, for a start, Sir, top hand firm, play the ball
against a firm left side in the V, mid-on to mid-off. I'll
bring a basket o' balls to the nets in ten minutes sir. Just
check Mrs Coote don't need anything.'

It was at Cambridge that I first started to live with the
greatest enemy of all my playing days – knee trouble. In
my very first term I found myself in the surgery of Dr
Windsor Lewis, President of the Rugby Club, wondering
whether I was fit enough to play against Oxford at
Twickenham. 'You must play,' he said. 'It will be
wonderful for you and great for Wales. It will easily hold
out.'

He was right, but a year later I was on my back, minus
a right knee cartilage, in the orthopaedic department of
St Bartholomew's hospital. In the second Cambridge

61

summer, 1961, four months after the operation, I badly twisted the same knee in a match against Richie Benaud's Australians at Fenners and apart from the University match, which I struggled through for my good friend the captain, David Kirby, I retired for the season. No Glamorgan at all.

My University matches against Oxford were a bit of a mixture, all three drawn. In the first, 1960, the opening bowlers David Sayer and Andy Corran were strong and fast. The man with the strange walk, as if someone had stolen his walking sticks, was Alan Smith, the captain. He opened the batting with David Green, later a powerful strokemaker with Lancashire and Gloucester-shire. Then there were three very straight-faced sub-continental wizards, the Nawab of Pataudi, Javed Burki and Abbas Ali Baig. Add to those the spin of Colin Dryborough, Alan Duff and Dan Piachaud, and the wicket-keeping batsman Charles Fry. It was a side as formidable as any Oxford had ever put out. Every one played county cricket and four were to play in Tests. By the Varsity match I had moved from batting at number three or four to opening with Roger Prideaux. Roger was a handsome striker of the ball, though he became more cautious in subsequent seasons when he settled with Northamptonshire in full-time county cricket.

I remember a moment when he grew up quickly. The South African fast bowler Neil Adcock sent Prideaux a bouncer which Roger hooked with a resounding crack to mid-wicket. As he completed the stroke Roger sent a schoolboy grin down the pitch to me. Adcock saw it and was not pleased. He bounced one again. Roger hooked. Four runs. The next one was one of the fastest balls I've seen and a bouncer. Roger began the hook shot as the ball crashed into his knuckles and flew up into the wicket-keeping gloves of Johnny Waite. Roger's face was drained of all colour. He had seen his god, and learned the Fenners lesson that whereas a Test fast bowler would not want to bowl flat out there, over after over, on an unhelpful wicket, he would not expect an undergraduate to fill his boots with runs to his embarrassment. One four an over, or at the most two, was permissible in that school.

At Lord's Cambridge were bowled out for 153. Oxford scored 310 based on the admirable technician Javed Burki, 79, and the wonderful virtuosity of Pataudi, 131. Astonishingly Cambridge held out with the help of rain. Happily, the freshman Lewis played one of the most inspired innings of his lifetime ... c. Burki b. Duff 95.

If Roger Prideaux learned one lesson at Fenners, I learned another at Lord's. Why no century? Why hole out again at mid-on? I was not short of advice. The umpires were Dai and Emrys Davies, the former Glamorgan players. 'Take it easy Tony bach,' cajoled Dai when I was at the non-striking end. 'Get them in singles Tony,' Emrys whispered in his delightfully quiet way. Charge! Down the pitch I went, mainly because I was running out of partners quickly, to the leg-spinner Duff. Out! I had to retreat past Dai Davies. 'Tony bach. I'll crack that stump across your arse. A hundred it was there for you.'

The 1961 match was a dull draw. Poor David Kirby, our captain, was forced into no-man's land on the last day with time only for Oxford to win or draw on a good pitch, but not for us to win. The late star of the light blue effort turned out to be my fiancée Joan, at the Tavern Bar terrace. She was in the company of Roger Michaelson and the captain of University boxing, Roger Bannister. They were being harangued by a loud Oxford man who was yelling up at the Cambridge dressing room, hoping to prompt a declaration.

'How grey, Cambridge. My God, how grey!' he roared over and over again. When I was out, I went over to join Joan, Roger and Roy. The Oxford man was still in full flow. 'How bloody grey, Cambridge. You're not light blue, you're grey. Bloody grey.' He was tipsy. I was prompted to try to explain how, if we declared, only Oxford could win. He turned on me bellowing, 'What do you know about it little man?' Whereupon my loving fiancée swung a mean handbag at the fellow's chest and rendered him permanently silent.

I had a hard word with her to remind her that a cricket blue, especially at Lord's, does not come down from the team dressing rooms to end up fighting at the Tavern Bar. But the lads loved it. 'Well done, Joanie,' they said. 'We were in behind you.' Bannister and Michaelson! If they had joined in, now that would have been some punch-up.

By 1962, my year as captain, a number of fine young cricketers had come up – Edward Craig, Mike Brearley, Richard Hutton, Raymond White, Tony Windows and Richard Jefferson, all county players and all good enough to stay in the game as long as they liked. Unfortunately for us, Richard Jefferson fell over an academic trip wire and went down after one year. We had batting enough but not enough penetrative bowling. A rather more aggressive approach to the University match by the captain might have troubled Oxford more, but I got myself confused. I was batting at the time the declaration was to be made. As Glamorgan players could later testify, I could never work out a declaration from the crease. For Glamorgan, Don Shepherd used to work out the equation of time and minutes and then wave me in. Sometimes I got myself out on purpose so that I could write down my long-division sums on paper. The other distraction was the fact that I was nearing the University match century which had eluded me two years before. I was afraid of repeating the 1960 disappointment by holeing out in the nineties: entirely selfish, but I found myself seizing up. I got the hundred, declared and we drew. I am sure we would have drawn whatever I had done, but I always regretted my lack of clarity at that stage of the match.

Early in the term I made the decision not to select the freshman of reputation from Repton School, Richard Hutton. His bowling action was unusual and rather unattractive, his personality appeared dour and unsmiling, his batting was a lumbering exercise mainly on to the front foot. Even allowing for the guess that he was just not a good net-player and that he was shy, I still could not see him an automatic choice. After a couple of matches against the counties, I had a letter from Richard's father, Sir Leonard, asking if he could take me out to dinner. I accepted. He took me to a small basement restaurant in the Market Square. It did not take me long to discover what father and son both hid behind clear blue eyes and a simple slow conversational style – the most bewitching dry humour.

However, Sir Len's basic message was: 'My son's a good player y'know; he's a good player. He can bowl a bit y'know, and he can catch; and he can bat ... what you want to do is ...' the long pause, the wide blue eyes, the face opening up as if it was revelation time.

'Yes, Sir?'

'Go in for stockbroking,' he said.

Soon Richard proved that he was indeed a good player and a delightful man. His arm action was high and he hit the seam; he could use a new ball with some life; his batting was still rather plunging but he held good slip catches.

Mike Brearley was Secretary and vice-captain. Brearley, Edward Craig and I were excellent demonstrations of three cricketers taking different routes into postgraduate life. Brearley and Craig were an astonishing couple because they kept on getting Firsts in their examinations, playing high class cricket and also finding time for many other interests – Edward played the piano well and learned German for fun! Mike played the clarinet and had a half blue for lacrosse.

Edward played for Lancashire and for the Gents against the Players, but he was a committed educationalist. He went straight to Churchill College, Cambridge, to become a don and retired from cricket. 'Have you really hung your boots up so soon, Edward?'

'I have not hung them up, I have nailed them to the wall.'

Mike gave up cricket and wobbled between cricket

65

and a life as a University professor. He turned his back on cricket and then turned around again. He went to America and to Newcastle University, then left to captain Middlesex and England with conspicuous skill. A.R. Lewis, who never believed that he would play cricket for long after Cambridge, wallowed in it, loved every irrelevant minute of it, and when he was done with county cricket, 12 years later, found that all he was qualified to do henceforth was to build his second career on the game by writing about it and broadcasting.

Edward Craig came to Fenners with the reputation of having scored more runs for Charterhouse than Peter May. His defence was excellent because, as he put it, his geometry was sound. To the good balls he would push out with a rather hefty front boot and close the gate between bat and pad with precision. The bad ball nearly always went for four. Among the favoured strokes was a short-arm square cut and a clipping cover drive, no fancy stroke, well on top of the ball as taught by his father in the garden at Formby.

Mike had conspicuous success against the 1961 Australians when he was not out after our first innings and then, when we followed on, he opened the batting and was not out a second time too. He was the wicket-keeper with safe hands. It was a pleasure to watch them bat in their many fine partnerships, both thoughtful, chanceless, but overflowing with humour. Indeed, when we fielded together in close positions we spent a lot of our time giggling.

Edward was forever wanting to prove that the teaspoon with which he was stirring his tea did not exist. Only Mike could understand his argument.

Mike's elegant strokeplay was later to be seen to huge effect for Middlesex and he became one of the finest of modern captains. It was possible to see the signs of this at Fenners. He was always the man who enquired, thought the matter through to the root and took positive action even if it went against convention, or, I suspect, especially if it did. He was direct with people, often argumentative, suspicious of formality.

I was keen to have my Cambridge team photographed at Lord's wearing scarves knotted and tucked inside the light blue blazer. I liked that. It reminded me of misty old pictures. Mike argued that it was unsuitable because it was hot and unnecessary. It had no sense. He was right, but, of course, dreamy-eyed nostalgia won. He perseveres. Even today he fights the tie as an accepted apparel because it is to do with protocol and not personal comfort.

A small issue, but I was not surprised that when he came to captain England he led a social revolution at the same time. He took his players to better financial arrangements, and into more positive argument against administrations of the game. He fought the cause of the common cricketer and gathered devoted support. He himself refused interviews with the media if realistic fees were not offered. His conviction was that the reporter was earning money from what he, Mike, did, so why should he not write the article or the book himself. He did, very successfully, and from such an argument began the proliferation of books by players.

What Mike Brearley had in his Fenners day, sure to stand by him, was humour and the common touch. He never adopted a stylized Oxbridge posture, it would have been abhorrent to him. He was clever, determined and a stimulating companion. You could see the determination in his batting. It was a sadness to me that Test cricket never saw the best of it, which was probably ground down by the battery of fast bowling which he had to face.

Strangely, when Mike Brearley was captain of Cambridge after me, he had problems with Edward Craig, friends as they were, because Edward lost all incentive for playing cricket, for going through the same mental exercise yet again. I recall him coming to play against Glamorgan at Margam Steelworks ground and Mike was simply trying to keep Edward going until the University match. Maybe Edward was entitled to have his mind on other matters. He was placed in the First Class in three triposes. Mike took a First in Classics and a good second in Moral Sciences. They were both a delight to play with and our friendships persist.

In fact, after a lengthy break in communications between us, Edward Craig came down to my house in Glamorgan with golf clubs for a short holiday. This was another game he had worked out, geometrically or otherwise, because he had a single-figure handicap. We were just about to leave the house for the Royal Porthcawl course when Edward, who had been tinkling at the piano said: 'Get your fiddle out Lewis.' Ten minutes later we were deep into a book of Beethoven violin and piano sonatas. We never made Royal Porthcawl that day.

In his forties Edward suddenly began to play cricket again, the game which he had dropped so brusquely. 'I unnailed my boots from the wall,' he said with a wry smile. He turned out frequently for the Quidnuncs, the University Old Boys. I accepted his invitation to a Fellows' dinner at Churchill College recently – the same wide eyes, the same humour.

I did suffer as the result of playing at Fenners, but that was not the University's fault. I went back to the pitches of Swansea and Cardiff and tried to play my stylish cover drives to balls which turned square from the first ball on the first day.

Swansea particularly was dusty and horrendously slow. Glamorgan's pitches were fixed to turn. Entertainment of almost circus variety was possible and there was always a deluge of catches popping up to short leg. I swore to Wilf Wooller that I was definitely playing for the wrong county. Leicestershire had asked me to play for them. Mike Turner the secretary had introduced me to Mr Bentley, the Leicestershire chairman, and I had been to see a house. I was to work in France at Mr Bentley's hosiery business in the winter and play cricket in the summer.

The nearest I came to that was in 1961 when I charged down the pitch at Toey Tayfield at Swansea and was stumped by yards. Gilbert Parkhouse sympathized with me. 'I'm afraid it's tough down here. I'd love the England selectors to come and play on these.' I despaired.

My cricket went backwards. I had to devise a way of tucking the bat in behind the front pad, not letting it flow freely forward; letting the ball come, nudge it to the off, tuck it around the corner to the leg. Thirty-five was a substantial score at Swansea in those days.

If I had my time again ... I would still play all my career for Glamorgan. Whatever the wicket, I was Welsh and felt it passionately. We had identity, something inside which would make us too proud to play badly without self-recrimination.

But those turners had ill effects. Glamorgan batsmen never attracted the Test selectors' eye often enough for their talents, and Jeff Jones, the fastest bowler ever to come out of Wales, was often left out of the side. Once Peter May came all the way to Swansea to see Jeff bowl and was astonished to find his Test hope was twelfth man.

Also Don Shepherd, one of the finest bowlers I have ever seen, did not get his desserts, which in my opinion should have been a long run in the England side, because it was thought that he could only bowl on these dust heaps. Far from it. He was a superb bowler on anything: full stop.

So I looked back on Cambridge without regretting the times I had tossed my wicket away through overambition. Life at Fenners had been magic. I wanted it never to end.

Then, early one misty morning, when the dancing at the Christ's May Ball had stopped, when the final champagne cork had popped, I walked in crumpled dinner jacket to the College gate, turned with Joan and took the last, long look at the First Court. I listened for a second to a distant band and set off for a match at Lord's. I would not be coming back. I felt lost: disassociated; not feeling the slightest tickle of anticipation of what was to come, just the numbness of glorious days passed.

9

Last of the Amateurs

So, right from my second county match, Wilfred Wooller, known all over Wales as The Skipper, had told me that he wanted me to captain Glamorgan one day, and that it would mean being an amateur. A few counties had made a professional their captain, but it had never happened in Glamorgan. 'I've written off to Christ's to see if we can't get you up to Cambridge. As an amateur you'll get your expenses but no match fees. Stay close to me, I'll show you the ropes.'

I was just 17. I had scored 28 runs in three first-class innings. Blushingly at first, I became not one of the boys. At lunch times, dutifully blazered and often with tie, I sat with club committeemen, either in their private dining room if they had one, or on a table away from the professionals. At Old Trafford, Mr Wooller and Mr Lewis, the only two amateurs, went through the players' dining room, where they were tucking into steak and kidney pie, to join the Lancashire committee who always lunched with some formality. Impeccably uniformed waitresses offered aperitifs and handed out menus indicating choices of meats hot or cold and often salmon. If an amateur had the misfortune to lose his wicket during the morning's play he could settle into Stilton and port with abandon. The welcome was generous; the company excellent. At first I listened to quite loud arguments about cricket. Silence got you nowhere at Old Trafford. 'Speak up lad,' I was once told. 'D'tha know nowt?'

On the major grounds the amateurs had their own dressing rooms. There was a particularly spacious one

70

upstairs at the Oval. It was just for the Skipper and me: a wall of coat pegs each, wicker armchairs for viewing the game, dressing table with clothes brushes, a basket for used hand towels. At 11.25 our personal attendant announced: 'The umpires are out and your team is ready Skipper.' And along the corridor we walked. The rest of the team tagged along behind. My first time there was in 1960, the end of the season, Alec Bedser's last match, and also the Skipper's last match before retiring, 22 years after his debut.

The Oval pitch was green and lively. We batted badly in the first innings. The Skipper stormed into the professionals' room and cursed them. He returned shouting across the dressing room at me: 'And in case you don't know it, it's the duty of the bloody amateurs to lead from the front.' He had been top scorer with 32 out of 101: I had got 5.

We followed on. The pitch was still seaming wickedly and I was in the process of scoring the longest 10 in the history of cricket, trying like a man blindfolded to lay a bat on the bowling of Alec Bedser, Peter Loader and David Gibson. It was 85 for 5. In came the Skipper. As he took guard, Peter Loader, Surrey's quick bowler, announced that he was going around the wicket. He then raced in and let go a very fast bouncer. The Skipper, six foot six, 16 stone and no hooker, turned his back on the ball, ducking his head out of sight. It hit him a thumping blow on the shoulder. Next ball Loader did the same: Wooller took it on the shoulders again and it ricocheted high in the air to Arthur McIntyre, the wicket-keeper. Loader swaggered down the pitch after this one and stared. He waited until the Skipper looked up and said, 'I've waited a long time to pin you Wooller, you bastard. You won't retire; they'll be carrying you off.'

He snatched the ball and hurried back to his mark. I was witnessing war. Bouncer after bouncer sunk into the Skipper's back and side. The repartee was hot. Wooller, the Test selector, shouted at Loader: 'God. I thought you were quick. How the hell did I ever pick you for England.

71

And you've just proved that you are a coward, Scrubs, hitting the guy who can't hit back eh!'

'I haven't finished with you yet, you big ...'

I shrank beside the umpire Eddie Phillipson. I expected the double-decker buses to stop outside the Oval and workmen to down tools on the gasometers. Loader was on his way again. Whack! Another bouncer. Thump! The ball hit the Skipper's turned back. A few balls later I was out, caught by Micky Stewart off Dave Gibson, and I left like a lad removed from a horror movie half-way through to save me from a harrowing experience.

The records have it that we were out for 137 and lost by an innings. The Skipper saw off Loader. He got 30. In our amateurs' dressing room John Evans, the physiotherapist, began to treat the scarlet blotches on the big man's body with swabs of lead and opium mixture. So this is first-class cricket, I thought.

The Skipper eased over on his side. 'Well tried, Tony,' he said. 'You didn't get many, but you stuck it out. That's what you've got to do when you're captain, when you see great pros like Hedgy and Watty playing for their lives the other end.' Bernard Hedges had got a tremendous 57, and Allan Watkins 23.

It was the first time that I learned how deeply Wilf Wooller had set himself to follow the example of Glamorgan's outstanding pre-war leader, Maurice Turnbull. 'He was an autocrat,' the Skipper recalled. 'Maurice brooked no nonsense. But he drove himself hard. He led; he took full decisions; he took full responsibility.' John Evans continued bathing the bruised body. 'That's why I'm glad you got that rugby blue, Tony. There's got to be toughness down there inside – take the knocks. D'you know, Maurice Turnbull took all the responsibility and the raps. The players just got on with their jobs. I learned some valuable lessons from him.'

I became aware of the inheritance. Wooller and Turnbull, Cambridge rugby and cricket blues, both Welsh rugby internationals; Turnbull an England crick-

eter too and a Welsh hockey and squash player; Wooller
squash for Wales and soccer for Cardiff City. I never saw
Maurice Turnbull because he was killed in action with
the Welsh Guards in 1944, but I did know other amateur
pillars of Glamorgan's brief history.

When Glamorgan became a first-class county in 1921,
Mr Norman Riches was the county's captain. In my
second XI days in the fifties he used to umpire. I
remember once going back to my stumps, missing the
ball and being plumb l.b.w. The bowler's appeal was
rejected by Mr Riches. Some overs later I stood alongside him at the non-striking end. 'Lucky to get away with
that Tony,' he said. 'Don't do it again or I shall give you
out, but d'you see,' he smiled, 'stroke-makers get two
chances with me. Blockers go first time. The game is
being ruined these days by infernal blockers. So learn
your lesson. Keep playing your strokes. Oh, by the way,
it's the same for both sides, so don't think I'm cheating.'

Trevor Arnott led Glamorgan in 1928. In later days,
when he was in his seventies, he would leave his beloved
Monmouth and make a pilgrimage to the game. However, he was never out of touch, because he wrote highly
eccentric letters or postcards to me right through the
season, often using three or four colours of pen for variety
of emphasis. 'Sorry could not get down for Worcester
game. "Great victory." Have been taking evidence re
five poachers who stole the school cricket nets to net our
salmon, so could not go to Sophia Gardens. Good luck to
the lads. "Kick high and follow up." Yours ever.
Trevor.'

Another historic figure of Welsh cricket was Johnnie
Clay. His presence at a Glamorgan match in the years
after he had stopped playing in 1949 was almost
spiritual. He would not stay for long; he would not say a
great deal, but you felt that one of the great household
gods was still keeping watch, guarding and guiding the
club he had done so much to make. He was tall, thin and
grey-haired, an elegant man, slightly stooping, padding
unobtrusively into some corner of a Glamorgan home

73

match. He was a horse-racing man. On Derby day he would arrive with a tip and stake the bet for the professionals. He cared greatly for individuals, but never fussed.

During a Glamorgan match at Neath, I was depressed because I was not scoring runs. Once again I was out quickly and went to the nets, persuading some small boys to bowl at me. Mr Clay walked over with a bit more purpose than usual. He came to the side of the net and asked me what the problem was. I told him in despair that I thought I was playing for the wrong county. 'We have slow turning wickets. I go to drive the ball and it's just not there. Coming to Glamorgan from Fenners is impossible,' I bleated. 'Do you mind if I bowl a few,' he said. He was in his sixties. Off came the jacket of his sports suit, and with a hitch of the braces, he went back to bowl. I hadn't seen the beautiful, upright action since the championship year of 1948. I was only ten then, but I can still see Mr Clay, a tall off-spinner, moving into his delivery with both arms held high to the front, peering over the left shoulder, and the ball flighted even higher.

I had never faced his bowling, nor even seen him bowling since then. The first half-dozen balls dropped embarrassingly half-way down the pitch, and then, one by one, they crept up to me. Some turned sharply. Suddenly, in one split second of illumination, I saw it all. His arm came over high and quickly, the ball looped high but still buzzed, and dipped quickly. I played forward ... and it wasn't there. I could see what all the fuss had been about J.C. Clay, how he got over 1,200 wickets for Glamorgan for less than 20 runs a piece – dragging the batsman forward, making the ball loop, turning it square. He did not tell me how I should play spin. He just explained what he was trying to do. He described how he used to practise, even at home, spending hour after hour in his outdoor net at his beautiful home in St Hilary in the Vale of Glamorgan, bowling and bowling. They say he used to walk through the streets of Cowbridge squeezing a tough rubber ball.

'I wanted strong fingers. I always tried to spin it. I always wanted to get the batsman forward. The most difficult man to get out was the man who waited for the ball, or came out very quickly to the pitch of it.'

We practised a little longer. I was far from perfect and he was perhaps 25 years off his best, but I always felt that the beginning of my competent batting against spin began with the understanding of what Mr Clay had been up to most of his life.

J.C. Clay, Wykehamist, landowner, successful businessman, was the true amateur. Indeed he was prepared to tell the England selectors in 1935 that he did not wish to waste any more of his time being twelfth man for England. He had been called to the first four Tests, but not included in the side. Only his family persuaded him to turn up in hope at the Oval for the fifth. He played and bowled well. His only Test.

By the fifties it was unrealistic to expect many cricketers to be financially independent of the game. From as early as 1949 there was a classic example of how professional captaincy could work in Warwickshire. Tom Dollery led his team to the County Championship in 1951. Len Hutton had become the first professional captain of England in 1952, although he was never the appointed captain of Yorkshire. Yet even that county, which stuck hard by tradition, put the professional Vic Wilson in charge in 1960.

There were two popular ways of retaining amateur status. For instance, Ossie Wheatley, after taking over the Glamorgan captaincy from Wilfred Wooller in 1961, was attached to an advertising business. His public prominence was useful to his partners. I went the other way. County clubs took the occasional amateur on the payroll as assistant secretary or secretary. I was briefly the assistant secretary of Glamorgan. Both methods brought cries of shamateurism. Compared with the Johnny Clays of the world, of course we were. However, I could still argue that I was not paid to play cricket. In that one year, I worked through the winter on a membership campaign for Glamorgan, travelling up and down the country with a professional fund-raiser. In the summer I played cricket. I got £800 for the year. The professional received £800 too, but just for the summer's work. They were at liberty to find jobs in the winter. They certainly earned a good deal more than I did per annum.

Wilfred Wooller was paid only as secretary too. In Derbyshire there was Donald Carr, in Hampshire Desmond Eager, Trevor Bailey in Essex, all secretary-captains and amateur cricketers. Inevitably the pretence ended. The dying rites of amateurism came in 1962 with the last of the famous series of Gentlemen versus Players matches, the traditional event at Lord's in June, then the echo, played in more lighthearted mood, at Scarborough in September. I played in both of them.

For the Lord's match, Ossie Wheatley, Peter Walker and I travelled together from Glamorgan's previous game. We were good friends, always spending a lot of our spare time together, but on this occasion we had to split. Peter got out of the car on the Edgware Road and set off for the professional's hotel; we joined the amateurs at the Great Western at Paddington.

On the morning of the match the press paraded photographs of Colin Cowdrey, Ted Dexter and the Reverend David Sheppard, asking which would lead MCC to Australia the following winter. Cowdrey had been the original choice to lead the Gents but was ill; the Reverend David Sheppard had volunteered an interruption of his ecclesiastical calling and was thought sure to get the captaincy if he got runs in this match. Dexter was actually leading the Gentlemen, but many believed him to be an aloof outsider. I felt I was an irrelevancy, although I had scored over 1,300 runs for Cambridge by July. I guess I was one likely to benefit from the experience.

No one knew that this was the very last Gents v. Players match to be played at Lord's. There was no nostalgic reference to the series which had begun in 1786.

I wish I had kept an official scorecard.

It is worth recording the teams: Gentlemen – Rev. D.S. Sheppard, E.J. Craig, E.R. Dexter (captain), M.J.K. Smith, R.M. Prideaux, A.R. Lewis, R.W. Barber, D.B. Pithey, T.E. Bailey, A.C. Smith, O.S. Wheatley. Players – M.J. Stewart, J.H. Edrich, P.H. Parfitt, T.W. Graveney, P.J. Sharpe, P.M. Walker, F.J. Titmus, F.S. Trueman (captain), K.V. Andrew, N. Gifford, D. Shackleton.

The match was drawn; David Sheppard got a solid century and Ted Dexter was made captain for Australia. A.R. Lewis, batting at six, mustered only 2 and 10 before falling to Shackleton and Titmus.

In the following November the announcement came from Lord's that amateurs and professional would henceforth all be known as cricketers.

There was one small flourish to be enacted before that happened, the Gentlemen against Players match at Scarborough in September, another annual encounter but played before holiday crowds with nothing at stake. It was always relaxed and fun. My Scarborough Festival memories are among the richest I have.

The amateurs stayed in the Grand Hotel, a giant, Victorian stone-built edifice perched on the cliff tops. Lifts took people down the steep slope to the level of the promenade with its amusements, its theatres and long beach. The professionals stayed at the Balmoral, which we called the 'Immoral', now deceased.

The Festival was managed benignly but firmly by Tom Pearce, the former Essex captain. There were usually three matches, T.N. Pearce's XI against the Tourists, MCC v Yorkshire, and the Gentlemen against the Players. The Gentlemen, who, of course, had no fee for playing, had their hotel bills paid, wives included.

Play was from 11 o'clock until 6 o'clock and the Scarborough brass band played off and on in their little bandstand all through the day. There was often some casual cricket, but you could not fool a Yorkshire crowd for long. Also there were first-class runs and wickets at stake, the guarantee that players were trying.

The Scarborough ground is open, fresh with sea air and yet intimate. On one side is a spectator bank built into a natural slope and along the path at the top was a small line of bars. In the days when the taste was for a lager or two, we called it Denmark.

For lunch we would walk across the field to small marquees draped in bright colours and prettied with potted plants and flowers. There was no rush. It was a social, even sartorial perambulation; no autograph request was turned down because of haste. A dry sherry or two, a gin maybe, before luncheon, earnest conversation with guests of the festival, civic dignitaries, workers for cricket, representatives of the splendid Scarborough Cricket Club, the aroma of hydrangea and colourful geranium, ladies in wide-brimmed hats, Stilton cheese, a glass of vintage port and back to the game. Just outside the marquee you could give a sympathetic nod to the third cornet player whose valves had been full of spittle throughout the lunchtime recital.

The other formality of the play was at the 6 o'clock close. Players and umpires stood to attention, hands rigidly to sides, while the band played 'God Save the Queen'. Then, it was amateurs back to the Grand and into black tie each night for drinks in the Pearce's first-floor suite. Dinner guests would join there and Mrs Stella Pearce would issue the orders for escorting this or that lady to dinner ... down the wide central staircase into the palm court: To the left, the trio would be playing, piano, violin and cello, out in front sat the cricket lovers, sipping their drinks and staring at the ensemble which descended to dinner at the famous Cricketers' Room. It was a glittering ritual repeated nightly.

Regular attenders were former Yorkshire players, Norman Yardley, Don Brennan and Brian Sellars of the severe countenance and intimidating reputation. 'Na' then y'Welsh bastard. What d'y make of this bluddy lot then?' – his usual greeting.

Always there was Major Leveson-Gower, nephew of

the famous Shrimp Leveson-Gower. The Major was diminutive, balding and bespectacled and was famed for his faultless remembering of Bradshaw, the railway timetable – he was what was called a movement officer in wartime – and also for standing on tiptoe and peering down the fronts of ladies' evening dresses. Greta Bailey, Trevor's wife, as mischievous as any, would fabricate some journey of extreme complexity which she was due to make on a Sunday of course – 'Tell me, Major, I would like to be at a meeting of the Lowestoft Womens' Circle, a week on Sunday, at half-past two in the afternoon.'

'Ah!' the little major would exclaim loudly, moving in close for a peep. 'Now then! You would need the 06.13 from Scarborough, changing at Malton, for the 07.00 for York. There is a Sunday goods train with two carriages for passenger accommodation from York to Scunthorpe ... then Scunthorpe to Grimsby, down to Boston for the 11.04 ...'

'But why can't I go straight to London and out to Lowestoft from there, Major?' Greta would ask, moving even closer.

'Ah! But you see! You'd arrive cross country in Lowestoft at 14.07, eight changes, and from London not until 14.24. Cutting it a bit fine for your meeting don't you think.'

Besides which, it was much more fun for the Major. As Colin Ingleby-MacKenzie prompted the ladies to wear dresses more and more revealing as the Festival went on, the Major's train routes got even more amazingly complex.

The Cricketers' Room took three or four large tables, some 30 diners maybe, and around the panelled walls hung a framed photograph of every amateur who ever went there to Festival cricket.

After dinner, the younger brigade made a speedy retreat to the Balmoral, where dancing began in earnest, where professionals and amateurs were all cricketers. It had always been the natural order of things.

Trevor Arnott would often send me one of his erratic postcards to the Grand at Scarborough.

Monmouth
Tony,
I hope you enjoyed Scarborough. Lovely Festival. John Clay and I once played there when there was plenty of grouse, york ham, etc. John Clay and I played there when the late Lord Harewood was alive. It was the year when I drove Jack Mercer after we had defeated Notts. at Swansea. We had to pull up in Nottingham for petrol. We had some dinner etc. We saw in the paper that the local press had referred to us insulting Nottinghamshire prestige at Swansea as the band did not turn out (Red Rose won the Championship that year). Yours ever, Trevor.

Eventually the cricket at Scarborough became irrelevant. It lacked seriousness and cricket looks a poor game when it is frivolous. It did take on fresh importance from 1971 to 1981 because a devoted patron emerged who believed in the old Leveson–Gower maxim, 'sportsmanship and fun at the seaside'. This was Sydney Hainsworth, Chairman and Managing Director of Fenner and Company of Hull, who put up the Fenner Trophy for competition over three days in limited-over matches, much more in the vogue of the day.

Unfortunately the first-class season, with its spreading competitions, elbowed into the Scarborough time of the year. Sydney reluctantly heeded the changing times. He ended his patronage of the Festival with a story by Lord Willis. Lord Willis sent a script to J. B. Priestley and asked, 'Should I put more fire into this play?' Priestley answered, 'No. I should put the play into the fire.' That is what Sydney did to the Fenner Trophy.

Indeed, the official abolition of amateurism, when it came, meant that amateurs like me, who had struggled financially in order to retain that status, were at last paid for playing. Sir Jack Hobbs made a most understanding comment. He said, 'It is sad to see the passing of the amateur. They were a great asset to the game, much appreciated by all of us because they were able to come in and play freely, whereas many professionals did not feel they could take the chances. Now, times are different and I can understand the position of the amateur who has to make his living. You cannot expect him to refuse good offers outside cricket.'

Thus amateurism melted into changing times, and cricket lost a lot which it has never replaced. It lost the man who was not dependent on the whim of a committee for his livelihood, who had style and presence and who was not easily deflected from the purpose of nurturing good cricket. Most importantly, I think, he was the man who could afford time to attend to the aspirations of the professionals without envy, without putting himself in a position of professional competition with them.

It can be argued that my own amateur life had been contrived and therefore artificial – false. However, I must tell you that I have been forever grateful to Wilfred Wooller for imposing it on me. It was no more artificial than assuming military rank, but you had to be worth it.

My true acceptance, by Wooller, as a worthy amateur tough enough to play first-class cricket came at the Flying Horse Hotel, Nottingham, one Saturday night when the Glamorgan team were celebrating. Peter Walker had won a case of champagne for taking the most catches in the month. We added Guinness to make black velvet. There was a lounge area, a recess opposite the hotel reception. The team sat around, the Skipper stood at one end, in front of an ornate fireplace, and I was in front of another fireplace opposite him. We were about a dozen yards apart. Suddenly he called 'Tony'. I looked up. He was lifting a hefty onyx clock from the mantel-piece. Then he shaped up like a scrum half, swung his arms back, and sent a massive pass across the room to me.

I caught it full on the chest bones and the weight knocked me over, backwards. I heard the laughter as I disappeared, half-way up the chimney of a mock Adam fireplace. The face of the clock fell open and a spring popped out! I was winded, but staggered up. With my own imitation of a rugby scrum half I winged it back to our giant leader who simply plucked it out of the air and replaced it on the shelf as if it was a small travelling clock. There was applause from the team. A sip or two later, when the incident had passed, I went off to the gents lavatory. God, that clock gave me a crack, I thought.

Suddenly, I was not alone. A large shadow fell across the porcelain. The Skipper. He slapped me on the shoulder, almost knocking me straight down the urinal.

'Bloody great,' he said. 'You got up and threw it back. Now they know what you're made of.'

There was a pause for nature. Suddenly he said, 'Call me Wilf.'

Amateurism perished at a time when the nature of authority in all departments of life changed. Rank or position gained through inherited wealth, public school or Oxbridge was being questioned at every turn and no longer sat easily in a country soon led to comprehensive education. Yet it was simple to see that the traditional educational institutions still bred men who could lead with independent spirit, men who stood above the carpings of a cricket committee, who had the bravado to chase a victory when others played safe; men who were hard but fair, and honourable and sporting in victory or defeat.

In fact I do not think that the Glamorgan players, with whom I had grown up, or by whom I had been coached, seriously objected to the shamateur status. In a way they were happy to have their amateurs so that they were free from responsibility.

I know that the senior Glamorgan players, Bernard Hedges, Don Shepherd and Jim Pressdee often said that they felt sorry for me, having to carry on irrelevant conversations with committeemen over lunch. However, their key question about an amateur captain in the late fifties and sixties was 'Can he play?' There were still those in county cricket who were captains only because they were amateur but were not very good players.

Amateurism disappeared overnight. I would not have argued its retention, but 20 years later I can see that its best qualities of independence and unselfishness have not been replaced by anything half as good. When amateurism went, cricket then became, in the minds of all eleven men in the team, a cash business. It is the worse for it.

10

Full-time Cricketer

Deciding to play full-time cricket after coming down from Cambridge in the summer of 1962 was not difficult because there was nothing else I looked likely to do better. My third-class BA degree would convert painlessly enough into an MA after five years, upon payment of £7, but probably it meant that I myself would convert into a third-class schoolmaster.

However, most young men, given a chance, would give cricket a go. The life is fun; there are new friends to be made; another town, another brewer to be sampled. It is a tiring job, fielding all day, travelling all evening, but you are carried along by the never-say-die spirit of an itinerant theatre company. You love the applause. Leave the field at Hove with your bat aloft, acknowledging the clapping for your fine play, and the seven hours by road to Swansea for the next day's play seems like seven minutes. Nor does the greasepaint ever come off cleanly. This is why a cricketer at the end of his career is deeply hurt when a committeeman taps him on the shoulder and tells him that it is time to go. It is the severing of his emotional bond with the game and its life-pattern.

My father had relinquished hopes that I would become a solicitor. Occasionally I still thought of playing the violin in a professional orchestra, but mostly I imagined playing for Glamorgan. So, I left the 1962 University match and travelled to join the Glamorgan team at Bath for a match against Somerset. I had a £500 overdraft in the bank but my fiancée, Joan, who had gone home to Neath, teaching to save for a year, had collected £350 in the bottom drawer! By the end of this same Somerset match, the savings and the fiancée had gone.

It was hot, sunny weather. Glamorgan were in the field. My captain, Ossie Wheatley, sent me to third man with the instruction, 'Take a look at that while you are down on the boundary, A.R.' He pointed to a young lady, dressed attractively under a black, wide brimmed straw hat which shielded her face. Nice shape, I thought, good legs. I had got within 20 yards when the brim of the hat lifted suddenly, like a visor. It was Joan. 'Hi,' I said. 'Thought you were at home. Great to see you.' I should have detected by the firm-footed stance and the folded arms that she was at battle stations.

She marched a dozen yards infield, over the boundary line; embarrassing, in front of hundreds of Somerset spectators perched on temporary stands in that quarter of the ground. She then made her speech. 'If it is your wish to take the Bishop of Portsmouth's daughter to the Christ's Marguerites' cocktail party and not me, then you can jolly well marry her.' Next, in a ceremony cheered loudly by the Somerset fans, she removed her engagement ring from the third finger, drew back her arm like a javelin thrower, and hurled it at me. Spectators were now on their feet clapping as she turned on her high heels and left.

First-class cricket is best played with a clear mind and I cannot say that I concentrated on a single ball bowled from then on. There is something distinctly uncomfortable about fielding with your engagement ring back in your pocket.

I saw her drive away in a gleaming new Mini – she had blown her savings.

We were married three weeks later.

I had drifted into first-class cricket on a golden wave. It had mostly gone right. I was now cossetted by predictions of playing for England, even captaining. Yet I failed to ask myself important questions – how badly did I want to succeed?

The answer, with hindsight, is that in those early years I was never single-minded enough about first-class cricket to ensure continued personal success. The life was good; the life was fun; but only for two or three days a week was I a dedicated professional player. There was far too much to see and experience in the world to lock myself into a mere game for six days a week. I used to stand in the outfield at the Oval and look longingly at the City, imagining fascinating business being enacted; I would race away from Lord's with Peter Walker to a Promenade concert. Once I shouted out with cramp, curled up on the floor with the promenaders, but luckily in the middle of a blast of brass and chorus in Belshazar's Feast.

I collected antiques. I used to buy silver, usually in unfashionable corners, in order to sell when Glamorgan were at the smarter resorts such as Hove, Cheltenham or Harrogate. I was often with the dealers by 9.15 in the morning to make my turn of profit before net practice.

Not surprisingly, I got to know John Arlott well. He stayed with me sometimes in Wales, though his landlord-in-chief was another collector, Wilf Wooller. I bought my first antique furniture with their advice in Bowns of Pontypridd. I helped John too by looking out around the cricket circuit for Sunderland Plate and Stevengraphs. These interests and the sheer joy of being in a most generous fraternity had me meandering through three poor seasons without dreadful worry but without consistent batting form either.

There was a serious cricket factor too. It was a scramble to get together a technique to stay at the crease on Glamorgan's poor pitches, let alone hit the ball for runs. I was also an infuriating perfectionist. What a cheek I had, when I was not prepared to give cricket every ounce of my attention. If I was playing badly I would be happier getting out than fighting on. This also was the result of too many people expecting too glossy a career from me. There is nothing more delightfully perverse than to play as badly as you want rather than as

86

perfectly as they insist. Don Shepherd, Glamorgan's senior player for so long, always used to tell me that if I had been short of money and had been forced to score runs for the next tin of baked beans, then I would have succeeded right from the start.

Professionals do not look kindly on players who are cavalier about their game. There were always bitter objections in the fifties when an amateur schoolmaster came into the county team for August and some devoted professional had to go down to the seconds. In Gloucestershire in the sixties there were mutterings about the captain C.T.M. Pugh, an old Etonian, who scarcely batted well enough to hold a place but was there to preserve the tradition of the amateur leader. In fact some Gloucestershire professionals supported him – they saw Tom Pugh as a brave man, who listened carefully to his senior advisers, but who never shirked to play the game his way – others were damning.

However, in Glamorgan, for me there was always firm advice from Don Shepherd, Bernard Hedges and Jim Pressdee who had coached me in nets from an early age. They would never allow anyone to toy with the game at which they worked so devotedly.

Glamorgan's pitches were ill-prepared. Cardiff Arms Park looked rough, turned sharply and often kept low. St Helens, in Swansea, had light dust rolled into the top, and the very first ball of the day would turn a yard. At the other grounds there was no regular county cricket, so pitches at Llanelli, Neath, Pontypridd, Ebbw Vale and Newport were always heavily watered to keep them safe. This helped us to get results at home but it also spun away the confidence of young batsmen like Alan Jones, Alan Rees, Bill Slade, Euros Lewis and me.

Every pitch was slow. I can remember thinking that at Swansea a half-volley is no longer a half-volley. Batting became an exercise in waiting for the ball and 'working' it with the spin. I could see that, even though I was not spending enough time at the crease to employ this new method. I would play forward and pop the ball into the hands of short square-leg. In order to avoid that, there was the slog over mid-wicket which usually was caught. Off-spin was the problem; oddly enough, the ball that left the bat was less lethal. It did not mean to say that I scored freely all around the wicket off left-armers, but I did late cut and dab the odd ball square through the covers.

I made a study of those batsmen who did manage a long innings in these conditions. All had one move in common – the forward defensive stroke was played with the front pad, the bat tucked in behind the leading leg. Sometimes, when a ball of full length pitched outside off-stump, Gilbert Parkhouse and Bernard Hedges swept it to leg. Jim Pressdee spent a lot of the time whipping the ball hard off the back foot. Bernard had a very individual shot, best played by a short man as he was, a short-armed pull shot, right elbow tucked into the body, off the back foot, over mid-wicket. I took note that the play of all three of these good players involved improvization.

Unfortunately, after struggling on slow pitches for a game or two, Glamorgan batsmen found it difficult to bat away from home on hard fast surfaces. Caught Dawkes bowled Jackson; caught Booth bowled Flavell; caught Parks bowled Thomson – these would be among the popular early exits taken by Glamorgan batsmen groping with extra speed and bounce away from home.

It was only when I lost a lot of pride, some four seasons later, that I was prepared to bat badly but stay at the crease. The death-wish receded and I was prepared to get scruffy 30s and untidy half-centuries.

I would have been a better player for another county with more runs to my name, but would not have been half the cricketer in the end.

Meanwhile the Welsh crowd bayed. The college boy was overrated. 'What do you think of Walker dropping that catch, Lewis?' a loud watcher asked at Neath.

'Oh! I wouldn't think it was a catch, it went quickly, I'm glad I wasn't there myself,' I replied.

'No. It would 'ave 'it you straight in the bloody mouth.'

Winter jobs were important to county cricketers. They always struggled to find regular out-of-season employment. Cricket was not the 12-month-a-year pursuit which it became after the Kerry Packer revolution in 1977. In the sixties, cricketers were still locked into the feudal practice of touching forelocks to committeemen and businessmen during the summer in the hope of getting a job and a pay-packet in the winter. I remember hearing of Ray Illingworth and Brian Bolus selling fireworks, which everyone thought was the perfect seasonal employment if followed up with Christmas cards and Valentine cards. John Snow and Alan Knott very publicly signed on the dole.

Most dispersed in September, some to the most menial tasks. It never made sense. For example, how could a Glamorgan captain expect Eifon Jones or Jeff Jones to walk down the steps in summer with the self-confidence to perform great deeds when Eifon had spent the winter digging holes in the road for the Swansea Corporation and Jeff reading gas metres in Bridgend?

I leapt at a job as an account executive with an advertising agency. I was very much the foot-in-the-door cricket personality who bore art work under his arm muttering, without confidence, 'London creative skills, Sir, at provincial prices'.

However, it was when Glamorgan were playing Essex at Leyton in mid-August 1965 that the message came of the advertising agency's closing of the Cardiff office. A fortnight to the winter labours and I was out of work. I immediately shared the news with the gentleman to my left on the pavilion verandah, Michael Melford, who was there to report the game for the *Daily Telegraph*. I had once written an article for him on Welsh cricket in the *World of Cricket*. 'Would reporting rugby appeal?' was his instant reaction. 'Yes. Anything,' I volunteered. 'There's only a fortnight before the season ends.'

Five minutes and one telephone call later I had the offer of a job from Kingsley Wright, Sports Editor of the

Daily Telegraph. Welsh rugby reports, £5 a match, 4p a mile and £2 subsistence: freelance – no work, no pay. I have always been indebted to Michael Melford for his generous help and because he linked two of my loves in one occupation, games and writing. It was much more than just another winter job. I knew it.

To complete my luck, floodlit rugby was spreading quickly around South Wales. There were many mid-week matches, and so I was on the telephone all the time to Kingsley Wright assuring him that every next encounter should not be missed by the *Daily Telegraph* readers.

'There's a surprising interest, Kingsley, in tomorrow's game at Abertillery.'

'Who's at Abertillery, old boy?'

'The Metropolitan Police, Kingsley.'

'Good grief, old boy, we can't take that.'

'But there's this policeman, d'y remember the one who saved the dog in the pond in Richmond, Kingsley? He's on the wing.'

'No. Forget that one, old boy, absolutely irrelevant.'

'But it kicks off at seven o'clock, Kingsley.' That would be my last desperate throw. Copy in by 8.30 was gold dust to the sports desk. Kingsley was never enamoured of the 7.30 kick-off with play dragging on until 9 o'clock and copy floating in right up to edition dead-line.

However, Kingsley Wright supported me. He knew that I needed every tiny fee and often eased up in conversation – 'Alright, Tony, old boy, now let me just take a look at the Welsh page lay-out again. And it could stay in the London. Right! Go and see your Metropolitan Police in Abertillery. Give me six paragraphs in all, 45 words a paragraph ... but not a word more d'y understand?' Apart from the *Telegraph*, I would wait days, weeks and months for the telephone to ring. Maybe an article for the *Welsh Rugby* magazine or the *Cricketer*. Freelance journalists have independence, they can work at home, they can be their own bosses, but they do need the telephone to ring.

BBC Wales phoned. It was Tom Davies, radio Sports Producer, asking me to the studio in Park Place, Cardiff, to perform a report on the rugby game I was seeing for the *Telegraph*. 1 minute and 15 seconds; which, I recall from the fear of going over, was 227 words.

I used to read these words out solemnly until one day I was forced to busk a bit. It was the most important experience. I was retreating quickly from a Llanelli match at Stradey Park to the BBC studios in Swansea. I was held up in heavy traffic; the programme, *Sports Medley*, was getting closer but the studio was still a long way away. I made a telephone call and warned Tom. He told me to try to get there, but use a telephone box report if I failed.

I settled for a telephone report some ten minutes before the programme started, but when I got to a telephone box it had been vandalized. I drove on. A second box was out of order. I drove on. I reached the third as the programme went on the air. The phone worked but the box had no lights and it was dark outside. I was through to the Cardiff studio, and, in pitch blackness, dashed outside and held up my script in the beam of my car headlights to memorize the scorers. When I got the phone back to my ear, John Darren, the presenter, was saying, 'A lot of points, Tony Lewis, I guess the going was good and firm.'

I blurted out my scorers and chatted for about a minute and a quarter or thereabouts. The verdict from Tom Davies, was that, give or take a few seconds, it was one of my best reports, but who would have the guts to go into the studio with a list of scorers only every week?

It so happened that one Saturday evening after rugby I encountered one of the country's most brilliant broadcasters, Alan Gibson. It was in Bristol. I had been asked to report on a Bristol v. Cardiff match. Alan presented the Saturday evening *Sports Report*. I arrived with my 227 written words.

'No,' he said kindly but pointedly. 'We don't write

reports on this programme. What I'd like is the scorers – write those down – but then tell us in your own words how the game went and what you thought of it.' A flood of sweat gathered under the armpits, but Mr Gibson did seem quite positive; there was no chink for debating it. So, sitting tensely, I did what I was told.

'Very good,' he said afterwards. 'Just what we want. Very natural.' The tiny penny then dropped. If I wrote my 227 words in talking language, not in the *Daily Telegraph* sentences full of sub-clauses, then I would sound more natural. An enjoyable career outside cricket was starting.

There was one other occupation in the early freelance days which raised an eyebrow or two in the cricket world. Joan, my wife, left teaching and opened a boutique for ladies in Rhiwbina, a suburb of Cardiff. A new vogue of youthful, bright fashion had sprung from Carnaby Street in London. It had spawned a new generation of young designers and hopeful shopkeepers who became so popular that the traditional wholesalers based on Great Portland Street had to dance quickly to keep in step. Our Popsie Boutique was the first boutique in Cardiff.

So, in the winter months, I found myself sitting at trade fashion shows in London, appraising the latest designs of Mary Quant, Jean Muir, John Varon, Tuffin and Foale, and even Laura Ashley, who was then selling from her house in Carno, mid-Wales. I can remember sitting at a Mary Quant show next to a big London buyer.

'I like that,' she turned to say.

'Yes, lovely cut,' I volunteered. 'Nicely waisted without being too severe, don't you think?'

'I agree.' She looked down at her order form. 'I think a gross in a 34, a gross in 36 ...'

I turned to Joan. 'What do you think of this little number ... apart from the model, I mean, who's got a great figure?'

'Well, I think it would look nice on Mrs Paine, don't

you. We could afford one in a 34, that's her size. Perhaps one in a 36 as well.'

Two ticks on the sheet and the business was done. In fact we used to work hard, often having garments packed while we waited and driving them back to Cardiff, so that I could genuinely boast of the latest London fashions on your provincial doorstep. I was not a lot of use to the boutique except for helping fetch and carry at fashion shows and leaping into black tie to compère them.

In the tiny boutique, I tended to put off potential customers when my wife was in London buying and I was left behind the counter. However, there was a day of bumper takings when a fey gent insisted that the six suspender belts of assorted colours would all fit perfectly. He bought the lot.

Popsie Boutique was easily our best money-earner. Then suddenly came two daughters, Joanna and Anabel, and that particular game was up.

The mood of the Glamorgan side was set by Ossie Wheatley, the captain from 1961 to 1966. Physically he had charm and authority – well over six feet tall, blond, flapping hair, a deep rich voice and the most genial company. He felt strongly that cricket matches were there to be won; always go for the 10 points to win and then they would be interesting to watch and to play. The 2 points for first innings lead did not appeal. By his warm approach to opposing captains he persuaded them too to approach the game in his way. His declarations were fair; he would call for a spurt from any batsman if he felt their efforts were not dovetailed to the whole purpose and he set a high personal example by his outstanding bowling. His 715 wickets for Glamorgan in his six seasons cost only 18.67 runs each.

He was a good enough swing and seam bowler to get wickets on Swansea turners. He was unathletic and lumbered in to bowl, head rolling, but, at the crease, he had the perfect sideways-on action, the strong pivot of the taut front leg and the perfect wrist position to bowl his stock away-swinger. His in-swinger, or rather, the ball that drifted in late, was performed with exactly the same arm action but just a late, hardly perceptible roll of the wrist.

He consistently dismissed the best batsmen in the country. For a while Roy Marshall, one of the most dangerous strokemakers in the game, was one. Roy confessed over a beer one night that he had made a mistake about Ossie. 'When he came in plodding, with that blond hair coming down over his eyes and his head lolling from side to side, I thought to myself, this fella can't bowl, but I kept on getting out.' Unluckily for Glamorgan Roy then decided to play Ossie with exaggerated respect and a defensive straight bat before cutting loose. This he did at Cardiff in 1964. We had just beaten the Australian tourists in an exciting game at Swansea. It was hot and sunny. The scorecard read: R. Marshall, 180. Ossie Wheatley was a good enough bowler to play for England at a time when Flavell, Coldwell, Rumsey, Larter and White were getting their Test chances, but his lumbering fielding style must have gone against him.

However, there was in Glamorgan a fast bowler who did impress the selectors, Jeff Jones. Jeff bowled left-arm over the wicket with a lively, long-striding action. His body arched into a magnificent coiled spring before the delivery, and when it uncoiled he was genuinely fast. This speed could be engendered from a short run-up. Batting against him in the pre-season nets at Neath could be frightening. He was tall enough to get high bounce and the sound of the ball smashing into the wooden indoor pitch echoed ominously.

Jeff was a natural for MCC abroad. He offered a touring captain a change of angle and real speed. He could bowl ferocious bouncers. However he never managed the art of swinging the ball into the bat, unless the ball was brand new. To get his speed he fell away to

94

deliver the ball from near the popping crease.

I recall Colin Cowdrey, on his way to West Indies in 1967, writing to me to ask if I had any helpful observations to make about Jeff's field placings. I suggested that Colin took a view himself from first slip or from his wicket-keeper to discover the instant that Jeff stopped swinging the ball in from off to leg. Immediately, backward short-leg had to be put across to slip or gully. If he waited too long a catch could easily fly off the outside edge. It was the lack of the in-swing which stopped him from entering the Alan Davidson, Gary Sobers class. Jeff's ferocity as a bowler contrasted with his delightful nature and quiet humour. A superb team man.

When he was quick he was very very quick. There was a day at Swansea in 1967 when Worcestershire were in brutal form with the bat. Swansea pitches were by now excellent. At last, soon after lunch, we got a wicket, but that only sounded a fanfare for Tom Graveney to tip toe down long terrace steps the familiar slope of the right shoulder, the cap peak slanting upwards. Formidable! I went to Jeff. 'The ball is a bit rough now, but slip three or four quick overs at T.W.G. will you Jeff?'

'There's no one I would like to roll over better. Gimme the ball, skip.' Both Tom and Jeff had been part of Colin Cowdrey's successful tour of the Caribbean.

Tom played right out of character. In the first place he played back instead of forwards. He was nearly always on the front foot; I had seen him with my own eyes hook Wes Hall and Charlie Griffith for sixes off the front foot. Jeff stormed in again. He was fast. Again, back went Graveney. Playing and missing. Next came the deliberate positioning of a square leg. Whack! The bouncer went in and was perfectly lined. This was Jeff's strength; the ball lifting sharply from outside leg stump could cramp the batsman and get his bat handle and gloves, elbows and head in a terrible tangle. Tom Graveney tried a hook, but the ball was on the splice of the bat

95

and up into square leg's hands. Graveney, c. b. Jones 0
for 2.

'Great Jeff, c'mon. Let's have a few more overs at this
speed and we could get out of this trouble.' He took his
sweater. Laughed and said in the soft gentle voice which
belied his ferocity. 'I enjoyed that captain.'

One of the bravest innings I ever saw was against Jeff
Jones at Grace Road, Leicester, in 1965. The batsman
was David Constant, now a Test umpire. It rained on the
first day; only two hours play was possible. Leicester at
the close were 64 for 6. The last four wickets put on 63.
117 all out, Ossie Wheatley 6 wickets for 54. We also
struggled on a lively pitch, the ball lifting and seaming,
but slowly enough for the occasional readjustment of
stroke. The stand between Jim Pressdee (38) and Alan
Rees (43) gave us a substantial advantage. 185 all
out, the wickets falling to Cotton, Marner, and Greensword.

Last day. The pitch now looked dry though still
grassy. Jeff Jones ran into bowl to Maurice Hallam. It
was a flier. The ball leapt up off the surface which had
clearly hardened yet still carried moisture. It whizzed
past Maurice's nose. David Evans, the wicket-keeper,
consulted with his slip fielders and retreated 30 yards.
Six of them lined up quite close to the boundary. In came
Jeff Jones. Again the ball took off, and Maurice Hallam
was felled by a blow to the heart. Next ball, Maurice
flashed, got a nick and shouted 'catch it' back to the
slips. Peter Walker, standing well over six feet, had to
jump to take the catch left-handed at first slip. It was
frightening to watch.

Brian Booth went next, then Peter Marner, both
caught behind. In came Stanley Jayasinghe, the popular
and talented Ceylonese batsman. He adopted alarming
tactics. As Jeff Jones was bounding in, Stanley was
walking down the pitch, sideways on towards him. In
went the ball, short. It flew off the greasy surface and
then there was a crack as it struck the Jayasinghe hip
bone. Stanley was a very thin man. This was a case of

ball on bone without the benefit of any flesh padding between. He went down with a wail of agony. After a considerable time he was able to turn over on the ground and, looking up with a large smile, he took a cricket sock out of his left pocket. 'Do you know! Damn ball missed my thigh-pad.' Unbelievable! Fancy taking on one of the fastest bowlers in the country, on the fastest wicket in the world, with a sock for a thigh-pad! His Ceylonese team-mate Clive Inman completed a 'pair'. Jeff Jones had taken 5 wickets for no runs.

Meanwhile batsman number 6, a short man, was being pounded in all parts of the body but still got behind the ball and prodded it away. David Constant batted left-handed for Kent and then for Leicestershire. He was always a struggling player, but no one suspected that he was so brave and determined. Four wickets fell at the other end, Greensword a noble 14, Julian 2, Barratt a heroic 11, Savage 1 and Cotton 0. David went into bat when 4 wickets were down for 2 runs and was not out 9 at the end. Leicestershire were all out for 40. Ossie Wheatley took 2 for 29 and Jeff Jones had the astonishing figures 13 overs, 9 maidens, 11 runs, 8 wickets. He was terrifying.

Glamorgan's best uncapped bowler was Don Shepherd. 2,174 wickets at 20.87 runs each. A superb career. He was a devastating match-winner, season after season. Don was brought up the hard way in cricketing terms. He was on the Lord's ground staff, pulled the heavy roller, bowled at members for a shilling and sold scorecards: the strictest apprenticeship. He set a perfect example of discipline and behaviour to everyone. He had standards which helped Glamorgan to be neat in appearance and clear-thinking at play. 'Treasure your action,' I can hear him advising young bowlers. 'Never believe that it will look after itself. Keep sideways, look at the batsman from behind the left arm, pivot, follow through. Check it all the time. Your action is your most precious possession. Keep its rhythm.'

He bowled off-cutters at medium pace. He was frugal.

97

He loved control. Don's action was high, handsome and as regular in stride and turn of arm as a metronome. He was, above all, thoughtful and competitive. He read batsmen well. Don did not play for England because someone believed it was necessary to have a bowler who fitted into the classical category of slow off-spinner. If you asked a batsman of the sixties which bowlers he would hate to meet in a match, many would have included Derek Shackleton of Hampshire, Tom Cartwright, then of Warwickshire, and Don Shepherd. Shepherd was the only one not to get a Test call. Perhaps his success on Welsh turning wickets led selectors to think that he would not be as effective on good pitches. If so, they were wrong.

Glamorgan were, above all, good fun. We were a highly muscial outfit. Once upon a time it was all Welsh hymns and folk songs. My first memory was of Willie Jones and John Evans, our loyal friend and physiotherapist, standing on chairs in the bar on a Saturday night singing Oes Gafr Eto. Almost everyone knew the words of the Welsh favourites. Don Shepherd with a couple of pints down could be found in a corner forlornly trying to pitch E flat to start up a rendering of the hymn tune Llef, proving again that only the Welsh express great joy in the minor key.

David Evans was by far the most moving tenor voice, but the most flexible was Alan Jones. Alan could sing every traditional air bang in tune, but when pop music was introduced to our dressing room by our Bajan Tony Cordle, then he was able to trip easily through an obligato accompaniment to Delilah. We were never a choir of perfect pitch, but once Tony Cordle had got permission to carry his record player into all dressing rooms and to hotels at the weekends – of course, there was no Sunday cricket until 1968 – then music was a large part of the Glamorgan scene.

Visiting county players who were in Swansea for a weekend were easily led by Alan Jones and brother Eifion down to the Fountain pub in Pontardulais where the 'Bont' male voice choir used to sing after official choir practice. Delightful Welsh harmonies would float through the bars and into the West Wales air. I have seen Australian touring teams silent and appreciative, Colin Cowdrey sitting on the bar applauding, Mushtaq Mohammad trying to join in, Colin Milburn feeling his way into the bass parts. Those nights in Pontardulais offered those who came with us rich and genuine memories of Wales at its best.

Glamorgan were humorous and happy, a fine side at a Saturday night party, a fighting outfit on the field in a tight spot. Bernard Hedges used to hold urgent conversations with his bat in the dressing room 'Come on clicky-ba, you not 'fraid of that nasty massa Trueman'; Peter Walker, apart from early depressions about his play, was the centre of good humour in the dressing room. There was the night the club van, emblazoned with daffodil, was stuck in a farmyard outside Cambridge ... the odd night of champagne at Raymond's Revue Bar ... the earnest pints with Middlesex at the Star ... the 'we never close (for the weekend) spirit' at the York Hotel in Derby ... an opening bowler climbing into Christ's College, Cambridge, in the early hours, a 30-foot drop, an ankle badly swollen by the fall, having to explain to Ossie Wheatley next day that he could not continue the match against the University because he had fallen off the kerb going to Mass ... all these and a million more moments which bound us together off the field and therefore on it.

In one way we county cricketers of the early sixties were the cheated generation. We had been brought up on Hutton, Compton, Edrich, Washbrook, Evans, Bedser, queued up to watch the 1948 Australians, clamoured into county grounds with thousands of others, and now when we ourselves had made the grade there was no one watching. Administrators of the game huddled in their meetings at Lord's trying to work out a remedy for falling gates. In 1963 a new competition was announced, the Gillette Cup. A one-day match, 60 overs each, no bowler

99

allowed to bowl more than thirteen overs.

The Glamorgan players thought it was unimportant: all the intrigue of the three-day game would be lost; it would be all defence in the field, no scheming. Deadly boring, and batsmen could slog without being blamed for rashness. It was paper hat and red nose time just to try and raise a few pounds. It was like playing Monopoly the short way, dealing out the properties first. When Glamorgan's first match came around we decided to rest some of our first-team bowlers; Ossie Wheatley and Don Shepherd relaxed as I, Ossie's vice-captain, took the side into that experimental circus ring. Nowadays, county players are rested from the three-day matches in order to be fresh for the one-day bashes.

Average county sides peak about twice a decade. Wheatley's Glamorgan came second in the 1963 and third in the 1965 championships. I contributed more to the second than the first because 1965 was a personal turning point. We won 12 matches, Northants won 13 and so did Worcestershire, the outright winners. We beat Yorkshire in two days at Swansea, Jim Pressdee took 9 wickets for 43 runs in the first innings, and Don Shepherd 9 for 48 in the second. The crucial tilt at the top came in a match against Northants at Cardiff in early August. It was a match of tremendous tension, a low-scoring contest. Northants 185 and 141, Glamorgan 189 and then, caught with the ball lifting after heavy morning rain, we lost the leading batsmen before lunch on the third day. After lunch the pitch was good again, but there was no loosening the firm hold taken by the bowlers, Brian Crump, Albert Lightfoot and Jim Watts. They were in fine form and so were their close-catchers. We lost by 18 runs and our Championship hopes disappeared.

I got more purpose in my play that season and my batting average was at least out of the twenties into the thirties. By the end of the following season, 1966, it entered the forties. I got five centuries in the County Championship, including 223 against Kent, and over

2,000 runs. Golden days were returning when the selectors asked me to attend the fifth Test against West Indies at the Oval as twelfth man.

'Good to see you getting runs regularly, Tony,' said Peter May. 'Take in the atmosphere of Test cricket and keep it up.'

Unfortunately there was no MCC tour that winter.

11

Rugby Come-back and *Valete*

It was like this. Bill Morris, Pontypool's rugby speedy left wing, capped by Wales, taught with Joan, my wife, at Whitchurch Secondary School in Cardiff. 'We need a full-back at Pontypool,' he told her. 'Ray Cheney's gone to Cardiff. Get Tony out of retirement. We'll pay his travel.'

I had not played rugby for three years, since the early university days. Come-backs are only for cowboys. Never come back. It is one thing to be John Wayne in the movies, disappearing into the hills, honing the skills of shooting a colt 45 left-handed with a dazzling draw and heart-point accuracy, it is another to withdraw a modest rugby skill from public scrutiny and then re-impose it on paying spectators at Pontypool Park.

Consider my last act in first-class rugby before this come-back. Cambridge University, 15–13 ahead of the Racing Club of Paris at the Rabat Stadium in Morocco, two minutes to go. Line-out on the University line, won by Brian Thomas. He held, fed to Trevor Wintle, who winged one of his howitzer passes to me almost on the dead-ball line.

My angle was good, my kick superb; it screwed its way to safety and was even drifting into touch at the half-way line. Alas! It was fielded by the Racing Club's full-back, a gentleman called Michel Vannier, M'Sieur Drop of French International fame, who ran straight across the half-way line to the centre of the field. He dropped a goal. The whistle went for full time. We lost.

Can there be a come-back after that? Even John

102

Wayne would have stayed in the hills. Two days later our small charter flight stumbled on the runway. We skidded and swirled onto the grass. I was in the front up against the cabin, in the aisle seat. On the inside was my giant friend Brian Thomas. He panicked. Claustrophobia! He lashed out with his elbows, striking me a direct hit right in the eye. When the plane rocked to a standstill, he clambered over me as he did through international packs in the seasons to come. That was it. No more rugby. I decided then that a spinning plane in Casablanca was the swan-song.

However, here came Bill Morris with this message from Clive Rowlands. Clive and I had played out many a war in schooldays, Ystradgynlais Grammar School against Neath, and plenty of Welsh Secondary School trials too. Pontypool, I thought – great pack, helluva side to play for. So I went, and put on the Pontypool red, black and white shirt three years after Vannier's drop.

At first I was operating a little below the tempo. This is a painful way to play Welsh club rugby. You tend to run into bone-shaking assaults which are called tackles. After a match at Newbridge I saw my old school rugby master Roy Bish. 'Will I be alright? D'y think I'll make it back?' I muttered through swollen lips having run into the sharp end of Arthur Hughes.

'Yes. Easy,' he coaxed. 'It'll take a game or two. Just train to quicken the reflexes. But I must say your tackling has come on.'

Ah! This was right. Thereby hangs the ultimate demise of my first-class rugby career. Pontypool had two half-backs, skilled in all else but tackling, D.C.T. – Clive-the-Kick – 'Top Cat' Rowlands and Benny 'I make'em swoon in the aisles at St Luke's' Jones. Talented boys. Clive read the game well and kicked to perfection. Sometimes he fed Benny with long passes and Benny had a quicksilver eye for an opening. A dodging run from him would be well worth the turnstile money and bring roars from the crowd which otherwise looked so peaceful in the rural beauty of Pontypool Park.

103

It was when a big, strong opposing back row burst from the back of the line-out that the Rowlands-Jones partnership dissolved. They went their own way or sometimes annoyingly ran alongside the onslaught, shepherding them into my back yard with a 'Take 'im Tone, yewers'.

One Saturday afternoon, after Christmas, Clive got the ball from a line-out well inside our half. He moved to the touch-line to kick, but his way was blocked. He turned to the open side and was blocked, but lobbed a hopeful pass to Benny. Benny, no doubt mentally clocking up the time lost, counting the seconds before the Abertillery back row dropped their visiting cards, began to run backwards in my direction. I saw his face go white, he had the hunted eye of a fighter pilot who had just spotted three Messerschmitts in the rear-view mirror. He bailed out. He lobbed me an even slower and higher pass than the one Clive had sent him.

The last seconds of my first-class rugby career were a kaleidescope of green and white Abertillery hoops as their unholy trinity hit me – Malcolm Lewis, a great club stalwart, and two Welsh internationals and British Lions, Alun Pask and Haydn Morgan. They arrived, simultaneously, all horizontal, none of them in touch with the turf, as I was kicking left-footed for the far touch-line. I knew as I kicked the ball that it was safe to touch. All else is vague.

My first bedside visitor came on the following Monday, Wilfred Wooller, secretary of the Glamorgan County Cricket Club. 'You bloody fool,' was his sympathetic greeting. 'Broken bone in your ankle six weeks before the cricket season. You're half bloody mad ... and I suppose the only reason you're not completely bloody mad is that you were playing *for* Pontypool not *against* them.'

12

Glamorgan Captain

Captaincy of a county, I discovered, was not like being managing director of a company which had hierarchy and guidelines. Nor was it regal and distanced from the subjects, loyal or otherwise. It was more the tribal chieftain; I battled through the same daily jungle as the rest, without preference or protection. There were strong wills to challenge mine. I saw that it was possible to be the special target of someone of my own side, stirred by envy or some other contrary quirk, as well as being the bull's-eye for the opposition. I loved it.

Captaincy in Test matches is easier than the day-by-day captaincy of a county. The county captain lives with all the problems, all of the time – at least he did in my day before the recruitment of cricket managers. Doug Insole, captain of Essex, always gave as example the leg-spinner who knocked on his hotel bedroom door at midnight to groan, 'Skipper, I've lost my googly.'

There was the player who could not think straight because he could not pay his mortgage, the one who got homesick as soon as he crossed the Severn Bridge, the one whose Christian conscience would not allow him to play on Sundays in the John Player League.

In 1967, when I succeeded Ossie Wheatley as Glamorgan's captain, I realized that my own survival was the first objective. The captain decided almost everything. I remember the first 60 seconds in the job at the Neath Indoor School in early April: it went something like this – no, it is too wet for outdoor nets ... no, I did not bring the new balls down from Cardiff ... yes, you can have a

105

meeting about the car mileage allowance, but in the lunch-break ... yes, you can nip out for fish and chips at lunchtime, but be back by two o'clock ... no, if you want to discuss higher basic salaries, let's have the Chairman of cricket here ... yes, Alan Jones can pad up with Bernard Hedges and Roger Davis ... and someone make sure that the hot water switch is on in the showers.

I was lucky that I had always been a captain, right from schooldays – Neath Schools, South Wales Schools, Welsh Secondary Schools, Neath Grammar School, rugby and cricket, Cambridge University. It was my second nature. For five seasons I had been Ossie Wheatley's vice-captain. I had no difficulty in being loyal, but also I had the feeling of lying fallow; the captaincy, when it came, was the original seed planted by Wilf Wooller 12 years earlier.

Ossie finished when he was playing well, but he had to look to business interests outside the game. 'Six years is enough,' he said. 'You can build up a side and take your tilt at the championship if you are lucky, but after that it is usually time for more youngsters, more rebuilding.' It was exactly as I found it. I also led for six seasons.

Unfortunately, in the first two seasons my own batting hit a shattering low, a runless trough with no way out. Dramatically I had reduced myself from the young man who had scored more runs than anyone in the country in 1966 to one who snicked his way to an average in the low twenties for two seasons.

Why do new captains find their form dipping? Where did the runs go? In the first place I made a naïve mistake. I expected my batting to carry on from where it had left off the season before. I was absorbed in the make-up of the team, in everyone else's form. In the pre-season nets, I remember going without concentrated net-practice myself. Cricket is a cruel mistress, toy with her at your peril.

However, even though I was not scoring many runs, I left every day's play exhausted and satisfied that I never stopped concentrating and had contributed a great deal.

106

The fellow who batted under my name was someone else, or so it felt.

During England's tour of India in 1984–5 I wanted to take David Gower for a beer and tell him what was happening to his game. It was his first tour captaincy. Before the fifth and final Test his batting average was 11. I had watched David put a mass of thought into England's effort for months. He had suffered one or two filthy umpiring decisions, but he looked tentative at the crease; his footwork was imprecise and the half-cock shots got him out. I wanted to tell him about Bernard Hedges and the lesson he taught me during my own dreadful first season of captaincy in 1967.

Mid-season, we had lost to Derbyshire by an innings and 3 runs in two days at Cardiff, so on the third day we had practice on the same used pitch. This was a humiliating process. It was essential that I had a long knock. In 20 minutes batting I got out half a dozen times to weak shots. I was desperate. If anyone had said that I was not trying I would have called them a liar, anyone, that is, except Bernard Hedges, a humorous but wise man. He came to me from slip, impatiently. 'Look skipper, you're wasting our time out here. You may think you are trying, but you're not trying an inch. Now listen. It's harder when a touch player like you loses it, because you can get half-way to the pitch of a ball and still work out some sort of a shot and get away with it, but I'm telling you, you've got to get your feet going and to do that you've got to be thinking positively. Hit the ball somewhere. Okay, now try to get 12 runs to win the match off the next over.' I did not hit every ball with the middle of the bat, but I got the 12 runs easily. Each over he set new targets and I got them. Two games later I got my first century of the season, 128 not out against Pakistan at Swansea.

The next time I felt ambivalent about my batting was when I captained England on the tour of India in 1972–3. There was a huge leadership job to be done for the team, on and off the field, and the odd innings against the West Zone or North or South did not appear important on the day. I was still exhausted by the thought put into it, but only the Tests mattered. I put the Bernard Hedges theory into practice again and got a century in the Kanpur Test.

David Gower looked to be going through a very similar experience. I wanted him to set himself positive objectives in his batting. Maybe to hit Sivaramakrishnan out of the attack, or to refuse to play a maiden over. David Gower was not the sort of player who could graft his way to form; he would never get his lazy feet to move that way. It was not coincidence that David at last got runs when he had most to play for. He had purpose, though strangely it was in a defensive role. At Kanpur, when England had only to draw to win the series, he watched his middle order falter. India looked like forcing England to follow-on. David Gower's acute fear of failure made him positive. He had an objective. Scoring 78 in the first innings and 33 not out in the second, he managed to identify with Gower the batsman.

Once I realized that I needed batting objectives I was fine. I could respond to the tense state of the game, to the sight of Wilf Wooller sitting at the sightscreen, I could bat to save the lives of my daughters against the fastest bowling. It would have been much simpler to have been like Colin Cowdrey – always motivated by the art of batsmanship itself.

Athough struggling with the bat, not surprisingly my captaincy improved, but in this too there were swift lessons to be learned, especially in my second season when Glamorgan came third in the championship table. At Folkestone we lost a match to Kent by an innings and 77 runs. It was the game which virtually decided which of us would be runner-up in the championship. We were bowling and fielding respectably when without warning we were mutilated by the Kent tail. Alan Ealham got 94 not out and, much more annoyingly, Alan Brown, not a recognized batsman, slogged 81. These two reduced us to a shambles in the field. I had lost a grip. Every time Alan

Brown slogged the ball, there was no one waiting to field it, a clear sign that the link between bowler, captain and fielders had broken down. Worse than that, I had resigned myself to the shambles. Ossie Wheatley was playing and he recommended that he should bowl. He restored order. He bowled outside off-stump to a blanket off-side field, Don Shepherd returned too. Out of the chaos, order came, fielders were keen again, and Brownie was run out. Ossie proved the lesson which Don was always preaching.

That was the lesson always preached by Don Shepherd. 'Control is priceless,' he used to groan over a pint of beer on a Saturday night. 'Why did you change the bowling at Worcester last Monday? They got away, didn't they? Control. Tie 'em down; don't overattack, make them hit the ball to your fielders. Batsmen can be idiots. They'll get themselves out half of the time.' Understanding that, tightened my whole approach.

When I came to captain Derek Underwood on tour in later days, I saw that he hated giving a run away as much as Don Shepherd did. They both bowled their spinners at a similar medium pace. They were both fiendish to play on wickets that helped, but both knew that on decent surfaces they could concede runs, especially behind the wickets. Neither was happy over-attacking. They got as much pleasure in having a batsman tied down, and holing out to a desperate attacking stroke as they had from knocking back a stump.

My relationship with Don Shepherd was to be crucial for Glamorgan. He was the pessimist, I the optimist. We probably made one balanced person between us! Don was from Gower peninsula near Swansea and spent his young days on those delightful beaches throwing pebble skimmers into the sea. He always claimed to have been ignorant of cricket as a schoolboy at Gowerton Grammar School, yet he felt he was born to bowl.

While on National Service with the Fleet Air Arm he attended the Worcestershire nets and, at their sugges-

109

tion, after his service took up the cricket apprenticeship
on the Lord's ground staff. He was a fast bowler then. He
came back to Glamorgan – in 1952 he took 120 wickets
with seam and swing, yet by 1956 was taking 168 wickets
in the season with medium off-breaks mixed with the
occasional cutter. In 1970, at the age of 43, Don was top
of the national averages, the only bowler to get 100
wickets.

He was extremely proud of his profession, meticulous
about punctuality, appearance, respect for spectators
and loyal to captains. He was the senior professional of
Glamorgan through Ossie Wheatley's captaincy and
mine. If there was trouble in the camp, you knew about it
when the barracks were smouldering not when they were
in flames. I am sure that Don would have loved to be
captain. Indeed he led Glamorgan to a brilliant win over
the 1968 Australians. I think he should have captained
Glamorgan when I resigned in 1973, just as caretaker. It
would have prevented the eventual chaos.

Every captain brings his own personal qualities to the
job. I offered independence, because I never relied on
Glamorgan Cricket Club for my living; my freelance
writing and broadcasting in the winter was far more
profitable. I believed in encouraging an atmosphere in
which players thought their own game through and
enjoyed themselves. I understood batsmen, which I still
believe is essential: not all bowling captains do. Don
Shepherd's caution was good ballast, but the overall
approach was an attacking one, with more than a touch
of adventure.

Somerset, seven wickets down, were once blocking for
a draw at Neath. We were into the last half-hour. I told
Don Shepherd, who had been bowling, to take his
sweater. He had not looked like removing Geoff Clayton
and Peter Robinson, two of the most dour defenders.

'Who's going on?' inquired Shep.

'I'll have a go,' I said.

Suddenly the ball jammed in his fist. It just wouldn't
come out.

'You aren't bowling? You're not serious?'

'Yes, it's leg-spin time,' I jested, knowing that Shep had no time for people who trivialized the bowling art.

'No! No!' he said, the ball still locked in his hand and his head now rolling in agony from side to side. 'But ...' he suddenly released it, turned, and walked into a cloud of red mist at mid-wicket.

I had last bowled my optimistic leg-spin in first-class cricket four seasons ago, and had taken three wickets in twelve years since my debut. But when we walked off the field that day, just five minutes before time ran out, Colin Atkinson, the Somerset captain, marched down the pavilion steps, veins standing out furiously from a scarlet forehead. He walked past me to have words with the last of my three victims, Fred Rumsey. The scorebook read, Lewis 4.1 overs, 0 maidens, 3 wickets for 18 runs. A win for Glamorgan.

There were more difficult decisions to make than that. When I took over, David Evans, our wicket-keeper, was approaching his 34th birthday. Eifon Jones, the reserve, was 25. David had perfect hands, was wholly reliable and unflamboyant, and a first-class team man. The mood in committee, and certainly of Wilf Wooller who still, long after his playing days, led the cricket argument in the club from his secretary's office, was that the time had come to play Eifon who could not be kept waiting much longer. Eifon had joined the staff as a batsman but had developed as a keeper in the second team. David's batting was courageous but limited. Should batting tilt the decision towards change? My own feeling was that the best wicket-keeper should play even though England had spent most of their time choosing Jim Parks before Keith Andrew. However, because he spent all his life in the reserves, I had never seen Eifon in the first-class context.

The physical act of telling David Evans that he was dropped was hard enough. He sensitively predicted a sudden end to his career. I was never so positive about that. As it happened, Eifon Jones did become Glamor-

111

gan's regular wicket-keeper. A year later, in 1969, we won the County Championship and he caught 68 and stumped 6 and scored 753 runs at an average of 31, batting at number seven. He was a pugnacious competitor and a clear cricket thinker. I constantly asked him for his view. Yet, with all the hindsight, I could not say that he was a better wicket-keeper than David Evans. It was one of those brutally hard decisions in professional sport, as in football, when only one goalkeeper can play. The injustice was that David, who had to wait an age for Haydn Davies to pack up, was now suffering a premature guillotine himself. It is always a savage cut which severs the deep affection which a man has for his game and his county, indeed, for David, a Welsh speaker, for his country. He was hurt. I must be honest, so was I, to have had to be the decider. He became ill: I was taught a lot about the aspirations of professional cricketers and their families.

In 1968 counties were allowed to recruit one overseas player by immediate registration. Without any particular planning we struck lucky. Majid Khan had belted an amazing 147 not out against us at Swansea the year before, but who could tell from this slogging innings that he would be technically sound enough to be consistent in the County Championship? Majid was 21. The other overseas signing, who had qualified by a year's residence, Bryan Davis from Trinidad, was 27. He had opened the batting four times for West Indies against Australia in 1964.

Glamorgan made an early error. They put these two in the same twin-bedded digs in Cardiff without it occurring to anyone that a devout young Muslim, kneeling to recite the Koran, might not fit the domestic habits of a Trinidadian who preferred cola with his rum and some bubbling social life. It took some time for this difficulty to come out. I only mention it because it was probably being experienced by other county clubs at the time. Gary Sobers had come to Notts, Barry Richards to Hampshire, Greg Chappell was with Somerset, Farooq

Engineer with Lancashire, Graeme McKenzie with Leicestershire, Mike Procter with Gloucestershire, Rohan Kanhai and Lance Gibbs with Warwickshire, Mushtaq Muhammad with Northants, Alan Connolly with Middlesex, Lee Irvine with Essex, Intikhab Alam with Surrey. These were the best known of the new signings.

As a cricketer, Majid settled immediately to confirm his class, but Bryan Davis, opening with Alan Jones, appeared to be unused to the ball moving a lot off the seam. His backward defensive stroke was played with open chest, feet facing to mid-off. Movement late off the pitch often beat him. Half-way through his second season I decided to move him down to number five. He was a little resentful. Firstly it was a tumble of ego for a Test player, especially one who had come to county cricket hoping to re-establish his chances with the West Indian selectors. Relegation in Glamorgan meant diminishing chances back home. These were tough days for the overseas players. They had come as glamour boys to be the stars and they felt the sceptics chirping at them when they failed.

Bryan developed into a superb cricketer in the middle order and a quite brilliant first slip. Our batting order had thus been adjusted to read Alan Jones, Roger Davis, Majid Khan, A.R.L., Bryan Davis, Peter Walker, Eifon Jones, Tony Cordle, Malcolm Nash, Don Shepherd and Lawrence Williams. I had no idea that we were good enough to win a championship in the following season, 1969.

It was interesting in 1968 that the first county cricketers union should be formed, called the Players' Association. I was one of the rare cricketers who did not join. My job as captain was one of representing the players to the committee and also the committee to the players. I was the middle of the employment sandwich, even a conciliatory influence when disagreement was strong. I did not see how I could be committed to one side or the other.

These were the first official rumblings of a more aggressive playing fraternity. The formation of the Cricketers' Association did not lead to the Packer revolution ten years later – that was engineered by Test players – but the Association was in a position to move firmly, especially in the aftermath of the High Court judgement in favour of Kerry Packer against the TCCB, towards minimum basic wages for professional players, and it became a watchdog in matters of restraint of trade by the counties. Perhaps, indoctrinated by Wilf Wooller, I was cemented in the old concept of the amateur captain standing alone. Not belonging to a union certainly fitted my love of independence, the need in winter or summer all my life to be freelance.

Glamorgan were struck by an historical performance in 1968. It was right at the end of August. We were tired and jaded: we might get to second or third in the championship, but Yorkshire were already safe at the top. The highest hopes were dead. It was at Swansea. Notts batted well and it would have been a quiet sort of a day if it had not been for one or two middle-order players, generous not to name, who sensed a declaration coming from their captain and selfishly blocked to make sure they would be not out and so improve their personal batting averages. They were using up valuable time. A wicket did fall. Down the long flight of steps came the furious Notts skipper.

Unfortunately for Glamorgan, that skipper was Garfield St Auburn Sobers. A benign Sobers is not an animal to taunt, and a mad Sobers is a species to be avoided. What happened next is history. Sobers, played sizzling drives, and then struck the bowling of Malcolm Nash for six sixes in an over. Leather missiles cracked off the bat into the sky, sights not seen along Swansea Bay since the German Blitz in 1941 when anti-aircraft guns fired hopeful shells at the Luftwaffe. If Sobers had been defending us in 1941 I'd have had a few bob on the ball.

Malcolm Nash was experimenting that day. Normally he bowled medium fast swing, left-arm over the wicket.

He was a most dangerous bowler with the new ball; he took almost 1000 wickets for the county before he retired. However, Malcolm, like other left-armers, had noticed that a young man called Underwood had burst onto the cricket scene and into the Test side with a load of wickets bowling left-arm spinners at Malcolm's speed. So on this fateful day which took him into the history books, it was Nash the left arm around the wicket, Underwood lookalike, purveyor of spinners, who bowled to the angry Sobers.

There have been historical reconstructions of the six-ball sequence. I took no particular notes, because I did not know until the sixth ball that we were about to slip into history. For my part, I can confirm that none of the 36 runs came from error of field-placing! We retreated. I know that Roger Davis did take a catch just alongside me at long-off, but he fell over the line with it; I did tell Malcolm that he could go back over the wicket and bowl his usual stuff up in the blockhole if he wanted to – that was after the third or fourth six; but other than those vague memories I am just left with images of the ball being blitzed with a coil of the body and lash of the bat to all directions. Mercifully for the spectators who were surging back and fore across the terraces like herds of frightened sheep, Gary struck the sixth six up past the bulbs of the rugby floodlights, down King Edward Road. He walked off, Notts 394 for 5 declared, Sobers 76 not out. Malcolm always took this assault on his bowling with tremendous humour, but no doubt he was relieved to be joined in 1985 by an Indian left-arm spinner called Tilac Raj who, in a match for Baroda against Bombay, was hit for six sixes in an over by Ravi Shastri.

In 1969, Glamorgan won the county championship for the second time in their first-class history. There was a strong element of design about it. In the occasional chats with Wilf Wooller and Tom Taylor, Chairman of Cricket, when I called into the club office during the winter, the theme was always the need to get runs quickly in the first innings of a three-day match. It was so easy to dawdle on a good surface.

The points scoring system introduced in county matches in 1968 was sure to support this approach. These were 10 points for a win, but bonus points were awarded within the first 85 overs of a first innings. For batting there was 1 point for every 25 runs over 150: for bowling, 1 point for each two wickets taken. Therefore, a maximum 5 for bowling, but the batting points were limitless.

What I enjoyed about 1969 was that we had only eleven regular players, a little help at the end by Ossie Wheatley and an over or two of leg-spin by the Cardiff Club bowler David Lewis. We were free from injury and no one was wanted to play for England. You need that luck. Glamorgan's members deserved a championship. There was always a loyal following, and the more Welshmen in the side the better. The Welshness gave it purpose and pride particularly when the game was going badly. A strong Welsh contingent gave the supporters identity too, and so when we began our August charge on the title the crowds piled into the grounds, and we were the talk of the pubs and clubs.

The last time a Glamorgan side consisting of eleven players born in Wales took the field was in August 1955 against Warwickshire at Neath, my second county match – Wooller, Parkhouse, Pressdee, W. E. Jones, A. Watkins, B. Hedges, J. Pleass, A. R. Lewis, D. Ward, H. G. Davies, D. J. Shepherd. However, there was a side which played against Yorkshire at Harrogate which was all Welsh-born except for David Evans, fluent Welsh speaker, born in Lambeth but brought up in Ammanford.

Glamorgan is effectively the Welsh team, but I do believe that the local produce of all nationalities should join in – Peter Walker, Bristol-born and brought up in Johannesburg, Tony Cordle, who left Barbados in his teenage and settled in Cardiff, or later Rodney Ontong who came from Cape Town on a long apprenticeship before becoming captain. I am opposed to watering down the pride in the locality with average players from outside. The most harmful concept is of Glamorgan as just another professional organization toiling with a bunch of mercenaries in a commercial league. Success is vital, but the way to get it is to spend time and money on research and development of the game throughout Wales. Let the Welsh lads see the way to the top uncluttered.

1969 was a delight because every player had moments of inspired contribution of which he could be proud. There were no passengers. We also proved that winning cricket is played closed to the bat. We were lucky to have four fine close-catchers, Bryan Davis at first slip, Majid Khan at second, Roger Davis at short square-leg and Peter Walker at backward short-leg.

Peter Walker had the control of these men. He could adjust their positions, a sort of fine tuner. I relied on his instincts because he was the best close-catcher I had ever seen. Even now, looking back, and having seen many more, he is still the best. He practised daily, often cajoling a player to hit him a burst of catches off the bat, or, if there was a slip-catching frame on the ground, he would flip ball after ball into the net, with a left-handed throw or right, always varying the angle of rebound. He advanced the theory that the best catchers had balanced eyes, which set the rest of us off to the mirror to see what the lop-sided cricketers looked like. He was brave. For many seasons he stood at short square-leg, the most frightening position on the field. He fielded equally well on the off side at slip or silly point. The outfield was child's play for him. He was very tall, well over six feet high, and he would meticulously work out how far apart his feet should be to give the fastest take-off over the widest arc.

I have memories of many brilliant catches – Willie Watson, stunned to see a firm turn off the legs in Peter's hands at short square-leg at Leicester, Tom Graveney stretching well down the pitch at Pontypridd, nicking the ball from bat to pad and suddenly seeing Peter moving alongside him and diving across his path from silly point, taking the catch two-handed off Euros Lewis's bowling.

In this glorious 1969 season, we were unbeaten. We won 11 matches, one more than Gloucestershire who were second; our batting plan worked; we took the highest number of points, 67; we were eleventh in the bowling with 73; our 250 points total was 31 ahead of Gloucestershire; Prince Charles was invested as Prince of Wales; my second daughter, Anabel Sophia, was born; the run for the championship gave my batting the positive motivation it needed, I was in the runs again. Should life be so sweet?

We began the Championship season with an oddity. We were awarded 10 points against Hampshire at Bournemouth before no more than half a dozen eye-witnesses. I want you to read first the account of *The Times* correspondent, my good friend Alan Gibson. 'When the umpire shall call "play" the party refusing to play shall lose the match.' This, referring both to the state of play, and to intervals (including the fall of a wicket) was set down in the Laws of Cricket as revised by the Marylebone Club in 1830. It has always been, and remains, the basic assumption of any match at cricket.

I suppose the result of this match should be recorded as: 'Glamorgan won because Hampshire refused to play.' Not that they refused in any deliberate sense. They had simply gone away under the impression that the match was over.

To set the scene: at the beginning of the day Glamorgan, faced with Hampshire's declared total of 337, had scored 256 for seven. A.R. Lewis, the Glamorgan captain, slightly surprisingly, decided to bat on. He was presumably hoping for a few more quick boundaries from E. Jones, who indeed got a couple of lusty ones. But when Jones was caught and bowled, after 20 minutes, Glamorgan declared, which was sad for Williams who was just beginning to get his eye in.

The Hampshire second innings had not really begun to take shape when the rain started. It was slow, persistent, dismal rain. Lunch was taken early. The rain drizzled on. We longed for a storm to end the futility of hanging around. Duty, not hope, kept us miserably waiting.

The public, such of them as were present, was given no indication of what decisions might be taken about the future of play, and gradually drifted away. At four o'clock, sitting in the little pavilion and contemplating a cold, flat beer, I saw the Hampshire team leave, changed and off to the next engagement. I concluded that all was over, and ordered a taxi.

Perhaps five minutes later the Glamorgan team came out of their dressing room, also changed, packed and ready to depart. A. R. Lewis spoke, casually but sensibly enough, to the senior umpire, Wight. Lewis said: 'I suppose it is all off?' Wight replied to this effect: 'There are more than two hours to go, the rain is not heavy, the wicket will be playable almost as soon as it stops. It is far too early to abandon the match.' Someone said: 'Does Marshall know?' Wight replied: 'I have not been asked.'

In this decision Wight was, in my view, unquestionably right, and his fellow umpire, Budd – a former Hampshire player – was strong in agreement with him.

So Glamorgan stayed on the ground. Efforts were unsuccessfully made to contact the scattered Hampshire team. At five o'clock the rain had almost stopped. The umpires made an inspection and ordered mopping up operations. Satisfied with these, they decreed a resumption of play at 5.30.

Glamorgan, unnecessarily, changed back into flannels (or thereabout: Walker was partly revealing a fetching pink undergarment) and took their places on the field. Budd, the bowling umpire, called 'Play'. It was all quite properly done. There was no unseemly hurry. Cordle marked out his run.

119

And then, at 5.31 – believe me I do not exaggerate – the flimsy drizzle developed into serious rain. A batsman might have been justified in walking off, but there were no batsmen. Glamorgan stoically stuck it out in the field (Walker had taken up an aggressive position within the return crease), Wight looked at his watch, measuring every agonizing second, and after the necessary two minutes turned back towards the pavilion.

Glamorgan had taken 10 points for a win, because the other party had refused to play. This gave them 12 points to Hampshire's seven, though I suppose it is arguable, and will be argued, whether a side failing to come up to the scratch is entitled to any points at all.

No criticism can be made of the umpires. The weather was good enough at 5.30 to resume play, and though it rained shortly thereafter both sides had played through heavier rain in the morning. The question why Marshall, the Hampshire captain, was so confident that the game was over, is more difficult. I was assured by the umpires that they had said nothing whatsoever to give him such an impression. My own guess is that it started from one of those well-meaning busybodies who are sometimes found at cricket grounds. A glance at the foreboding sky, a wave of the hand, and 'all off!' – and it percolates to the dressing room. Still, it is a captain's job to make sure.

Shortly before Glamorgan took the field for that last time, Derek Shackleton looked in at the ground. His wife said, 'It's all over Derek. You've wasted your time.' He took one look at the situation, the men with the squeeges on the pitch, and said 'It's nay of the sort. Where's the lads?' Later, when it was over, he said 'Ee.' No more. Just 'E.' Then Glamorgan said 'We don't particularly relish the points, but after all that's the law.' 'It's the law,' said Wight, at once worried but certain. What Roy Marshall said, when he heard, can only be conjectured but not printed.

It was quite a day.

So it remains to be answered why Roy Marshall thought the game was off, and what happened next. This is where I can help.

Roy and I met in the Hampshire dressing room, which was heavily steamed up because hot water baths were being taken by his team who were changing. We agreed, so I thought, to call the game off after tea if it was still deluging. Roy thought that the game was now off and we would simply make the official announcement after tea.

It was Don Shepherd, proper professional, always doing it by the book, who asked me, 'Is the game really off?'

'As good as,' I replied.

'Have the umpires told you it is off?'

'No, but Roy and I reckon there's no chance.'

'Go and see them,' said Don. 'They're not in the pavilion, they're in a little hut along the boundary. It's best to check.'

I left the beer I was taking with Alan Gibson and my colleague from the *Telegraph*, John Mason.

The umpires, Peter Wight particularly, was adamant, that they were the final arbiters, and that the game was still on. I sent one of the Glamorgan team to chase after Hampshire. Gone. I went to the Hampshire match manager to tell him the tale. The enemy had fled! Ten points.

In the middle of August, Glamorgan were embarrassingly still carrying those ten points near the top of the table. Hampshire had begged a court of appeal and got it. The judges sat at the committee tables in Lord's, and opposite me were the many representatives of Hampshire's case, secretaries, players, lawyers, managers. There were the umpires too. I was the sole Glamorgan advocate. Hampshire's volatile argument lasted most of the morning. Eventually, near lunchtime, I was asked for my version. I said that I had come only to advocate the removal of the ten points from Glamorgan; we were at the top of the table and did not want to be remembered as the team which won the title by some anachronistic law.

It fell silent. Formally we were asked to wait outside. The adjudication was that there had been a misunderstanding. The umpires were complimented but the match was made a draw, Glamorgan forfeiting their ten points. I think by the instincts of the professional jungle Roy Marshall felt outfoxed and sore. Time will have persuaded him that we were both starring in one of the better modern farces.

Our serious charge for the championship title came from two powerful wins over Gloucestershire who had led the county table from mid-June to mid-August, sometimes by as much as 60 points. It was a cruel time for them and I am sorry it had to be their fate. Glamorgan had a very close relationship with Gloucestershire, Somerset and Worcestershire. We used to be involved in a full second XI programme home and away every year and fit in friendly practice matches at the start of the season.

The first ball I ever faced in professional cricket was from a tall, intimidating man, with tanned, wrinkly skin, who bowled from around the wicket. It was 1953, I was fifteen. It was a wet wicket at Pontypool Nylon Spinners' ground for Glamorgan and Gloucestershire seconds. I stretched forward and drove this first ball through extra cover for four. 'Enjoy it son, you'll never do that again,' came a curly West Country voice behind me. The next ball bit outside of the stump and hit me in the ribs. The next pitched, turned and went between bat and pad over leg stump. At the end of the over Jim Pressdee came down the pitch to talk to me.

'Ever seen Tom Goddard bowl before?' I looked up, saw that leather face reimposed on one of my prized cigarette cards. I shuddered at the boldness of that first stroke.

Gloucestershire and Glamorgan always shared wet Mays, turning wickets on small grounds, Lydney or Stroud, Neath or Ebbw Vale, a surfeit of off-spinners and batsmen born to play the sweep. In that 1969 showdown there were those of us who could go back to encounters of the early fifties – for us Alan Jones, Peter Walker, Don Shepherd and I; for Gloucestershire, Ron Nicholls, Arthur Milton, Tony Brown, the captain, David Allen, John Mortimore, David Smith and Barry Meyer. It was a pity we had chosen the same season to chase the title. However, we played superbly and they below their best. We beat them at Cardiff and at Cheltenham and went to the top of the table.

We were lucky to complete the home run at Swansea and Cardiff with wins against Middlesex, Essex and Worcestershire. It is like a fantasy now, as if I was not there at all. Yet I do recall the leadership of two captains, Brian Taylor of Essex and Tom Graveney of Worcestershire. Both believed in playing games towards the end of the season in exactly the same mood, and with the same object of winning, as those played at the start. In other words, they did not believe in obstructing us by playing defensively, just to let everyone see how they had stopped our progress.

I left Tom 284 runs to win on a 'shirt front' pitch at Worcester, with a very short boundary on the pavilion side and oceans of time, and, even before they set out for the runs, he said it was such a fair declaration that they would go for the runs right down to number eleven. A lot of captains promise that but do not produce. The Worcestershire boys did. Brian Brain came out swinging the bat and fell bravely 29 runs short of the target.

Then, at Swansea, Brian Taylor's side got to the last ball of another declaration match with his last two players, John Lever and Ray East, facing the final ball of the game. John Lever played the ball to deep backward point, they raced down the pitch. The ball was a couple of yards from Ossie Wheatley when they decided to chance a second run to get a tie for 5 points. It was a good bet for them. Ossie had dropped out of full-time cricket. He had come back to help us at the top of the table. He was never known for his agile fielding.

However, once the ball went into his hands and stuck his throw was fast and flat to the root of the stumps. Eifon Jones completed a run out and amazing scenes broke out. Crowds ran onto the field, singing, cheering. I was called up for a papal appearance on the balcony. Yet, as I went up from the dressing room, I saw Don Shepherd, the old pro, rolling his head and lamenting, 'It's not over yet, you know.'

In the next match, against Worcestershire at Sophia Gardens, an astonishing innings of 156 on a broken pitch by Majid was enough to create the victory. I have not seen a more brilliant innings. Don Shepherd took his 2,000th wicket, we drank champagne, Tony Cordle and Malcolm Nash and Don were splendidly in the wickets, Peter Walker was in the runs, I got a 'pair', and when the last Worcestershire wicket fell we were champions at last after 21 years. As the team streamed off and the crowds gathered I looked for Don Shepherd and he for me. We hugged each other briefly and walked off together. We had hit near perfection – his caution, control and devoted professionalism and my own musketeering instincts with a team of many skills and adaptability, incredibly without physical injury, and without too many egos getting in the way of an overall design which called for unselfishness.

The lesson for us was that our almighty pursuit of batting bonus points had led us to so many winning situations; the value of runs scored quickly in the first innings of a three-day game was made obvious. It always was and still is the way to play in the County Championship – bonus point system or not.

To represent the joyful reactions of Welshmen throughout the world, I will publish only one letter of congratulations from a friend.

From Dr Byron Evans, 59 Cathedral Road, Cardiff.
My dear Tony,
And it came to pass that at 15.09 hours I was listening to an ardent cricket fan's heart in the Outpatients' Department of Cardiff Royal Infirmary when Bert, the Hall Porter, burst in

and said, 'We've done it. We've done it.' Whereupon the patient said, 'Mi heart is b-gg-red now and, if I may be so bold, you're b-gg-red too. I will come back next week.' Congratulations and my best wishes.
Yours,
Byron

Then, of all the telegrams from past players, civic dignitaries and supporters all around the world, none was more treasured than that from Balmoral Castle in the investiture year. 'I am delighted by your splendid win, especially in this particular year. Many congratulations. Do it again next year. CHARLES.'

Next year we disobeyed the royal request. We came second.

Black Day

Sophia Gardens, Cardiff. 29 May 1971. Violent convulsions had taken over Roger Davis's body. I was in the gully; the Warwickshire batsman was in the way, but I could see his legs jabbing and jerking in that death-trap at short square-leg.

I had not seen the ball come off the bat or hit him, but cricketers recognize the sounds – the middle of the bat, the crack of solid leather on the skull, and the silence; no yelp, no hopping about and cursing, just an unconscious, twitching body lying there and a ball rolling mildly away as if to say 'What me?'

Everyone rushed to help, but was helpless. Over the years for Glamorgan I had seen ugly knocks – the teeth smashed out of Bernard Hedges, a broken nose for Brian Lewis, concussion for Billy Slade and I had helped carry Peter Walker off the ground at Leicester when a ball had been whacked into his kidneys; but this was not like any of those. This was beyond our basic first aid. 'Don't move him' was the only sage bit of advice.

I ran for proper help and was met in front of the pavilion by Phil Clift, the county coach. He set off to organize doctor and ambulance, but by the time I returned to the middle there was a doctor out there who had come out of the members' enclosure. He was examining the body which was now completely motionless. One of the umpires, Bill Alley, turned my way. 'Worst I've ever seen, skip.' I glanced over the shoulders and saw Roger's face moving from purple to dark blue.

'He has stopped breathing,' the doctor formally announced.

'Give him air. Have we got an ambulance? God, he's stopped breathing.' Almost in unison players moved and uttered like a Greek chorus.

A second doctor arrived. Yes, Roger Davis had stopped breathing. 'When did you eat last?' the second doctor asked us quickly.

'Just had tea,' someone replied.

'He may have choked on his food,' he rather mumbled as he knelt, lowering his face to Roger's to begin mouth-to-mouth resuscitation.

Again I could not look. About a minute later, though it felt like ten, I heard, 'He's being sick ... his colour is coming back ... he's breathing.' I joined in for another look. Roger's cheeks were still bluish; he looked dreadful, but he was certainly breathing.

After 15 minutes or so it was decided to carry him off. By the time bearers had laid him down on a bench in the umpire's room on the ground floor of the pavilion, his eyes were open, though they stared straight ahead without understanding.

How could we go back out there and play cricket after that? Poor Neil Abberley, the batsman who had hit the ball, was pale, rubbing his hand across his forehead and eyes as if to wipe away the cobwebs of a nightmare. Everyone felt the nausea. However, just as we were making our way back onto the field a slight drizzle began to fall from an innocent sky. It had not rained all day, but now, with merciful timing the drizzle thickened. We walked back to the dressing room and did not bowl again for 45 minutes.

The accident itself had happened in a flash. Warwickshire had just gone in to bat; it was late afternoon, and I was pacing around the gully area wondering if we had enough runs to make a game of it; bowled out for 191 before tea, and Warwickshire with seven Test players in their side. Mind you, the Sophia Gardens pitch always gave the bowlers hope, and especially this one, because it was damp in patches after rain on the previous day.

Malcolm Nash was bowling with the new ball from the river Taff end. Neil Abberley, facing, was the sort of player we fancied getting out caught off bat and pad at short square-leg. We respected his patience and quiet authority when he was well set, but in these opening overs we had to crowd in there. He tended to commit himself to the forward defensive push and hardly employed a back-lift at all.

Malcolm was just the sort of bowler to give him trouble. He delivered the ball from left-arm over the wicket and swung it as sharply as anyone at a whippy medium pace from the off to the leg side. So the swinging ball might find the edge of the bat and pop up off the pad into the hands of Roger Davis or, even finer, to Peter Walker at leg-slip.

As I have mentioned before, Glamorgan's close field in those days set itself – Bryan Davis at first slip, Majid Khan at second, Peter Walker at backward short-leg and Roger Davis at short square-leg. An instinct for anticipating where catches would fly next made them the best judges of how deep they would go, how wide or how close. They played it like a chess game in their private club. Glamorgan owed them a lot in the three seasons of success which had gone before.

But short square-leg is not like any other position. This fielder not only has to dive inwards and sideways for the false strokes, he also has to duck and dive away from some of the most savage shots in cricket, the hook, the pull and the sweep. All the while he is fighting the instincts of the cat on a hot tin roof, he should be well balanced, feet apart and weight slightly forwards. If fear or panic takes him back onto his heels he is locked there, unable to move to anything. So the best catchers are the brave, positive thinkers, but they are bolstered too by their own technique for covering up in times of trouble. Peter Walker was the best fielder I had ever seen at short square-leg and he had an emergency routine like a boxer. As soon as he sensed one of the big hits coming his way he would guard the front of his face with straight rigid

128

Not the loaves and fishes!, in 1969, Glamorgan beat Essex on the last ball of the game and the Welsh crowds sense that a second County Championship is at hand for Glamorgan

Not the team mascot. In the Neath Grammar School XI at the age of thirteen

Competitive start with Neath Cricket Club, winners of the South Wales and Monmouthshire League, 1955. Back row: Jim Bown, Ken Jones, John Williams, John Collins, A.R.L., Peter Lester, Mel Chapman. Front row: Granville Davies, Terry Shufflebotham (captain), Jack Kemp (President), Stan Trick, Les Harris, J. W. Jones

Rivals then, friends now. A.R.L. batting in the 1960 University match at Lord's, watched by wicket-keeper Charles Fry and Abbas Ali Baig at first slip

University openers, still together at the Scarborough Festival. A.R.L. with Roger Prideaux (Kent, Northants and England)

Leading Cambridge for the first time at Fenners, flanked by outstanding academics and fine cricketers: Edward Craig to my right, Mike Brearley on my left

Racehorse trainer Ian Balding, a
friend and former University
rival *(above)*

Short back-and-sides, bull and
big boots at RAF West Kirby
(left)

Cambridge full-back; attracting
the attention of Newport wing-
forward Brian Creswell at
Rodney Parade

Nervous moments before the 1959 Varsity match. Back row: Mr R.C. Williams (Ireland); F.C. Inglis (Oundle and Caius), M.R. Wade (Wyggeston G.S. and Emmanuel), R.L. Makin (Bedford and St. Johns), J.J. Rainforth (Oundle and Emmanuel), P.R. Mills (Rutlish School and Caius), A. Godson (William Hulme's G.S. and Christ's), G. Windsor Lewis (immediate past captain, Trinity Hall). Front row: M.T. Wetson (Marling G.S. and St. Catherine's), K.R.F. Bearne (Rydal and Clare), K.J.F. Scotland (George Heriots School and Trinity), S.R. Smith (captain) (Eltham College and Emmanuel), V.S.J. Harding (Marylebone G.S., and Christ's), D.A. MacSweeney (Rockwell, Tipperary and Christ's), D.R.J. Bird (St. Paul's and St. Johns). Seated: J.C. Brash (Fettes and Christ's), A.R. Lewis (Neath G.S. and Christ's) (*above*)

Happy days with 'Glos' in 1958/59. Back row: T. Day, E. Martin, G. Dance, T.H. Millington, R. Upham. Middle row: R. Morris, T. Lewis, A. Ricketts, R. Timm, B. Hudson, L. King, W.M. Patterson, R. Smith. R. Chamberlayne, S. Davies. Front row: H. J. Balchin, A.T. Voyce, B. Green, P. Ford, C. Thomas (captain), A. Alcock (President), A. Holder, G. Hastings, D. Ibbotson, Rev H. M. Hughes (Chairman), A. Hudson. Seated: K. Ibbotson, M. Booth (*below*)

Wilfred Wooller in 1948, the year when he led Glamorgan to their first County Championship *(left)*

Championship county, Glamorgan, in 1969. Back row: Eifion Jones, Bryan Davis, Malcolm Nash, Lawrence Williams, Roger Davis, Majid Jahangir Khan. Front row: Tony Cordle, Peter Walker, A.R.L., Don Shepherd, Alan Jones. Also played – O.S. Wheatley 6 matches; D.W. Lewis 2

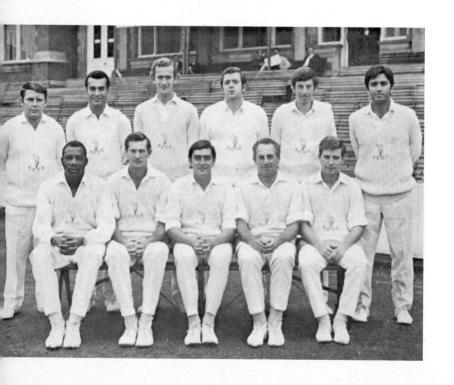

End of the amateur. Batting for the Gentlemen against the Players in the last of the traditional fixtures at Lord's, 1962. Keith Andrew keeps wicket; Phil Sharpe at slip

Ossie Wheatley, Glamorgan captain from 1960-1966. Robin Hobbs backs up; David Constant adjudicates

'Treasure your action,' I can hear him say. 'Never believe it will look after itself.' Don Shepherd, who took over 2000 wickets for Glamorgan

Bernard Thomas's contribution to England cricket has taken him to strange parts! In India he tends Mike Gatting's rear. Tim Robinson can't watch

Peter Walker, the best catcher I ever saw

Mrs Gandhi meets the England team before the first Test in Delhi, 1972. Chris Old is nearest the camera, then Geoff Arnold, Barry Wood and Roger Tolchard

Chatting with Rinku, who as Sharmila Tagore is one of India's best loved film actresses. Wife of my good friend Tiger, the Nawab of Pataudi

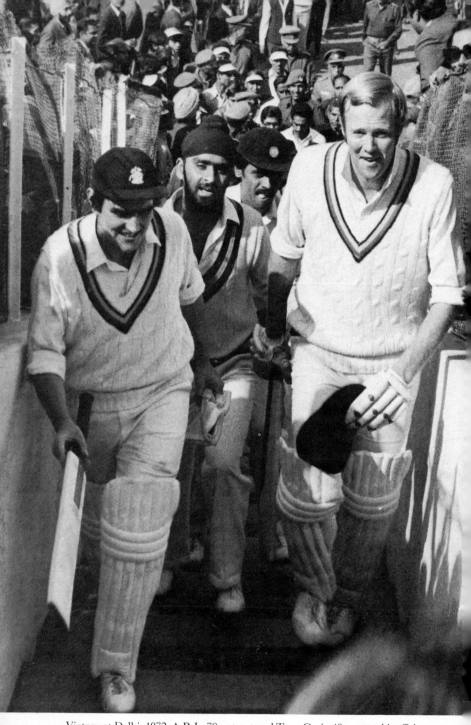

Victory at Delhi, 1972. A.R.L. 70 not out and Tony Greig 40 not out hit off the runs to win. Bishen Bedi follows and Venkat

The captain's job in India is …
trying to get a word in *(above)*

Agit Wadekar, India's captain,
and I agreed to stop close
fielders cheating half way
through the series *(left)*

His Excellency Zulfikar Ali
Bhutto, President of Pakistan,
with the Test captains, both
Glamorgan players, Majid Khan
and A.R.L.

"Goodness gracious me,
a maneater!"

"But all white men
look alike to me"

Pat Pocock fidei defensor, on guard at the Brabourne Stadium

Entrepreneurial days in the sixties. Joanie opens the Popsie Boutique to bring
Carnaby Street to Cardiff

In Bridgetown, Barbados, with Gary Sobers and Clyde Walcott. (Enjoying the one about E.W. Swanton and the rope?)

Mike Denness becomes England captain in the West Indies, 1973-74. He is a guest at the Arabs cocktail party in the Coral Reef Hotel. Emma Balding to his right and Joanie to the left.

At home in Glamorgan with Joanie, Jo and Bella

forearms and cover his head with his hands. If he had more time still, he would do all that and pivot quickly, spinning around to make his back the target rather than his front.

There is one more stroke, more lethal than hook, pull or sweep. In the professional game it is called the whip. It is played with a straight bat. The batsman shapes to on drive, off the back or front foot, then at the last split second he turns his wrists and whips the ball through mid-wicket or square-leg. When it is played off the front foot it is hard to anticipate the stroke at all and when a batsman has little back lift, as Neil Abberley had, fielding at short square-leg becomes Russian roulette. Thus Roger Davis, drawn in by one or two of Neil's early hesitations on a slow pitch which had little bounce, was lured into the trap of standing too close. All it required was a ball of full length, swinging into the legs, and an expert whip shot off the front foot to knock him senseless. The ball apparently struck him behind the left ear as instinct had him turning away to his right.

That 45 minutes break in the dressing room was a doleful affair. Everyone agreed that Roger had been too close. Where was the captain? What about the close-fielders club? Don't captains put a fielder in that position just out of habit these days? Do they genuinely work out that the ball will go there? Isn't it just rubber-stamp time, when the skipper says 'Ah! Yes. Time to attack. We'll have two slips, a gully and two short-legs.'

There was no argument, but it was worth putting the captain's view that a great number of chances did pop up off the bat and pad to leg-trap. It was a combination of two factors, the pitches which too often in England produced uneven bounce and lateral movement for the seam bowlers, and the l.b.w. law which allowed wickets to be taken by balls which pitched outside the off stump and came back. The batsman was safer if he plunged forwards to take the ball on the bat or pad far enough down the pitch to avoid an l.b.w. judgement. Worse still for the batsman, there was the experimental l.b.w. law in practice which stated that a batsman could be given out if he 'intercept a ball pitched outside the off stump and which would have hit the wicket and in the opinion of the umpire he made no genuine attempt to play the ball with the bat.' So the batsman, on responsive pitches, spent most of the days stretching forwards with intent to play the ball. This set of circumstances was bound to bring the short-leg position into play frequently.

A defence for the batsman was put forward. More and more, a ring of close fielders was set around a batsman just to intimidate him. Very often their presence was not justified by the bowling or by the nature of the pitch. Therefore a batsman was entitled to remove that pressure by ignoring the fielders and hammering the ball through them, even at them, whenever he could.

Ambulance bells rang: Roger Davis was on his way to hospital. Lawrence Williams and Malcolm Nash resumed their bowling. There was no short square-leg.

The first change bowler was Don Shepherd. After an over we could see that his off-cutters were biting enough for Roger Davis normally to be brought up to his specialist position. But who now? It was my choice and it had to be me. This was no heroic gesture, but I simply could not bring myself to ask anyone else. I eased in from mid-wicket and crouched a few yards from John Jameson's back pocket. From the start I felt a sluggish, an easy target. I moved with the stroke instead of standing still. My head moved, my feet moved and my left foot moved back, ready to perform the defensive spin-around.

At the end of the over Don Shepherd wanted a chat. 'Don't think I need a short-leg, skip. Tell you honestly, for the first time in my life my hand is sweating just seeing a man at short-leg at all. I can't grip the ball and if I can't drop on the spot I'm not going to get anyone out am I?' I thought about it between overs. If Shep's hands were sweating how would the other lads feel? He was always sensible and tough. His judgement was seldom faulty.

We met again at the start of his next over. We agreed

that the ball was 'doing a bit' and we had to get a man in there close to the bat. But he did not think it should be me. I went back to short square-leg to think. That is a joke. All I could think of was death.

Peter Walker marked a line on the ground where he thought I ought to stand. He kept chatting to me from backward short-leg, offering a crash course in short-leg fielding which I had never attempted in my career. John Jameson swept the ball a powerful blow over my head, down to the deep at square-leg. I began to feel as if I belonged! After one more over from Don Shepherd, Peter turned and said, 'Move over A.R. You'll get hurt if you stay there any longer, and I doubt if you'll catch anything there anyway. I'll do it. You do the backward one.' So Peter Walker went back to his old position, the place where he had lived with danger for a lot of his life, and now, having sworn that he would never return, was back in with the flak again. The sight of a proper fielder with the appropriate reactions for the position helped Don Shepherd because we began to work our way through the Warwickshire batting.

That evening, the players from both sides sipped a thoughtful beer or two on the pavilion balcony. Warwickshire were as horrified as we by the accident. I listened keenly to two pieces of advice, and took them home with me. Later, I sat in my study at home in Groesfaen, a large glass of whisky and water in my hand, looking to the Vale of Glamorgan for escape, but the first voice I kept hearing was M.J.K. Smith's. Mike, a former England captain of course, and an outstanding forward short-leg fielder himself, told me that Roger had been too close. I started to blame myself. Also, he emphasized how the chances that come at short-leg off medium fast bowling differ from those which pop up off the spinners. Obviously with the seamers the ball is coming quicker on to the bat and therefore much more quickly off it. It is suicide to get too close. I blamed myself more.

Then there was Wilf Wooller, another splendid short-leg fielder in his day and another captain who gave

131

thought to every detail of the game. His catches at forward short-leg for Glamorgan were legend. 'You've got to steel yourself,' he hammered out with a pointing finger. 'It's like war. Someone goes down and you've got to get someone else in there straight away. Crying about Roger Davis is going to make you a bad side.' That might sound unsympathetic, but I knew he was right. The overnight news of Roger was not good. We heard that he was suffering from brain damage and could not speak coherently. So, again rather forlornly, we prepared to take the field. Suddenly Tony Cordle, our Cardiff Barbadian, diverted all the attention to his corner of the dressing room and there were one or two laughs. 'I'm serious man, I'm serious,' he kept repeating. 'I'm your short-leg, skip,' he announced loudly, and as he said it he placed a white boxing helmet on his head.

The umpires were out; there was hardly time for discussion. I thought he would wear it for an over or two and then discard it because it looked so ludicrous and completely foreign to the cricket field. Out he went. Tony Cordle moved without question, probably with some relish, to short square-leg, and when he was not fielding there he handed his helmet to the umpires David Evans and Bill Alley. There was some logic in the argument which said that close fielders, who often wore abdominal protection, should also protect their temples. Wilf Wooller blasted in with his belief that the acceptance of helmets on the field simply anticipated injury, and the qualities of courage and skill would be gone. We continued with the easier option, and now I believe we were wrong.

Glamorgan lost that game to Warwickshire. We were bowled out for 90 in the second innings. Tony Cordle continued to wear his helmet through the season and took some good catches at short square-leg. Within a week of his introducing the new equipment, short-leg fielders in other first-class counties acquired headgear of varying styles, Barry Duddleston of Leicestershire, David Lloyd of Lancashire were two. The whole profession quickly identified with the Roger Davis incident: fear found its outlet.

Yet, thereafter, in 1971, Glamorgan were a demoralized side throughout the season in spite of Roger Davis's return to the first team in August. He did not open the batting, but, in the final match of the season at the Oval, the whole team sat on the balcony and watched him duck and hook Bob Willis at his fastest without a flicker of hesitation. We never thought we would see him take on the hard ball again, though Roger himself did not know what all the fuss was about. He could not remember a thing about the events of 21 May. Mind you, he did say that he never wanted to field at short square-leg again. He never did. Tony Cordle did that ... in a helmet.

14

Captain's Diary

MCC Tour of India, Ceylon and Pakistan 1972–73

The Party

	Age	Caps
A.R. Lewis (Glamorgan, Captain)	34	0
D.L. Amiss (Warwickshire)	29	10
G.G. Arnold (Surrey)	28	6
J. Birkenshaw (Leicestershire)	31	0
R.M.H. Cottam (Northamptonshire)	28	2
M.H. Denness (Kent, Vice-Captain)	31	2
K.W.R. Fletcher (Essex)	28	19
N. Gifford (Worcestershire)	32	10
A.W. Greig (Sussex)	26	8
A.P.E. Knott (Kent)	26	41
C.M. Old (Yorkshire)	23	2
P.I. Pocock (Surrey)	26	2
G.R.J. Roope (Surrey)	26	0
R.W. Tolchard (Leicestershire)	26	0
D.L. Underwood (Kent)	27	30
B. Wood (Lancashire)	29	1

Manager
D.B. Carr

Tuesday 28 November 1972
The day before departure. By train from Bridgend to stay the night in London. A strange feeling; unreal all day. It's been such a long wait. It is now four and a half months since I was chosen to captain this tour, but I still haven't put on an MCC sweater – that's the important

fact when you have never played for England before. Picked in July and still haven't played in November. It's the longest wait ever

I have asked Norman Gifford to act as the old-style senior pro on the trip. I believe in senior pros. Vice-captains are too ambitious. So I invest in Gifford, and free Denness from serious responsibility. Gifford does not expect to lead England one day. Denness does. Gifford slipped me a note during dinner which read: 'Have plans for you. Several pints await at Clarendon Court Hotel.'

By midnight I felt as if I had captained England for twenty years!

Wednesday 29 November
We are not a very well-known side. I was walking through the Heathrow air-terminal with Alan Knott. A cameraman asked Knotty, 'Who is Lewis?'

'Here he is,' said Knott.

'Ah! Good,' the cameraman enthused. 'Tell me skipper. Which one is Knott?'

My manager, Donald Carr, and I talked endlessly about the cricket to come. Our problem, from the start, is that no one has played Test cricket in India before. In fact, we only have two Test centuries in the side and both of those belong to Alan Knott, one against Pakistan and another against New Zealand. We asked him to join us. He played against the Indians in England and he set us off on the theories of coping with the Indian spinners, Chandra, Venkat, Prasanna and Bedi. Knotty thinks it is important to stand up to play them because they get more bounce than English spinners. Anyone plunging forward is lost, he thinks. We agreed that ideally the batsmen must remain calm and play the ball firmly, without slogging, through the four close fielders which they always set closely around.

A lot of cricket talked by everyone. The boys are certainly keen. I just had one more thought before dropping off to sleep. Was Geoff Boycott genuine when he cried off? I had chosen him to be my vice-captain.

135

Denness was not in the original party. I think he is too concerned with his own play, but I feel it a kind of duty to keep Geoff Boycott batting with all his dedication for England. He wrote to me to say that, as a young lad, he had had his spleen removed and that he now feared illness in India. He had asked Donald Carr and the Test and County Cricket Board to guarantee treatment in an English hospital if he was ill on tour. Apparently he was told that this was impossible. So he withdrew. Donald Carr has not mentioned it to me yet. Boycott wrote to me to say that he hoped one or two of us might make the Test match grade!

Bombay. It was dark inside the air-terminal, humid, swarming with people, shirt-sleeved, sweating, leaning, fussing, queueing, complaining or uniformed and looking plaster-cast official. Outside, warm currents and the acrid smell of old swamplands.

At the first cross-roads our bus stopped. A sharp rapping at the window took our attention down to the roadside to a dirty looking woman, who had the most beautiful face and who was going through the actions with her hand of eating from a bowl. In the other hand she cradled an undernourished baby with a blown out belly. Tired as we were, this was a shock. 'Why?' I asked the official.

'Already?' he smiled. 'You must never ask "why" of India.'

The Taj Mahal Hotel, handsomely placed on the sea front opposite the left-over symbol of empire, the Gateway to India, is cool, air-conditioned and luxury. My head hit the pillow at 5.45 this morning. At 6.00 a band struck up outside my window. Around the circle in front of the Gateway monument the military brass was launched on an hour's ceremonial rehearsal. Smart, tuneful but extremely unwelcome.

Friday 1 December
Thousands watch our first practice at the Bombay Gymkana. They were roped off about 50 yards from the

nets and they stood there babbling away, ten deep, calling out 'Best of luck uncle' if you went to chase a ball.

Farook Engineer offered me a lift back to the hotel in his small car. Barry Wood and Derek Underwood joined us. We were mobbed as soon as we left the pavilion. We battled, after some difficulty, into Farook's car. Suddenly I felt panicky. The car rocked as hundreds closed in on us. There must have been 50 strange faces grinning through the windows. They shut out the light. Next came noises from on top. They were on the roof. I had a feverish claustrophobia. The car could collapse.

Farook said, with a false grin, 'Keep smiling lads; keep smiling at them whatever you do; wave goodbye as if you love them.' Ever so slowly, the tiny car edged out of its black forest into the mainstream of the Bombay traffic. Sweat covered my whole body.

Tuesday 5 December
Hyderabad. The first day's play in India. MCC against the Board President's XI. First taste of Indian crowds. I kept looking down at my MCC sweater for a few overs, just to make sure it was me. We fielded. After tea my knee started to pain sharply: just the same as last summer. At least I know that it will be alright in the mornings. Ah well! Let's get through it day by day.

This was the noisiest day's cricket I've ever played. 35,000 were there. Most of the rowdiness comes from the enclosures of 'Squatters'. Their explosions, shouting, cheering, whistling, clapping seem to bear no relation to the play at all; at least not all the time. They were most frantic while Sunil Gavaskar was taking 15 minutes to get from 46 to 50. A roar began as every bowler took the first step forwards into his run-up. The crescendo turned each ball into a George Best dribble, drive and shot into the back of the net.

The firecrackers were loudest. These are small fire-works on fuses so short that the exact moment of the explosion can be controlled to the second. Derek Under-wood was stopped by a bang, stunned, half-way through his run-up as if he had been shot.

You could actually watch the arguments spread through the crowd, in a cascade of flying banana skins. Police rushed in with their lathis, whacking away. Strangely, it was easier than you would think to concentrate on the cricket because the eruptions often came while the cricket was quiet. Extraordinary, that. I suppose it was like playing at Old Trafford on a Saturday when you push forward defensively to yet another straight good-length ball from Jack Simmons and suddenly there is a roar which almost takes the roof off Manchester: Bobby Charlton has scored a goal at the other Old Trafford ground, down the road.

In short, it was one helluva hot, hard day. We straggled off the field exhausted to be welcomed by the manager, a man not known for his musical skills, singing a refrain from a song from his tour of India in the early fifties:

> When this bloody tour is over,
> What a happy man I'll be,
> When this bloody tour is over,
> No more India for me.
>
> No more bowling at old Vijay,
> No more toiling on the mat,
> I've had my fill of that Hazare
> Never passed the bloody bat.

Thursday 7 December
First impressions. Umpiring dodgy; poverty shocking; match drawn.

Just along from the Ritz Hotel, *en route* to the stadium, we saw rough huts along the roadside and tiny children without clothes playing like fleas around dirt holes. Old men sleep under blankets to guard fine houses which are in any case guarded by handsome walls. Holes in the wall are often shops. Old-fashioned machinery winds sap from cane and everywhere there is dust and dirt. At the time of writing the crops have failed and many parts of

India have a mammoth drought. Only two hours water is permitted in many parts, except in hotels and privileged houses.

I know who rules India: the sun is King. No one, especially cricketers, can escape it. It consumes energy, slows the mind and chars the skin. You can shelter from it, but never escape. You are its slave.

Friday 8 December

I particularly wanted to spend some time with Norman Gifford and Jack Birkenshaw because they know that they will not be playing cricket for a while. With two Tests, held consecutively within 14 days, I have had to tell these two that Pat Pocock and Derek Underwood are the first choices to begin with, so Giff and Birki have to be left out of the build-up matches too. It is not easy to break such news to cricketers, however professional they may be, and these two are very special. I hammered home the message that their most important contribution is to be always available to bowl to our front-line batsmen in the nets. We must learn to play spin well. Day and night Gifford and Birki must be bowling in the nets. When they heard this they were sad, but soon came back to tell us that they are prepared to offer a special service to anyone who admits to being a Test batsman! They have a new business card printed which reads 'Messrs Gizzard and Brickenshaw Ltd. – Net Bowlers'.

I completed my patrol with Jack Birkenshaw's room. I found him lying under the mosquito net, reading the *Leicester Mercury*.

'How is it?' I said.

'Well, just look at me captain. What a life! Tha' keeps me in bluddy nets all day, now all bluddy neet as well.'

Saturday 9 December

MCC v. Central Zone, Indore. I know why Sunil Gavaskar was joking down in Hyderabad. He said that the actual pitch in Indore will be turning on the first day, and the outfield will turn on the second day. He is right.

139

There is not a blade of grass anywhere; it is uneven and rock hard. Jack Birkenshaw suggested that we all keep spittin' while we are fielding so that it might green up by the third day.

In the evening there was a reception in the garden of our hotel (they'd never dare go inside). The Maharani of Indore was there. Talked to her for a long time about her love of books and music. She is lovely. She told me the story of her husband correcting their young son who is very keen on cricket – 'No, you do not call MCC our enemies; in cricket, we say opponents.'

Sunday 10 December
Bad day. Injury strikes. I have pulled a calf muscle in my right leg. I will miss the next game at least. I am depressed because I was pleased with progress. Chris Old and Barry Wood are also off the field with strains. Tony Greig has a strained side and Bob Cottom has blisters. We should have spent a few more casual days in Bombay at the start. Donald Carr agrees. MCC sides must get that right next time.

Friday 15 December
Excellent team meeting in Delhi on the way to Amritsar. The first Test is here next Thursday. Every member of the party contributed to the discussion. The conclusions were:

1 Indians are used to spin bowling and, against spinners, they score most of their runs square on the off-side, off the back foot. All their teams have expert spinners. They are obviously unused to fast bowling, so we should probably be best using at least one fast bowler all the time. Knotty wants to pick all four fast bowlers for the first Test.

2 Our spinners should bowl straighter, not wide of the off-stump, and not throw in too many variations at once. We should be careful of overattacking in the field, but gully is a key position to the seamers, deep,

140

and possibly two at a time.

3 Batsmen must keep cool when surrounded by Indian close fielders. Bob Cottam suggested that Bishen Bedi can be ruffled if we attack him.

4 In the field we should lie deeper than we do in England. The ball runs fast over the dry outfields.

The dominant feeling was a defensive one. We should make the Indians fight for their runs and we should be happy with a draw in the first Test. It would buy time until we are on top of our game in foreign conditions.

My calf muscle injury is serious. Bernard Thomas has made foam pads which fit under the heel inside my shoes. I am not to walk anywhere without the raised heel, not even from bed to bathroom. I have had sackfuls of letters from Indians.

Sunday 17 December
Govind, the bearer assigned to Donald Carr and me, has looked after touring teams for the Indian Cricket Board since the Commonwealth Tour 1950–51. Govind is round-faced, shortish and rather tubby. He looks well-fed, fit and about 40. He anticipates every problem and administers to all the players' needs in the dressing rooms with a smile. 'Delighted to be of assistance, Sahib.'

Tonight, while the party were out at a reception given by the Maharani of Indore and I was resting my leg at the Lantern Hotel and feeling glum on a hard bed in the half light, Govind came in, beaming as ever. 'I have fixed for Sahib a splendid banquet in Manager's room,' he announced with a bow. I followed him to Donald's room, which was the most spacious of the lot, though some way short of luxury, and there, sure enough, a splendid table had been laid. What could they possibly produce? Govind had organized fish, chicken, fruit and local beer. He was right; it was a banquet. He opened and closed the doors for the waiter, whom, I felt, had found some antiquated uniform with brass buttons and epaulettes and plumed headdress especially for the night, and Govind generally fussed around me.

'Sadly, Sahib, I lack money. With money I could buy a good job. Everyone has a price in this land. I think you call it the land of the back-hander.'

Govind was brazenly pro-British. His father had worked all his life for the British High Commission. 'I wish British still ruled India. Everybody knew where they were in those days.'

The beer went down well. For hours I was regaled with fine tales of the Raj, and the teller did well to keep the tear from his eye. I was a stand-in for his British fantasy and we were both actors. For the first time India felt old and timeless to me. A peep into the past had opened both eyes to the present.

Monday 18 December
We are now in the Oberoi Intercontinental Hotel in Delhi, the first Test two days away. Will I make it? I have stuck to Bernard's instructions. I still have not tried to run, and although I can walk with the padding, I feel the calf muscle pulling again as soon as I walk flat-footed around the bedroom.

Jim Swanton has joined the party for a short while. He brought a tape from Joan. She says she has written 12 letters. I have not received any. I mentioned this to Barry Wood who is very upset because his wife has not sent any either. I feel like writing to him myself.

A smartly suited Indian came up to me in the bar this evening holding a piece of string between his hands. He looked as if he was about to strangle me. I backed away. He smiled and kept coming. 'My name is Adya. Hold out your arm. He ran the cord from shoulder, around the elbow and down to my wrist. 'A 40 chest?' were his first words. He grinned at me and offered to buy me a drink. 'I am a sweater manufacturer,' he then admitted. 'I wish you a fine present. Oh! By the way. I have arranged business in Delhi to coincide with first Test but sadly lack ticket ...'

Tuesday 19 December

I hardly slept last night. I woke up knowing that I had to take a fitness test and felt, as soon as I flexed my calf muscle in bed, that I would miss the first Test. I even told Mike Denness in the lift last night that he would be captain of England before me.

At the ground, the team went off to the nets; I stayed with Bernard Thomas. I jogged for the first time since the injury ten days ago and amazingly felt nothing, but found it strange running with the high padding under the heel. I then did lots of stretching exercises under Bernard's direction. I then went in to bat for 40 minutes. Still felt nothing. Finally, on the outfield, Bernard got me to run flat out, wearing pads, thigh pad, the lot. A miracle. Where was the pain? He suggested that in the Test match I should try to run my runs carrying the bat in the left hand so that I would do my stopping and turning off the good leg, the left. He has decided that I would play. He is a magician, but will I be alright for five days? It does seem crazy that after waiting so long for a chance to play for England, 17 years from my first-class debut, that I shall be going onto the field with my right foot tilted up by a false foam heel inside my shoe, and tough adhesive strapping from my ankle to my right knee. The pain which hits my other knee every day now comes like an old friend.

So I sit writing this diary after the traditional dinner which England teams have together before Test matches. Alan Knott, the senior player, stood and said a few words to wish me well on my debut.

It is hard to avoid nostalgia. The Christmas carols are piping out from the hotel stereo, sending my thoughts homewards. I think of Joan and the girls and want them to be proud; of my father who bowled to me in the garden, and of everyone at Neath Grammar School and at Neath Cricket Club. A good day for Neath in fact. Only one other Welshman has captained England, C.F. Walters, and he was also from Neath Grammar School and the Neath Club.

Wednesday 20 December
Arnold bowls to Gavaskar and I have played for
England. This evening I telephoned Joan. Told her it
was strange to be Welsh and yet playing for England. It
was on the scoreboard – England: A. R. Lewis. All my
life at home, England has been the opposition.

Thursday 21 December
A. R. Lewis l.b.w. b. Chandrasekhar 0. What a debut! I
know Len Hutton did it in his first Test, and Keith
Fletcher was noble enough to own up to it too, but why
me?

I retreated, head down, through all those baying
Indians and when I flopped on the chair in the dressing
room, I could not believe it. I still don't believe it. Is it
really true? The England players were generous, but I
now have to face the past and the frightening future:
nought behind me and what next time? That's the
question. I have three or four days to wait before finding
out.

England have not batted well. The Indian spinners
have succeeded in pressurizing everyone with their ring
of five or six close fielders – Solkar, Abid Ali, Wadekar,
Gavaskar, Venkat, and even Parkar sometimes. Chandra
got a lot of bounce. The leg-spinner only occasionally
turned, but the top-spinners and googlies fizzed and got
up above waist high. Amazingly, Chandra has a with-
ered bowling arm which acts like a delayed whiplash. He
bowled Keith Fletcher with his faster ball, which was as
quick through the air and off the pitch as any seamer
could bowl it. He competes like a cornered cat, teeth
tightly clenched, only opening them to screech his
appeals for this, that or anything.

Oddly enough, the l.b.w. decision which got rid of me
for a duck in my first Test match was so atrocious I
scarcely felt any pain immediately. I walked back to the
pavilion after only two balls with sadness, but also with

144

disbelief.

We are certainly up against it out here. The crowds roar whenever the ball hits the pad and fielders all around leap in the air each time to appeal for a catch, an l.b.w. or anything. They annoy me. This is probably not the usual tour of India. Wadekar's team are acclaimed as world champions after beating Illingworth's England and Sober's West Indies away from home. This is their lap of honour.

Sunday 24 December
Is it real? Can it be true? A.R. Lewis is off the mark in Test cricket, 17 not out, and England are at least in with a chance of winning if we can get a good start tomorrow. It is Christmas Eve. I've never been 17 not out on Christmas Eve! It is very funny going down in the lift listening to piped music. Bing Crosby sings about roasting chestnuts on an open fire, Jingle Bells and Adeste Fideles. My thoughts are with Joan, Joanna and Anabel. What a Christmas present if England win the Test!

Monday 25 December
Can Christmas ever be the same again? England score 207 for 4 to win the first Test by seven wickets. Who would have thought a young, untried side could have done that? We are widely acclaimed. Champagne in the dressing room, telegrams rush in from home, and some of the boys travel back to the hotel on the roof of the team's bus, waving to the crowds lining the streets. Alan Knott gave everyone a warning smile. 'I'll stay in here downstairs. Four more Tests to go before I jump up there.'

The evening was a peculiar anti-climax, though no fault of our hosts. We spent it drinking beer and singing some feeble out-of-tune carols in the British High Commission Club, but still a unique Christmas Day.

Now, writing hurried notes in bed. I think of my own batting, 70 not out. I was six overs getting off the mark: it was almost forever. When I pushed a ball from Chandra towards mid-off – a long run, but I did not start out confidently. Barry Wood urged me on, but my legs were rubber and it felt as if someone was pulling back the wickets at the other end further and further away from me.

Greiggy played well, 40 not out. We did not attempt anything flashy. We gently 'milked' the spinners and their close fielders receded.

70 not out and the Man of the Match award! I wish I had known I was going to do that four days ago. Back in the dressing room I was still afraid to place my right foot flat on the floor, and my leg was still wrapped in adhesive plaster. I lifted the glass of champagne to the little man in the corner who was sipping orange. He winked back. Bernard Thomas had performed the Christmas miracle as far as I was concerned.

Wednesday 27 December
Calcutta. I have been too ill to speak let alone write, but at last I feel like living not dying. Whatever people tell you about tummy trouble out here, believe it. On Boxing Day I felt bloated and could not eat or drink. By the evening I was doubled up with pains, high up, just under the ribs. Then for 12 hours right through the night, I was vomiting until I could hardly stand up.

The plane trip to Calcutta has been a nightmare today. Bernard had given me a sleeping pill to get through it. The Test starts tomorrow.

Saturday 30 December
Calcutta. Grand Hotel. This is a most miserable room, windowless, with cold marble floors and cheap furniture. Yet it has been a day I will never forget. There are moments which you know are indelible. Today, walking out into the blinding sunlight to bat for England in front of 85,000 Indians at Eden Gardens, was one of them.

I was amused to hear before the start of this Test match that thousands of 200-rupee tickets had been printed in duplicate. The Indian official who informed

146

me showed no surprise. It was almost expected. Never ask why! Sure enough, outside the ground, as the England team arrived by coach, there they were, the thousands, even at nine o'clock in the morning, squatting on the rough ground. Apparently the fans pay a rupee for the privilege of sitting down in sight of small blackboards on which entrepreneurs chalk up the changing events according to commentaries on transistor radios. When a bowler appeals for l.b.w. inside the ground, the entrepreneurs outside yell owzat too.

I know I shall never forget the sensation of waiting in the England dressing room to go in to bat next. It is not a pavilion where you can see out, just a cluster of rooms tucked away beneath the open stands. You rely on interpretation of the shouts and roars to know what is happening. There are many false alarms. You can hear the sudden rise and fall of the roar. It is like holding a seashell to both ears. But there is no mistaking the prolonged delirium ignited by the fall of an English wicket. Bat, glove, cap – out you go, through the back slaps, the floating flowers tossed from the stands and the twists of rice exploding at your feet. The bull must be properly feted ... before being killed.

The Indian spinners have been in strangling mood again. Very few England batsmen fought their way out of the ring of close fielders to get double figures. You can sense as you take guard that the crowd expect a quick kill. This is so different from Delhi.

I walked out into the white heat over surprisingly green grass. Six fielders closed in to within a few yards of my bat. Chandra began his run-up and the most deafening chant matched each step. Mirrors flashed in the crowd behind his arm; pots and pans were clanging to the right and the whole stadium appeared to be into a crazy, rythmical war dance. Then, abruptly, as Chandra twirled over his arm, the 85,000 spectators were silent. I could hear the ball go brrrrr through the air.

It was hypnotizing. I almost had to say to myself, right, Tony, its your move next. Habit got my feet going

147

in the general direction of the ball and I fended it off. This game, more than the last, is being played close to the bat, and we are so lacking experienced Test batsmen to attack and break the shackles. I wish we had two players out here; John Edrich, especially because he is left-handed, and Basil D'Oliveira because he would be brazen enough to step down the wicket to straight drive Bedi and Prasanna. I hope this isn't too defeatist, but it has been a day of torture out there and it will be so difficult to turn the tide without aggression.

Monday 1 January 1973
I did not stay up to see in the New Year, but it is hard to relax. I can see, even in my bed, the massed chorus of spectators stretching high up in the sky at Eden Gardens. They may look like the heavenly host but they are at the devil's work as far as we are concerned. They never allow the action to become settled or calm. Someone stands up and bangs a large gong and so the whole crowd claps out his rhythm. Another pelts Pat Pocock with oranges, and so they all throw oranges. Tony Greig defuses it by pushing a couple of oranges up his jumper and parades like a 6ft. 7½in. drag artist. The throng outside the gates gets impatient with appealing for l.b.w.s by proxy and charges the barrier of policemen. When the ball hits your pad it is deafening – the Indian cricketers appeal, 85,000 spectators inside the ground appeal and so do the 85,000 outside, the ones with the duplicated tickets.

Each night we leave the ground and pass the squalid shanty towns. Small children with swollen bellies splash in mud pools. On the way home in the bus you can look down at the sweat on your shirt, and run your finger along blistered lips, and complain about the dungeon-like rooms in the Grand Hotel if you want, but it takes just a glance out of the window to let in the chill alternative.

Thursday 4 January
On a perfect pitch we got into a winning position in the

148

field. We were magnificent until we tried to bat. No excuses. We failed to score a piffling 190 to win on a shirt front. Misery. One-all. Should be two-nil.

England's demise was greeted by a wild Bengali rush across the ground. Frantic spectators swarmed up into the players' enclosure which was part of a raised stand in front of the dressing rooms. We had to jump over the side to get to cover. There was a terrible crush. Youths were pinned to scaffolding and began to scream horribly. The police behaved insanely. They began to whack those in the front row of the crush, the ones who were jammed against fences and could not move whatever pain was inflicted on them. Inevitably a youth's head was split open, and this drove the crowds even more senseless; it incited greater hostility, and they threw anything that came to hand at the police. The disarray just about summed up the day.

We recovered. There were some laughs at dinner. Derek Underwood told us how he was lying in the bath in his room this evening washing away the dust and dirt, and hoping perhaps to soothe the disappointed spirit, when the doors burst open and some Indian fans came in. 'Underwood, Underwood,' was all they said, as they directed their camera straight at him and clicked. He yelled them out. That was the ultimate humiliation of the day he thought. But it was not. When he came down to the foyer later on, he was confronted by the same happy little group of photographers, asking Derek to sign the photo of himself in the bath. *That* was the final humiliation.

Friday 5 January

Just before we left Calcutta for Bangalore today, we received a written threat. Only Donald Carr and I know about it so far. It claims to be from the Black September movement. They have threatened to kill one of our party. Surely it is a hoax. Yet the murders at the Munich Olympic Games are only four months behind us, when 14 Israeli hostages were first held and then slaughtered, and while not wanting to panic without reason, we have informed the Indian police. They have told us that security around the MCC team will be increased from now on.

Sunday 7 January

A big shock! Joan telephoned from Wales to say that she was driving back home from St David's, Pembrokeshire, when she heard news of Black September threats on the lives of the MCC team in India. Palestinians are thought to be seeking reprisals for the arrest in Britain of one of their Black September group. How did Joan find out at home? The British press agreed not to write it although they are now aware of the threat. I gave her all the assurances I could. She is a little happier, but there will be more wives on the phone tonight.

The team met urgently over a beer in the bar. Donald Carr has arranged for them to make calls home. It is an unreal threat, but as Keith Fletcher put it, it is unreal only until it is real, and then it is too late.

Tuesday 9 January

Lying under the mosquito net three days before the third Test reading *Night of the Scorpion* by Paul Scott ... only a side-light shining, but looking up through the flimsy net I see the fan waft and whir, around and around.

(Bedi bowls. Lewis races down the wicket and crashes a six over long-off. Chandra bowls his top-spinner ... Lewis lies back and cuts it in a flash for four to third man ... dreams, dreams.) Someone has got to do it.

The hot night stops me sleeping. Shall I use the air-conditioning which sounds like the old *Pembroke Castle* steam-engine stoking up at Paddington Station or perhaps, if I leave the bathroom door open, I can turn on the fan out there and that will do. The heat and the prospect of tomorrow's Test match worry me. Fear of failure. I have scored few runs since the first Test. I can feel the press vultures hovering. Whoever dreamed up the saying 'the game's the thing'? It may be in the end, but at this very moment, the night before a Test match, the mind races, the feet perspire, and sleep is a long way away.

Wednesday 10 January
Arrive Madras. All around us at the airport are the glistening helmets of soldiers. They carry guns. Behind them are police and airport security men. We are shielded from the crowds who have come to see us. A bus arrives just a few yards away from the airstrip and we set off for the Connemara Hotel. Sentries, armed and helmeted, guard the hotel entrance.

On the bus to the nets this afternoon we had the quaint experience of being accompanied by 'shotgun' riders. Machine guns were set up at the front and the rear of the bus. What is going on? MCC has had no further threat from the Black September group and everyone is content to think of it as a hoax. Security at the ground is collosal. Surely we are not expected to play a Test series in this atmosphere.

Back at the hotel this evening Bob Cottam wandered out of his room to look for his Northamptonshire team-mate Bishen Bedi who was also staying there. A security guard stopped him. First Bob's identity was checked out, then Bishen's, according to their room numbers, and finally, as Bob was setting off for his chat, the security guard was attempting to communicate on his walkie-talkie to the guard on Bishen's floor – 'Cottam, tall, big, MCC player is arriving.' Bob left. When he returned five minutes later, the guard was still yelling ... 'Hello. Yes. Kottum, yes, Kottum coming. Big MCC cricketer ... Hello. Hello. Kottum comes ... Oh! Hello, Kottum ... Hello. Hello. Cancel, cancel. Kottum is back.'

Saturday 13 January
Chris Old asks to leave the field after three overs of the Test match because 'M'trousers are stook t'me legs.' True. His whites turned to greys as the perspiration ran down his body. His tightly tailored trousers were wrap-

ped around his legs like soaking flags around a couple of poles.

Tuesday 16 January
We are losing this Test, I can feel it. The pitch is turning a lot and Derek Underwood is missing. Carelessly, he took too much sun on the day before the game and has a temperature. Norman Gifford took his place and is bowling well enough, but Unders can win a match on his own on such a wicket.

The umpiring is getting worse and today we had a major incident on the field. Agit Wadekar edged a ball from Chris Old straight to Tony Greig at second slip. Greiggy caught it well, about knee high, and threw it in the air. Wadekar stayed where he was, waiting to be given out by the umpire. The umpire then confused everyone by shaking his head, which often means 'yes' in India, and yet signalling with his hands palms down that it was not out.

When the England players had digested this for a second or two they went berserk. Tony Greig raced from second slip towards the umpire at the bowler's end with the ball raised in his hand as if he was Geronimo. While he was yelling away, Alan Knott threw his glove high in the air, and they were both supported by Barry Wood, who accused the umpire of saying 'not out'. The umpire said nothing of the sort. He said he had been unsighted by Chris Old's follow through. I placed myself between the players and the umpire and told them to shut up. I asked the umpire what was going on. He said that he wished to consult the square-leg umpire. He did and returned to give Wadekar out.

This sort of incident was inevitable because of the gamesmanship which has developed near the bat. The whole series so far has been played within a few yards of the crease and fielders are claiming catches off bat and pad which are very tricky to adjudicate. Tony Greig openly believes that if an umpire rejects an appeal then a show of disbelief will get him the doubtful decision next time, whether the batsman has snicked it or not. It is, by any description, plain cheating. But the same is happening to us. Either both sides must play fair, or both cheat, to have an even contest.

At the close of today's play I went into the Indian dressing room and confronted Agit Wadekar. Shall we play cricket for the next two and a half Tests, or shall we cheat? 'Let's play cricket,' he said. The whole Indian team nodded but wanted a guarantee that Tony Greig would not continue his acting performance near the bat. I pointed to Abid Ali, Solkar and Engineer as equal culprits. Solkar was even in the habit of appealing for l.b.w.s from the position of short square-leg.

Donald Carr was not at the game when it happened, but he had read the most unfavourable press. He called an immediate meeting. All the players agreed that the charade of pressurizing umpires was not to be part of our game.

Wednesday 17 January
India win the third Test. They go two-one up. Our demonstration of bad temper has made world news. It looks even worse when we lose. Donald Carr has publicly apologized to the Indians. I have had more words with Greig and with Knott.

We could be three Tests up now. We have got into three winning positions in the field, but our batting has failed. In this match, only Keith Fletcher (97) and Mike Denness (76) can be exempt from critiscism. Lewis scored 4 and 11. So we lost and the campaign suffered a mighty set-back. Our morale is down. I am proud of the fact that I am still on the field. Every day my knee turns on the agony towards tea-time, but I have soldiered on and I am still fit enough to give of my best, if only I can get going again with the bat.

The time is beginning to drag. There are 24 more days to go in India. We have done well to endure the toughest conditions, blistering sun and non-existent social life for four months. A pint down the local would taste rather special at this moment.

153

The captaincy has come naturally because I am so used to it, making decisions about something or other every moment of the day. I find it hard to concentrate on my batting in the zonal matches. Dennis Amiss has been telling me that he feels it takes six or eight Test matches to be settled in Test cricket.

Saturday 20 January

I received from home a cutting from the *Sun* newspaper. Everyone knows now about the Black September threat. The story appeared under Clive Taylor's name. He is upset, because all the writers travelling with us agreed with Donald Carr not to mention a word of it.

Clive came to my room to apologize, saying that he was responsible only for a few lines of it and that he guessed the front of the story had been filed from India by a cricket reporter called Prabu of the *Indian Times*. Clive says that he feels that the story should have been written as soon as the soldiers and machine guns arrived in Madras, when we were taken to the ground under armed guard every day and by different routes in order to confuse anyone who might be planning a serious attack on the side. It should have been written.

As it is now, the English writers have been made to hop about a bit by their London sports desks. Clive Taylor thought of resigning from the *Sun*. He is disappointed that his office wrote the story without contacting him. He feels that his relationship with the MCC party has been destroyed. I think it will be momentarily affected, but Clive Taylor has the respect of every cricketer in Britain. I've told him that.

Our show goes on. I called another team meeting to say that as long as I am captain there would be no over-acting in order to get an umpire's decision; no pressurizing of umpires. Few applauded. Donald Carr did. Are we both left over from a different age? We have become good friends.

Wednesday 24 January

The day before the fourth Test match. This hotel in

Kanpur is alive with soldiers and plain-clothes police-men. Again, no one is allowed to put a foot on our floor, nor can they even take the same lift-ride as an MCC player. It is disconcerting. Do they know something which we do not? Are we truly in danger? I suppose they cannot afford to take the chance of the threats being a hoax. The police told me that they are afraid of the students as much as anyone else in Kanpur.

The MCC boys went on an official shopping expedi-tion along a pre-planned route lined by the police and the army. Charming. Even so, the boys say they were pushed and pawed everywhere. After coming out of one large store Jackie Birkenshaw was missing. Someone eventually spotted him, pinned to the side of the bus by a couple of oxen harnessed to a cart. The captive Birki, aware of his audience in the bus, wagged an angry finger at the oxen. 'No. I've told you, no. Ah'm not signing now.'

We had a practice in the early afternoon – a good work out. Afterwards Bob Cottam raced first into the showers. 'Ah!' he said. 'Hot water.' He turned to hang up his towel, turned back and the water dribbled to a halt. He stood around for a quarter of an hour and eventually gave up. As he left he slammed the door ... and the shower started up again ... we stripped off, and then it stopped again.

Thursday 25 January
Wadekar wins the toss for the third time. India bat. Graham Roope and Jack Birkenshaw make their Test debuts.

Friday 26 January
Rest day already. Visited All Souls Church, which was erected soon after the Cawnpore mutiny on the sight of the cantonment where the sepoys killed so many Brit-ish men, women and children. Clive Taylor was with me.

The church gardens are quiet, but you can see the low

remains and the original outline of the barracks. We saw the well where a lot were killed as they ferried water to those inside. It was a bloody massacre. When Clive and I saw just how many were murdered – long lists of names beneath regimental plaques on the walls inside the church – we both agreed that we could imagine the screams of women and children, the cracks of round shot and musket shot. We wandered on without talking.

Monday 29 January
A.R. Lewis b. Abid Ali 125. Dreams into fact; down the pitch to drive the spinners over the top ... Bedi bowls and Lewis makes ground down the track .. he is not quite to the ball but it is a good pitch and, in any case, the shackles of the Indians have to be smashed by someone ... the ball meets the bat with the sweetest of sounds and flies straight back over Bishen's head, first bounce into the crowd. Not a bad way to get off the mark in a Test match!

The Indians chortled around me after that opening and edged in closer. Bedi frowned and wrung his spinning fingers tighter around the ball. The next ball was short. I went back and felt the same surge to destroy, to square cut it for four. Some instinct took over which told me that in my adventurous state of mind I would be safer batting at the other end! I settled for a pushed stroke between the close fielders, into the space at square cover, and a single. Five runs in an over was a luxury, and not only for me.

In the next over I faced from Bishen, again I went down the pitch and hit straight. He saw me coming once and slanted it quickly down the leg side. I darted back without playing a shot. I had practised going down the pitch to Norman Gifford in the nets many times. Norman would just hang on to the ball if he saw me coming. He would force me to leave my charge until the last split second.

Next ball, I was away down again, and drove a six over mid-off. The Indian close fielders disappeared and I was out of captivity. Soon Bishen had five men on the boundary – deep extra-cover, long-off, long-on, deep mid-wicket and a deep square-leg on the sweep. Solkar, the most brilliant of all their close fielders, was at long-on. Chandra was too quick through the air to treat the same way, but with him it is always more a case of waiting for the bad ball.

It was the first century on either side in the series. For England it was the first hundred in 14 Test matches.

There was an amusing moment when I got to a hundred. Lots of Indians ran onto the field with garlands and handshakes. However, the century had come with a single which took me to the other end. The student avalanche therefore hit Keith Fletcher. I looked down the pitch and saw him suffocating with garlands, all dripping wet, and beaten to a pulp by back-slappers. He walked up the pitch and said, 'It's OK for you mate, but I'm only five not out.'

Perhaps Robin Marlar in the *Sunday Times* caught, best of all, the atmosphere here in Kanpur, at least the mixture of student aggression and our own security forces: also, the sheer difficulty of playing cricket in this climate. He wrote:

The vultures sit, 16 to a tree, the big brown kites whirl and dive, hundreds of thousands of bicycles are pedalled through Kanpur's crowded streets, the cars hoot and are ignored, and not so far from the bridge where the massacred bodies were disposed of during the mutiny of a century and more ago, in the new Modi Stadium in Green Park, England are trying to square up a series watched by 14,000 cheerful but potentially dangerous students and most of the police force of Uttar Pradesh.

England got the best of a drawn match. I am happy about my innings but I have one huge problem, my knee. I wrote to Wilf Wooller today to say that although my pain threshold has leaped up, I cannot play like this for much longer. What do I do? A cartilage operation will take time, and there is a new season with Glamorgan ahead.

However, I resigned the Glamorgan captaincy last autumn because of the knee though no one knew it, and maybe I should have an operation when I get home. It is certainly agony. I wish the joint would lock and we would know it was finished. Quite honestly, I wish at this moment, lying on my bed in Kanpur, that someone would saw it off from the knee, century or no century.

Monday 5 February
Just before net practice, Donald Carr received a typed message to say that some players would be killed during this fifth and final Test. We had a team meeting. The boys do not want to play. They will only play if all the tall buildings around the Brabourne Stadium are evacuated. The police agree. Great start to a match which we must win to draw the series!

Tuesday 6 February
Wadekar wins the toss. The pitch is without grass. India get 250 for 4 in the day. Our mission is now just about impossible.

While we were fielding a lot of the England fielders kept looking up at the tall buildings around the stadium. Eyes alert for the 'jackal'. It is a poor mental approach to a Test match. It is mercilessly hot too. Laughter comes from fear. The boys reckon that Alan Knott is the only wicket-keeper ever to walk in with a bowler's run-up! No one is going to shoot him that way. Keith Fletcher too fidgets around at first slip. 'It's alright for you skipper,' he responded to one of my jibes. 'If he shoots at you you'll only be hit in the leg and you'll be out l.b.w. again.' His reference was to the long run of l.b.w. decisions which the Indian umpires delighted to inflict on me.

Sunday 11 February
The end inevitably comes. Drawn game. England loses the series one-two. I made my way to the top of the

stands to do all the radio and television interviews at the end. I felt sick. Agit Wadekar understood this well. He has become a good friend. We both thought back to the time when we had agreed to cut out the theatricals close to the bat, and we had both stuck to our word.

But the failure of three and a half months of effort made me feel ill. I do not care about the future captaincy of England. I have never felt ambitious for it. But we gave this campaign a massive amount of thought and effort and, if I was honest, I would say that we would have won three Test matches, having done the work expertly in the field, if we could have batted better. We needed more experience than we had on the tour. We needed Boycott and Edrich for solidity, and I feel that D'Oliveira was the man who could have given us character.

As I did my bit for the media, Tony Greig took MCC on a lap of honour. Greiggy has had an adoring audience on this trip. The side were cheered to the heavens and I am proud of them; they all gave everything. But what the hell is Greiggy doing out there with my team?

Monday 12 February
On the bus to the airport we take a last look at India. Jack Birkenshaw, next to me, sighs and says, 'Well, d'y'know skip, I only realized yesterday why I've had no luck with the girls on this trip. Every time I've asked 'em they've shaken their heads. I thought it meant, "No, clear off Birky you little Yorkshire git." But now I know, headshakes mean "acha". Yes Birky you handsome, honey-tongued Yorkshire devil, come and take me.'

We laughed a long time about this, and India was gone.

15

Majid Khan

My first sight of Majid Jahangir, as he then called himself, was in 1967 at the St Helens ground at Swansea. He was a member of Pakistan's touring team. It was August and the Tests had gone poorly for him. He felt his lack of good form deeply, because he came with a handsome reputation, and because to Majid, a serious-minded, 20-year-old Muslim, the Western world had nothing to offer except runs, catches and wickets.

His mood as he came out to bat on that bright sunny morning must have been the mixture of bravado and desperation which every cricketer knows. Minutes later he was hitting Roger Davis's off-spin for five sixes in an over to the pavilion end, high up onto the terraces of the members' enclosure. In 89 minutes at the crease he scored 147 not out, an innings begun and completed before lunch.

Glamorgan rather enjoyed it. Certainly, we did not grieve. Matches against touring sides had ceased to be the keen battles of old. County players would often be rested from these games in order that they could be sharp for one of the competitions which, as levels of sponsorship were creeping up, were becoming more important to the players. Majid was brilliant entertainment for the crowd, but it was impossible for any of the Glamorgan players to judge how good a player he was. It was a bit of a slog; a glorious, savage, talented slog.

A month later, the Test and County Cricket Board decided that counties could recruit one overseas cricketer by immediate registration. Wilfred Wooller, Glamorgan's secretary, immediately got in touch with Majid Jahangir's home in Lahore.

The Glamorgan players, when they heard this, were sceptical about the secretary's motives. Was he not an old friend of Dr Jahangir Khan, Majid's father, during their days in the Cambridge University side in the early thirties? The old pals act? How could he say that Majid was a steady enough player to make an impact on the county game? There were plenty of other Test players from whom to choose. By the time my Glamorgan team-mates, Don Shepherd and Peter Walker, and I were on the 1968 Commonwealth tour of Pakistan under the captaincy of Richie Benaud, Majid had already been signed by Glamorgan. So, at Rawalpindi we had our second look at him. He played two scorching drives, breathtaking stuff, and then, a couple of balls later, holed out to mid-on – ct. Lewis b. Shuttleworth 8. Shepherd, Walker, and Lewis went into a huddle. Had Glamorgan been landed with a dud?

The records now prove that doubts were never more brilliantly dispelled. Majid did more than play well for himself, he positively led the Glamorgan batting from 1968 until his departure after the 1976 season. He earned the respect of every opposition and of his team as well. He was the darling of the Welsh public. On top of his technique and the sheer eye appeal of his stroke-play, Majid possessed the pride of the Pathan. No pitch, not even the uneven strip at Sophia Gardens in Cardiff, would persuade him to throw away his wicket. He was at his most stubborn in a tight spot, and for the sake of the side would bowl too, even though he was always worried about a recurring injury to his back. (For the whole of one season he slept on the bedroom floor.)

Yet, in spite of the maturity of his cricket, he was, at heart, still a small boy playing games. He never treated batting as a work-a-day duty but responded to challenges, sometimes no more than schoolboy banter. For months he lived with the Lewises, and so we travelled together and became close friends. The greatest love of

161

his life at one time, outside his family and his religion, were movies and ice-cream. He was a masterly baby-sitter for my two daughters Joanna and Anabel. A man of few words, he would produce the ultimate threat if they were making too much noise. 'You girls. Watch TV or go to bed.' Well, at least they knew where they were.

With the same abruptness he announced to me half-way through the 1969 season, 'I will win you championship.' He meant it; he had set himself a target, and that would be all the incentive he would need to dig out the gold at the depths of his talent.

We once did a deal at Cheltenham, when Glamorgan had to beat and overtake Gloucestershire at the top of the table, that I should buy him two ice-creams for a 50, three for a 75, four for a 100 and so on. That evening he was furious and angry with himself for failing. 'I wanted six or even eight ice-creams,' he said. 'Big ones, double 99s. But I only had a taste this time.' Yes, I had walked around the ground with him to the ice-cream van and paid up – two ices for a brilliant innings of 69, which turned out to be the top score of the whole match on either side.

Next year, 1970, we played at Cheltenham again on a damp turning wicket. It was almost a benefit match for the spinners. I went out to join Majid at the crease when we had lost two wickets for 15 runs. David Allen bowled me a couple of balls that bit and turned and at the end of the over I wandered down to talk to Majid.

'We are going to get stuffed here if we are not careful, Maj.'

He produced his severe schoolboy frown. 'Not if you are buying ice-creams again,' he announced.

Gloucestershire had batted magnificently for 324, but even then we could see what the spinners were likely to do. Roger Davis had taken six for 82 on the first day.

'Of course I'll buy you ice-cream. I always do, don't I?' I answered.

'Right!' he pointed to me. 'Last year, I make mistake. This year I shall have lots and lots of ice-cream.'

We both 'gave it the charge'. In two hours, against the bowling of Smith, Brown, Allen, Mortimore and Bissex, we put on 176. I got 87 but Majid arrived back in the pavilion much later with two sixes, 20 fours, 157 runs in all and six ice-creams. We spun out Gloucestershire cheaply next time and smashed off the runs to win by 5 wickets.

Of course, the doubting of Don Shepherd, Peter Walker and me had long since gone. Everyone in the team was a Majid fan and I can still say, as I said then, he was the finest batsman I have ever partnered in the middle.

Once, at Derby, by way of a joke, Majid told Don Shepherd, known for his bowling accuracy, that he could play him without moving his feet 'You are no problem Don. Come to nets tomorrow and I will show you.' There was a lot of joking as Majid took guard on a practice pitch which was rain sodden and full of divots. The ball popped, lifted, turned, almost stood on its head, though sluggishly. Even so, the Pakistani maestro blocked it with ease, feet together, hanging out a dead bat. Soon he found his confidence, and turned his feet, which were planted together along the crease, slightly forwards towards cover. It opened his stance a little. He then proceeded to whack the ball with amazing timing and power through the mid-wicket area. Even Don Shepherd admitted that what we were witnessing was incredible virtuosity.

I heard Shep talking to a Glamorgan member a few weeks later at Cardiff. The member said, 'That Majid. I'd even pay to see him just take guard and stand there.'

Shep came back quickly, 'Yes. He's a better player with his feet together.'

It was at the end of the 1969 season that Majid played his most brilliant innings for Glamorgan; brilliant because it was jewelled with perfect strokes and also because it was an innings of desperate importance to the side. We were at the top of the championship table with two matches to go, and to spare ourselves the pain of having to decide matters at the Oval against Surrey, who were hotly in pursuit of us, we had to beat Worcestershire at Sophia Gardens.

From the start, the pitch played badly. The faster bowlers got the ball to leap up from just short of a length and pieces dusted out of the top on the first morning. Norman Gifford and Doug Slade, the left-arm spinners, rolled up their sleeves and settled for a long bowl. After just one over from each of them, Tom Graveney, the captain, reckoned, as he told me afterwards, that he would bowl us out for under a hundred.

As it was, Glamorgan got 265, but Tom's expectations were perfectly reasonable. It took a miracle to get us to that total, and that miracle was Majid Khan. He scored a brilliant, belligerent 156. Only three others made it to double figures. I still retain the sight of him gliding down the wicket to meet Norman Gifford's spinners and thinking that he could not possibly make it to the pitch of the ball. Norman was an experienced Test bowler and had the ability to push the ball through quickly and yet keep the loop of flight and the sharp spin away from the bat. Time and again I expected to see Majid stranded, but instead of that, Tom Graveney had to reinforce his cover field with two fast runners on the boundary who were there to sweep up what they could of Majid's blistering cover drives. The only element in favour of the batsmen in the whole game was the hard, fast outfield.

There were other outstanding performances in the match – Ron Headley's 71, Tom Graveney's 43, Norman Gifford's 7 for 99 in 36 overs, Don Shepherd's seven wickets in the match which took his mammoth first-class tally to 2,000, not to mention Majid's four slip catches. Worcestershire fought gamely, but Majid had done his bit to 'win championship'. Sophia Gardens was alive with celebrations and singing; the Championship was back in Wales for the first time since 1948. In fact, it was a marvellous team effort from start to finish, but this contribution of Majid Khan, at a time when other hearts in the side were fluttering, not least my own, explains the nature of the man who could race for the highest prizes in cricket and not go limp around the last lap.

All that was in the sixties. Now came the seventies. Surely these were going to be the years when the whole cricket world would be treated to the talents I had got to know so well.

Quite typically, Majid's decision was to accept an undergraduate place at Cambridge University. Of all the challenges which lured Majid, the reputation and achievements of his father were the strongest. Dr Jahangir Khan is a legend at Fenners. Along with Peter May, he was rated by Cyril Coote, groundsman and mentor to undergraduates for almost 50 years, as the brightest talent ever to have pulled on the light blue sweater. Cyril used to say, 'Ole Jahangir, Sir, 'e used to go out there an' bowl 'em out on a flat'un, just 'cos they reckoned it was impossible to pass the bat. D'y'know once, Sir, 'e stood on these steps of the pavilion and threw the cricket ball, standin' still, and broke the wicket at the near end.'

Like father like son. It was not long before Majid was scoring 200 in his first University match, and conducting at Fenners a resurrection of University cricket, causing students to rush from lecture rooms to the cricket once more as they had in former days. He was made captain of Cambridge in both his second and third years. In 1972 he led Cambridge to victory over Oxford by an innings and 25 runs, the first result in an University match since 1966. In that final term too, he decided to celebrate the completion of his examinations with a double century, and produced this to order in a match at Fenners, although not first class.

As captain he was the perfect leader for the young and inexperienced who needed to be instructed and led from the front. He disappointed the University only in that he failed, after a million attempts, to knock over the stumps with a standing throw from the pavilion steps. (Why did no one offer him ice-cream?)

In the winter of 1973 Majid, who had played both for Glamorgan and Pakistan, when not required at the

University, was suddenly involved in one of those treacherous, political decisions for which the Pakistan Board of Control is famous. While he was in New Zealand playing for Pakistan under the successful captaincy of Intikhab, the Board announced that he and not Inti would be captain against England in the home series to follow. The Pakistan team were upset and mystified, and Intikhab was shattered.

I was leading the England side, and when I got to talk to the Pakistan players I could feel dissent. It was the first time I had ever heard Majid's name buffeted by criticism; it was the first moment when I realized how a delightful cricketer of pleasing, rather old-fashioned virtues, could be mauled by the machinations of professional cricketers who treat the game, understandably, as their next plate of curry.

More than that, Majid had just been made captain of Glamorgan. I had resigned after six years. Injury to knees was the deciding factor, but there was also a feeling of mistrust which had grown up between players and the club, the captain inevitably squeezed in the middle of the sandwich, placating neither side, and both parties trying to eat him for breakfast. If I had been fully fit to play regularly I would have fought on. As it was, my painful knee injury, following an endless shoulder injury, persuaded me to resign and maybe come back when I could contribute a lot more. In any case Glamorgan's committee had prematurely and idiotically opted for a rebuilding process, and it was right for a single captain to see that through for the five or six seasons ahead.

I recognized, too, the growing ferment among professional cricketers all over the country. For years the cricketer had been underpaid. Top county salaries were around the £2,000 a year mark. Yet more and more cricket was being covered by television which attracted new sponsorship. How much of that cash was coming to the players? Not enough, that was certain. Clubs said that they needed it and so they did, but they were going to have to change their priorities by the end of the

166

decade, and it took a players' revolution to achieve it.

Out of this shifting morass of cricketers' disenchant-
ment I moved happily; into it went the young, brilliant
Pakistan Test player, straight out of Cambridge. Majid
said at the time that he did not want the captaincy, but
for the sake of the Glamorgan Club he would do it. He
plainly announced that he would lead on the field only,
and wanted no part of the first-team organization or the
constant speaking at dinners which others had done
before him. Fair enough. If Majid was a man for
challenges, then both in Pakistan and in Glamorgan his
time had come.

History now shows that his captaincy of Pakistan
lasted three Tests only, and his leadership of Glamorgan
ended in public disarray and private torture in 1976 after
two and half seasons. Again, I suspect that it is no
coincidence that the most significant happening of the
seventies, the Packer affair, was just around the corner.
Only the smallest blame should be attached to Majid. In
Pakistan and in Wales, those who set him up in those
positions of authority might just as well have put him on
the rack. Given time he might well have been a proper
choice, but in 1973, at least in Glamorgan, there was no
way in which a 26-year-old Muslim was going to be able
to communicate with a dissident and only moderately
talented Welsh county side. In these ways Majid Khan
was a victim of the seventies.

As criticism heaped up and the disloyalty both of the
players and of the Glamorgan administration which once
wooed him could be heard paraded on all home grounds,
Majid returned to his introverted self of the sixties. On
the field he thrust his hands deeply in his pockets, used
his shirt collar as blinkers and carried on as best he
could. His batting faltered and the public which had
crowned him in 1969 were now prepared to crucify. He
was culpable, as I was before him, of lacking the appetite
for one-day cricket. That is not to say that we did not try.
Soldiering through the seventies without a world-class
fast bowler was the current form of suicide, practised

167

mainly by Glamorgan and Yorkshire. Not even Field Marshal Montgomery attacked without the tanks!

Successive Glamorgan captains through the seventies have staggered helplessly under the load. I have felt a great sympathy for them. Players have demanded more, committees require success in order to sell the game, and the captain, far from being the leader of the club's cricket, has been thrust into a football manager's role; succeed or die. Majid, I will remember, as calm and determined under a brimmed, fading white sun hat, stroking the most ferocious or most cunning bowling imperiously to the boundary.

He walked out of Glamorgan cricket towards the end of the 1976 season. Wilfred Wooller, who had invited him, brutally voiced Majid's flaws on the terraces at every home match. It was Wooller more than anyone who drove Majid from Glamorgan.

Where next? The only cricket open to Majid was Pakistan's and, of course, Mr Packer's World Series. I talked to him several times in Australia. He was appreciative of the pay revolution, because the Pakistan Board had always offered their players a pittance even though they drew vast crowds. Indeed Majid was one who fought stubbornly for a better deal in his own country. However, World Series cricket, while it flattered him at first to be considered among the finest players in the world, did not provide a suitable stage. Eventually he was forced, like others, to take to batting in a helmet and play the game as a form of self-defence against an endless stream of fast bowling. Long gone were the rippling cover drives of Fenners and St Helens. This was highly paid entertainment, but the money was only to be earned by cutting and carving in the fast bowler's jungle.

I had a meal with Majid and his wife Seema in Sydney in January 1978, and he confessed that he would return to Glamorgan if they asked him, as long as the administration had changed, and if some of the players he had marked as mutinous had gone. But I knew that the day of the brilliant Pakistani in the faded sun hat, who wore

168

the daffodil so proudly, had passed; his amateur spirit
had been overtaken by the money-grabbing times and
the shame remains with those in Wales he left behind.

16

Retirement and Reflections

On Wednesday 24 July I went to Sophia Gardens to play for Glamorgan. By 10.30 I was back home again. I had retired.

Alan Jones, the captain, and Roger Davis were sheepish in the dressing room; they mumbled something about not wanting to leave out any of the youngsters who had all done well in the last match. I took my cue. Retire. What had begun 19 years ago in Tom Dollery's last match at Neath had ended. I did not see my career in heroic terms, but, as John Arlott was wont to remind me, there was nothing more romantic than the clean break. Cricketers very rarely leave the game as they would want. I did.

I had always laughed with my old RAF team-mate Peter Parfitt about his last innings for Middlesex. How he had wanted to bounce down the steps at Lord's, members standing and applauding him all the way to the middle: an acclaimed last performance at the game's headquarters. Instead Parf's last knock was at Sophia Gardens in Cardiff, late in the afternoon, after rain, on an empty ground. Nor even did he enjoy the solo entry on stage because he opened the batting: the limelight shared.

He was a popular player, and for fun the Glamorgan team lined up and made a corridor for him and clapped. He had to cross over giant pools of rainwater and as he struggled out, hopping from duckboard to duckboard, there was suddenly a slow resounding toll of the big bell up on the players' balcony. As P. Parfitt, Middlesex and

England, went to the middle for the last time, Fred Titmus steadily tolled the death knell.

If only we could write our own career scripts. I would never have included in my story the constant knee injuries; I would never have suffered the irony of twisting and damaging a cartilage at the very moment I was chosen for England as captain. Even more I would have written out the ultimate agony of having to cry off most of the 1973 home Tests under Ray Illingworth's captaincy, turning down the request of the England selectors to get back onto the field and to take MCC to West Indies in 1973–74.

So, drinking coffee at that kitchen table, with my wife, on the retirement morning in July 1974 there was never a second thought about playing on. Honestly, it was an immediate relief not to get out of bed in the morning praying that my knees were not hurting.

When cricketers retire or are sacked they are often too close to the matter. They are boring about their place in the club or county history: anxious that they have amounted to something. I hated statistics all the way through my career, ignored them, perhaps in too cavalier a fashion. Averages bred selfishness and also misrepresented a player's worth. For sanity, one needed only to compare oneself to a great player to find the necessary calm to go quietly.

The finest cricketer I ever saw was Gary Sobers, and I particularly recall the first time we met. Glamorgan were playing West Indies at Cardiff Arms Park in 1963. When Wes Hall marked out his long run, the Glamorgan side fell silent. No one had been so far to bowl at Cardiff; he was ten yards from the boundary fence.

Alwyn Harris was our opening bat, a brave and solid player. He did not appear to see the first three balls, the last of which bowled him. I was in next. I fiddled nervously with my batting gloves and thigh pad. I looked around the dressing room for a nod of good luck from senior players. Jim Pressdee was stuffing cotton wool into his cap ... and he was in number seven! Bernard Hedges was busy removing his false teeth, wrapping them in his handkerchief and depositing them in his blazer pocket. It was in the days when the instruction had come from Lord's for the outgoing to cross with the incoming batsman on the field of play so as not to waste time. From that day, the Glamorgan team always reckoned that Alwyn was so fast getting off and I was so slow getting on that we were the only first-class cricketers ever to cross in the lavatory!

I took my guard; Wes Hall was furlongs away. I surveyed the field placing. There was no one at all in front of me. Which meant that I was not supposed to hit the ball anywhere. I heard breathing and a light chuckle behind me, Conrad Hunte was at short square-leg. Every other fielder was at slip or leg slip some 40 yards back towards the River Taff. Big Wes raced in, his white shirt open. I saw a gold neckchain and crucifix, swinging back and fore against a black perspiring chest. His eyes were white and raging and his arms flailed. There was a red blur as the ball hissed passed the outside edge of my bat.

Those three balls were the fastest I have ever received. I missed all three because they swung away late in the air. After the over, as the West Indies fielders walked from one end to the other between overs, one of them stopped to talk to me. It was Garfield Sobers. He put a hand on my shoulder. 'Just remember, son, it's all relative, this speed. You stay out here ten minutes and you'll be in time with big Wes.' He glided off.

I did, it worked, I got 50. I also got out to the sudden change of bowling from fast to slow. I swept a ball right down the throat of deep backward square-leg. At the close of play Gary said, 'Well played, but the second part of the lesson is not to relax when you've seen the quicks off. That's why I ask Frankie Worrell to put me on.' He laughed and was gone.

Gary Sobers was generous and modest, despite his wonderful virtuosity. He played for his side not for himself. When he batted he had quite a loop at the top of his back lift, but the blade always came down straight.

He was a player of technique as well as power and flourish. It was almost a violent instinct tamed. He must have been born with the natural Caribbean urge to bowl faster than anyone in the world and lash the ball further. He was as good a new-ball bowler as he wanted to be on the day, left-arm over the wicket – a vicious late swing into the pads of the right-handed batsman, a ball that ran away to off, a bouncer, everything was in the armoury.

His wrist spin had clever flight, loop and turn. I suppose of all his varieties the orthodox, left-arm spin was the least penetrative, but that is not to say it was unproductive or expensive. Gary often bowled orthodox spin with a flat trajectory in order to keep the batsmen under control in one-day matches.

All these high-class individual arts were performed by a super athlete, always in balance. The power of his hooking and driving, the delicacy of his wristy glides and cuts, the all-round genius of the man, made him the finest sight, with the bat, the ball or fielding at short-leg. To me, he was the most brilliant, the most selfless and charming man who played.

The best county side I played against was Yorkshire. From 1959 to 1969 they won the County Championship seven times. My first county match in Yorkshire was in 1960. On the way up north there had been a lot of talk among the players about J.C. Clay, the Club's President, and how he used to say that he would never retire until Glamorgan had beaten Yorkshire in Yorkshire. Alas! He had to. He played from 1921, when Glamorgan became first class, and he retired in 1949, the year after our first County Championship title, but there was no joy for us in Yorkshire.

Bradford Park Avenue was forbidding; the football stand on one side, concrete terracing around, a high red wall along the boundary which gave it the name of the bull-ring, a Wuthering Heights of a pavilion with dark dressing rooms up on the first floor.

We arrived on the ground early to find lots of

spectators already in their seats, or at least, if not sitting, having already staked out their vantage points with sandwich boxes, tea flasks and the mackintoshes. Veteran commissionaires in black uniforms, white peaked caps and shining brasses, barred entrances to almost everywhere until membership cards were presented.

In the dressing room I changed next to Alan Jones, Billy Davies and David Evans. You might describe Alan and me as novices, Billy and David as only briefly experienced. It was sprog corner.

Wilfred Wooller was not playing, so Gilbert Parkhouse was captain. As Gilbert went out through the door to toss with Vic Wilson, in came Fred Trueman. Allan Watkins had warned us that he would be in. 'Spends more time in the opposing dressing room than his own, but he's great fun as long as you don't let him frighten you. It's a bit green out there but he can only bowl at one end.'

Fred Trueman sat on a table rattling off hilarious jokes and sharp comments about players around the counties. Then he turned his stubbly Desperate Dan chin in our direction. When he saw such a cluster of beginners, his thick eye-brows shot up and stayed like a black lintel above two wide eyes; the voice was loud and nasal. It was as if the bull had spotted four picknickers in the corner of a field and was pawing the ground and snorting at them.

Bernard Hedges introduced us. We shook the great fast bowler's hand. He was now talking to nobody but us.

'I 'it Peter May on 'is 'ead last week, tha' knows.'

Our mouths dropped open.

'Ay! An' that Colin Cowdrey ... ah'll tell thee: wun int'block'ole and wun in't Adams apple and it's good day, soonshine.'

Mouths fell wider.

'Graveney! Thomas Graveney? E's a front foot player but 'ee never get's on front foot t'me, tha' knows. Ee knows ah'd pin'im like a moth t'bluddy sightscreen.'

We were all now mentally on the back foot and still were, minutes later, when Gilbert Parkhouse returned.

'Sorry chaps. We've lost it. Vic's put us in. It's a bit green but ... oh! Hello Frederick.'

'Good day Gilbert. Put you in 'as 'ee. Just like a bluddy batter. Na'it's me who as t'bowl thee art, in't it.' He got up and pigeon-toed it towards the door and, as we watched the large swaggering backside go, he was still regaling us. 'An' that Dexter, Lord Edward. His bat's got more cracked edges than a broken piss-pot.'

He stopped again and turned towards us, as if from fatherly concern. 'Well, it's reet nice to welcome you young lads to cricket in Yorkshire. I'll be comin' down the 'ill from that 'igh red wall a bit sharpish.'

He went half-way through the door and turned yet again. 'Well good luck t'y'four. Ah'll see thee art there in t'middle then – wun by bluddy wun.'

F.S. Trueman voiced the Yorkshireman's belief in the divine right of Yorkshiremen, but like any of that side in the sixties, he could put his remarkable talent where his mouth had been.

Yes, if only you could script your own career. I would like to have rewritten a few chapters for some of my Glamorgan friends. I have written earlier that I would have liked the England selectors to have seen how worthy Don Shepherd was of Test selection. I wish Alan Jones had got a fair run in the England side. He was a solid opening bat of class as well as technique. In the mid-sixties the best bowlers in the country, John Snow, Ken Higgs and Harold Rhodes, all rated him highly. His one Test was against a mighty Rest of the World side at Lord's in 1970 where he failed to score many runs. It could have happened to anyone. No one deserves one Test only.

Perhaps the weakness in Alan's game was his fielding. He could only throw in overarm and if tucked away at slip he was only a 50 per cent catcher. Glamorgan did not find his fielding a handicap. His catching in the deep was reliable and he never gave away runs by his improvised throwing style. Alan was unlucky.

I was sad too to see the arrival of two overseas

175

batsmen in 1968 remove another friend from the Glamorgan staff without a benefit year despite his efforts from 1955. Alan Rees and I used to open the batting for the Welsh Secondary Schools and also for the Neath club. He was a brilliant rugby union player, winning caps for Wales as an outside-half in the early sixties. He went to rugby league with Leeds.

Alan was a stylish batsman, and a real fighter under pressure. For example, when Glamorgan beat the 1964 Australians at Swansea he was the top scorer in each innings, 48 and 47, and took the superb catch to swing the match, at mid-wicket, Bill Lawry out for 64.

There was another career casualty, medically this time, Jeff Jones. Jeff had played 15 times for England before his left elbow began to give trouble. He was in the England side when it went wrong. He returned from the MCC tour of Pakistan in 1968–69 almost before it was underway. So he was at his peak when he underwent surgery for an arthritic condition. Could he come back? To give it one sustained trial Jeff came with Glamorgan on a tour of the West Indies in 1970. He began gently and worked up occasional spurts off his long run. Immediately we could see that his action had changed. There was a kink in the arm. Was it a throw or had it reset that way after the operation? Don Shepherd, Peter Walker, Ossie Wheatley and I discussed it most academically for days and we watched Jeff's bowling from all angles, but in our heart of hearts we knew that Jeff was illegally chucking the ball. He had no idea himself; he believed his arm action to be exactly as it was before the operation.

I shall never forget flying home, having already fixed that I should sit next to him. The conversation in which a skipper tells a young England fast bowler that his career is over because he throws the ball is not one you will find in any Teach Yourself Captaincy book. It is serious; it has to be all cards on the table. It had to happen then, because he would be straight back in the pre-season nets with his aspirations high, excitement in every come-back ball he bowled. There was never going to be any more excitement for Jeff and I knew it.

He took it as nobly as anyone could. I did not know whether to cry or order a large brandy. We did neither at first: we just sat and stared ahead and listened to the aeroplane engines grinding home the awful truth. Then he dabbed at a stray tear with a handkerchief. I would like to have rewritten the end of Jeff's career.

So, for me, the first-class days were over. Much had changed – no amateurs and professionals, but more and more cricketers prepared to speak loudly from the barrack room floor. There was a stirring of player power. A lack of regard for tradition, a questioning of the chain of command, a casualness in manners and in dress. Cricketers began to look at other professional games and complain about their poor rewards. There was a limit to the changes which the Cricketers' Association could bring about because the county game struggled to stay solvent. However, as the game began to attract more and more television, and therefore lucrative sponsorship, it was clear that a fresh look was required at conditions of labour.

The Test cricketers later, in 1977, conducted their own revolution with their millionaire Kerry Packer, and although the Cricketers' Association disapproved of the Packer movement initially, there were seeds in their own garden which were given a favourable climate in which to grow. Articulate voices, like Mike Brearley's in the late seventies, turned the mood for argument into solid reform. Packer's victory in the High Court had left cricket's established administration on the ropes and in went the players armed with legal weapons. The dressing room talk, which was once about car mileage allowances and petty cash, now ranged over such subjects as the rights of the individual to compensation when dismissed by a county, restraint of trade and a minimum basic wage for all players. What apparently began with Tony Greig's mercenaries in 1977 in reality had been stirring in the grass roots several years earlier.

I did not see that the players' stronger voice equalled excellence and order. Nor do I now. Indeed when I found myself in that last summer of 1974, at ten o'clock in the morning, track-suited and standing under towering catches by way of practice for a game which was to begin at 11.30, I knew my days were up. The fun had gone, the values had changed the old order was passing away, and me with it.

17

Essays of Odd Appearances

Geoffrey Irvine, my business representative, rang up to say that Colin Cowdrey could not make it. That is how it started. The 35th Annual Reunion Supper of the Confectionery and Allied Trades Sports Association at the Baronial Hall, Dunster and Colonial House, Mincing Lane, London EC3. It was on 18 February 1977. Would I be the stand-in?

Why had Colin Cowdrey cried off? How long would I have to speak? Where is Mincing Lane? Who on earth are the Confectionery and Allied Trades? What other speakers?

I agreed. Mincing Lane was deserted when I got there, but the Baronial Hall was underground, a shallow banqueting chamber of many acres, 500 inmates sharpening up for a night under the Town.

I was immediately aware that no one expected me. I mumbled something to a cloakroom lady about being the guest speaker. She suggested the VIP bar on the left. It was awash with past presidents, weighed down by gold medallions which hung from their necks on royal blue ribands. No one moved in my direction. I lurked nervously. I went to the bar and bought a whisky and soda, sipped and turned, and sipped again and turned the other way. I smiled at someone who was not smiling at me and then leaned on the bar, yawning with relaxed terror. What horror greater than being an unrecognized substitute for a household cricket name who had scored a hundred hundreds? How could I face the liquorice-makers of Pontefract, the Quality Streeters of York and the Mellowminters of Cardiff?

I sniffed hostility. Globules of sweat splashed down-wards from the armpits. I felt like a small schoolboy who had entered the staffroom in search of a teacher who was not there. I bought myself another hurried whisky before the man in the scarlet coat banged a gong and an-nounced dinner. I made for the top table and did find the place marked A. Lewis, ex-capt. Glamorgan Cricket Club. There was quite a hubbub out behind the pillars, but it was impossible to see them because the tables stretched away into darkness under the low ceiling.

At dinner I was a model guest, asking lots of interest-ing questions about toffee clusters and how you spread out the nuts and raisins for fruit-and-nut chocolate. During a gap for the loo visit, I scanned my speech notes. Although nobody had talked cricket, I presumed that the lads out in front would be keen. Perhaps I should mix in the odd rugger tale.

The chairman of the Confectioners' Benevolent Fund Appeals Committee proposed the toast of the Sports Association and a response was made by the President. I was still sure that they did not know who I was, when the Chairman stood again and announced, 'Now, gentle-men, to the moment you've all been waiting for.' I flipped out my notes again, and memorized the first line. 'And I am not the one to disappoint you, gentlemen,' he continued. 'Pray silence therefore ...' I moved my chair back. '... for Nadine.'

A lady spun herself out of the darknes into the centre of the spotlight which wavered mid-floor. Her face was deathly white; she wore a short black dress, lots of feathers round her neck and ladders in her stockings. To taped music she began to strip. She relied heavily on audience participation. She sat, one leg cocked over the other, as an ancient retainer released a stocking from its suspender and peeled it off her leg. On the move, she raised the spectacles of a highly inebriate senior groping sweetmaker; she swayed back from him, grabbed her nude breasts, one in each hand and then, thrusting forward like a jouster with twin lances, jabbed her nipples in his eyes.

It was then, Nadine had gyrated herself into a half hour's frenzy, that I really began to worry how my story of facing Alec Bedser on a green pitch at the Oval would go down. So, when she had finished, I jotted down a potted self-biography. I walked behind the top table and placed it on the Chairman's plate. 'I am Tony Lewis. I have come to talk cricket. I insist on ten minutes break before speaking. I can't follow this.'

'Ah!' said the Chairman. 'Don't worry old fellow. Perfectly in order. That's who you are, is it?'

Nadine was a success. As she left, the white circle of the spotlight was strewn with her bits and pieces and with the flowers, napkins, and the menu cards of her dutiful assistants.

Follow that. Should I switch to the one about Nurse Thompson, the Sydney abortionist? What about the one that ends 'Sorry skipper, I should have kept my legs closed ...' Answer: 'Not you son, yer mother.' Hell, I thought, have I come to the right place? Wait until I lay my hands on Cowdrey. What am I doing here?

The Chairman stood. 'Sorry chaps. Don't know much about cricket but I will just read out some facts about our guest speaker.' Now that was a rave introduction.

There was gentle applause as I stood: Nadine had drained them. I went for familiar tactics, throwing out the names of cricketers and counties until there was a response. At last. 'Wot abart Keif Flechar?' In I went with all my Fletcher tales. Response better; most encouraging. Next I played the biggest card of all, dear old Fred Trueman. After a few Trueman stories, I quit while ahead. The applause was enthusiastic in places and kindly in others. I could almost hear them saying, 'Ah! That's who he is.'

I was sipping a pint and thinking how after-dinner speakers should go into the disposable shirt business when the Chairman took the microphone again. 'Now then chaps, settle down.' He turned a long arm in my direction to the left of the top table, as if to say, 'Big hand for Tony Lewis', but instead simply announced 'Colette'.

The spotlight hit the top table. All else went dark. Colette was making her entrance by high-heeling her way along the top table between liquers and coffee cups; a leggy lady, wearing little. She stopped in front of me, turned to me, stood challengingly astride my place setting and looked down. 'Give us yer tie, darling.'

I did not want to. I had just bought it at Turnbull and Asser in Jermyn Street for two *Face the Music* television shows I was doing in Manchester next day. But I did. Then, to the timing of the taped music she began to thread my tie through her G-string. Colette never gave it back, but then I never waited. I took the opportunity when her music struck up to beat a retreat. I last saw her lifting this nice young man's spectacles up on his forehead ... I ran out onto Mincing Lane, sweating into the chill mid-winter; the straight man in a sex sandwich, I had been indigestible.

18

What Am I Doing Playing Here?

Apart from the usual school trip to Paris and an Air Force rugby tour to Germany, all sorties abroad were to play cricket.

The first time I bent down in blinding sunshine to mark my middle-and-leg guard with chalk on a coconut matting pitch was in Gibraltar. I pulled my cap down over my eyes to view the bowler. He was short, thin, Gibraltarian and he was ordering ten other short, thin Gibraltarians to 'Go in, go in.' They did. They surrounded me, all about ten yards away, crouching with hands stretched out and cupped. I walked down the pitch to chat to my partner, Brian Roe, the Somerset professional. We agreed, we had never before experienced the ring of ten fielders. Poor misguided fellows they were.

I hit lusty blows, blasting the ball through this human necklace, but suddenly a ball shot up from just short of length, hit the shoulder of my bat and popped, approximately ten yards, into the hands of gully. 'It worked,' yelled the catcher to the bowler, as if they had spent months on the Rock studying home-made movies of my batting flaws.

'Good plan. Good plan,' they were mouthing towards the boundary where a solitary spectator sat behind the bowler's arm. I was annoyed to think that these complete strangers knew something about my batting which I did not know myself. After a shower, I changed from whites into shorts and wandered around the ground to sun-bathe.

I was approached by the loan spectator. 'I'm Welsh,' he said. 'I saw you get a "pair" against Yorkshire at Cardiff Arms Park in 1957. You were caught near the wicket by Trueman and Close. So I told these lads your weaknesses.' He gloated. It was not worth explaining the difference between facing Bob Appleyard and Ray Illingworth on a raging turner at Cardiff and the slingy little seamer who had rolled me over here.

'I'm in the Services here,' the Welshman went on. 'And you can expect the same next match because I am playing against you.' I escaped that particular humilia-tion. I sunbathed so long that day that I got second-degree burns and the only activity I managed for the rest of the brief visit was a straight-legged shuffle around the night clubs in the cool of night with a face glowing like a new ball. The team doctor had to play instead of me. I have been a 'shade' man ever since.

With the Combined Services I played cricket against Holland at Amsterdam and the Hague, and then, with the Cambridge side of 1960, coached Danish youngsters at Hjørring and, rather unsteadily, opened the batting against text book out-swingers bowled by All Denmark at Copenhagen.

My first long tour was to South America with MCC in 1964–65, a missionary visit with a long list of matches and school coaching appointments in Brazil, Chile and Argentina. Alan Smith of Warwickshire was the captain.

A major MCC tour was on in South Africa at the time. Previously I had been short-listed for two England tours but I felt no disappointment at being sent to an unlikely part of the world to play cricket which was professionally irrelevant. To me, all cricket had value because I never thought of it as my profession. It was my boat, my plane, my education and I could not believe my luck that it was to open a whole new part of the world for me.

Of similar mind, I think, was Bob Gale, the Middlesex

opener. He was a talented left-hander who eventually left cricket to become a partner in a firm of stockbrokers. Late one night in Rio de Janeiro we sipped gin and tonics on the roof-top bar of an hotel overlooking Copacabana Beach and we marvelled at the astonishing scenes below. There were a dozen highly organised football matches being played by youngsters on the narrow bank of beach with proper goal posts. The touch-line on one side was the calm, rather timid sea which lapped the sand as if it was afraid to transgress too far on the playing area. On the other side was the raised sidewalk of the main road. I had never imagined that Copacabana was such a beach of the people. On the sidewalk important-looking young men raced about with battery-run hand-lights. This was improvised floodlit football. They had to make sure that the football in their particular game never disapeared out of their beam. Brazilian boys twisted lightly over the top of soft sand, turning amazing patterns with the ball at their feet. Paying no attention to their skills was a rushing public, and a cacophony of car horns. Some buildings were architecturally decorative, even hand-some, but they rubbed shoulders with shanty-town squalor: obvious wealth, in the same square yard as appalling poverty – the most shocking social contrast.

'What are we doing, playing cricket here?' I asked Bob.

'Amazing isn't it,' was all he could say. 'Amazing.'

Next day we reported to the quayside in cricket whites and blazers and boarded a small craft called *Cardiff*. In bright sunshine, we chugged across a natural bay for about 45 minutes, to Niteroi. The ground was secluded, among tall trees; the pavilion was attractively set on a grass rise; lunch was taken on the verandah, served by Brazilian waiters in uniform with plumed head-dresses and white soft shoes.

Each day at close of play we sat with our hosts, sipped long drinks to see the sun down, listened to stories of old matches when the British presence in Rio had been stronger, when perhaps the Navy was in, when a particular generation of youngsters had thrown up outstanding talents; after which we sailed back to our hotel to dress for the nightly party.

Alan Smith and I had played regularly against each other since the University match of 1960 when we were on opposite sides. He was a talented sportsman which few would guess from his knock-kneed, loping walk. He got a soccer blue at Oxford as well as captaining the cricket for two seasons in 1959 and 1960. By reputation he was a true Corinthian, amateur in approach to his cricket, but serious about it. He led a talented side at Oxford but gave them dash, direction and discipline too. He kept wicket, batted well enough to go in first, but also loved bowling fast-medium seamers with a hopping action, almost delivering the ball off the wrong foot. He was at his most competitive when bowling, determined not to be underestimated. He led this tour well. I was later to find out for myself what a tricky balance between relaxation and law-abiding has to be imposed to keep a minor tour in its best playing form. 'AC' was master of the frown and grimace, but behind them he had a good sense of humour.

We did share an extraordinary experience or two. The first was in Chile. We left our base camp, the delightful Prince of Wales Country Club, nestling at the foot of the Andes with snow-capped peaks towering 20,000 feet above, and moved for a day and a night to Viña del Mar. We found a pretty, small ground, built into the centre of a race course. Inside the small wooden pavilion was a notice drawing attention to an unfortunate accident to a jockey some years before. He had been four lengths up, a furlong and a half from home, when the batsman hooked a long hop to square leg, the ball striking the jockey on the head and removing him from the saddle. Hence the club rule: 'Batsmen are requested not to take guard when a race is in progress.'

Our attention was drawn to the faded photograph on the pavilion wall of the last MCC tour match at Viña del Mar, 37 years before, and a side which included Pelham

Warner, G.O. Allen, J.C. White, and Lord Dunglass, otherwise Sir Alec Douglas Home and now Lord Home of the Hirsel.

Overnight we were billeted in private homes. Alan Smith and I were allocated to the leading member of the British community, even though, as an old Reptonian with yellow stripes on a navy tie, Mr Cran-Kenrick, ageing and on the point of retirement, would have preferred to house another Repton man, Richard Hutton. AC and I left in his huge, black, chauffeur-driven car.

Mr Cran-Kenrick had a habit of repeating the exclamation 'What!' every few seconds, before comments, during them and especially after them. 'Weather good, ay Smith ... what! ... what! ... what! ... what!' In fairness to him I think he had ill-fitting false teeth, and every time the lower jaw moved the top set fell on top of the bottom. If you think about it, 'what!' is the sort of word which public school men, skilled in speaking with the minimum of lip movement, might squeeze out easily and indeed the more the jaw was clenched to repeat it the more he was able to raise his top set of dentures back to where they belonged. Whatever; this was our host's habit.

We had been travelling in Mr Cran-Kenrick's car some time when AC enquired how much further to his home.

'What! what! what! Smith ... well ... er ... we've been in the grounds for ten minutes ... what! what! what!'

That was enough to silence us until the car swung around a wide curving drive towards a mansion. Dashing smartly to the entrance were two retainers in red. They had come to collect our luggage. AC and I had a couple of Aerolineas Argentinas canvas shoulder-bags, wherein a tooth brush each but no change of shirt, let alone anything to match the formality of our new surroundings. Not a tie between us.

Upstairs I found the contents of my airbag laid out on the bed in my spacious room – soiled handkerchief, camera, shaving kit, suncream, tour booklet, rubber band and pen. It was as if a mischievous schoolboy had been told to empty his pockets. AC and I padded between rooms to consult about dress for dinner. It had to be the same county blazers and open-necked tee shirts.

Sherry in the drawing room, silver racing cups, precious books and two daughters home on hols from school in England, both attractively dressed for dinner. Mr Cran-Kenrick led the way across the vast hallway to the dining-room. AC and I, a daughter on the arm, followed in formal procession.

So large was the dining-room table that we were all half a dozen yards away from each other and we were only occupying one end! Then the host produced a conversation-stopper.

'Where were you at school, Smith ... what! ... what! ... what?' he enquired with a piercing look.

'King Edward's, Birmingham, Sir,' replied my leader, tensely and quickly. It was as if he had been asked, 'When did you last see your father?'

'Good school. Good school, King Edward's, what! ... what! ... what! Now, Lewis. Where were you at school?'

'Neath Grammar School, Sir.'

Mr Cran-Kenrick went blank. I do not think he knew the names of any Grammar schools. His eyes hit the chandeliers and found no inspiration. He simply started his 'whats' treble forte and diminuendoed ever so slowly '... what! ... what! ... what! what! ... what! what! ...'

The cricketers slept well. In the morning I was woken up by a touch on the arm. A maid was at the bedside. She held a small bowl towards me. Was I going to be sick? Perhaps for the fingers?

'Would this be the right temperature for you, Sir?' she asked. The bowl came into sharper focus as I woke up. Ah! Shaving water, I thought. She helped.

'Your bath, Sir,' she said. 'Is it the right temperature?'

'Oh!' I plopped in a finger and let my head fall back with relief on the pillow. 'Perfect, thank you. Perfect.'

'And by the way, Sir.' She had not finished. 'Breakfast

will be by the pool at the east side of the house.'

I shot up again and saw her go.

In the bath I kept saying to myself. AR, what are you doing playing cricket here? I didn't scour the bath afterwards, as I did at home. Probably not done, I thought. In fact, I got quite confident – I left the plug in.

In Argentina the cricket was strongest. British business had followed the great flow of capital into South America which itself was sparked off by the opening up of the interior by British Railways. Unfailingly the Briton takes his bat and ball with him wherever he goes.

We spent most of the time in the old colonial Hurlingham Club, windows opening onto the eighteenth-green of the golf course. There was a solemn, bearded barman called Jesus. He witnessed a near miracle. Daily and especially nightly, Bob Gale had attacked the many variations available behind the bar with the alacrity of someone on a week-end tour of Ireland. Towards the end of the second week Jesus was treating Señor Gale as something very special indeed. 'I geev 'im zee beer, zee whisy, zee geen, zee everything and the señor still thirsty.'

Alas! With but two nights to go of a fortnight's stay, Jesus, one late evening, witnessed the total eclipse of his favourite customer. Ever so slowly Señor Gale sank lower, and ever so gradually the bar rose higher. There was a muffled flop. The elegant Middlesex left-hander was temporarily among the great left-handers in the sky. There was a resurrection, and only a day later, but then, when Jesus witnessed Señor Gale's conversion to pints of milk, the light of a great faith had gone out.

We travelled several hundreds of miles inland towards the Andes to play a one-day match against the Northern Camps. There I truly appreciated how much cricket is loved. Just imagine what an MCC visit means to men who spend every day of their lives working with the cattle on their estancias in the centre of Argentina. They live on cricket memories and the written word. The main street of Venado Tuerto was right out of High Noon. There

189

were horses tethered to wooden poles outside the saloon, gauchos waddling down the sidewalk in their chaps. Unbelievably, a sign above a small door said 'Churchill Club'.

'Hello fellas. What's it to be? Gin and tonics all round?' The man behind the corner bar had a handlebar moustache. In a corner was a pile of well-worn cricket kit, yellowing buckskin pads, including a pair of old style wicket-keeping pads which had flaps of extra protection along the outsides. There were Len Hutton autograph batting gloves, the sort with brown leather sausage fingers and a length of elastic which you wrapped around your wrist before fitting on the thumb.

We played the cricket on a polo field, on a pitch full of deep hoof marks. A good crowd turned up, many on horseback and every time the home side scored a run I could see the bottoms of the gin bottles glint in the sunshine all around the ground. Then there was loud cheering each time as if they would never see another run again. We won the match, mercifully with leg spin, or else the faster bowlers Richard Hutton and Richard Jefferson might have wounded someone seriously on such a dangerous surface.

That night, Alan Smith and I stayed with a Scotsman called McKay who had not been home to Britain for 25 years. He lived on his own. We dined superbly and were sipping brandy when McKay brought a firm hand down on the table. 'Right Smith. It's no good. I can't keep it in any longer. Tell me, why does a keeper like you stand back to a piffling medium pacer like Cartwright at Edgbaston?' Not bad viewing from the Argentine out-backs!

In 1968 I made my first visit to Pakistan. It was a team collected by Alex Bannister of the *Daily Mail*. We went as the Commonwealth XI. There were teeming crowds, stifling heat, mosquitoes swooping and biting in the night, curry and Islam, ox carts and muezzins calling the faithful to prayer at absurdly early hours of the morning.

190

Heavily garlanded with flowers we were ferried on an hour's tour of Multan, two players to a horse and trap, the driver up front. Thousands of people swarmed the narrow streets with donkeys, chickens, bicycles, Ambassador cars, lopsided buses and camels, but this did not stop our drivers from trying to race each other. Leading the Ben Hur type gallop was a car which had a public address speaker on top. 'Welcome greatest cricket players in the world. Commonwealth team comes to Multan.' I hung on to the open trap I was sharing with Mike Edwards of Surrey. He shouted to me. 'What the hell are we doing playing cricket here?'

We had arrived in Multan extremely slowly, but sanely, by train, overnight at about 12 miles an hour from Karachi. I had shared a sleeping compartment with the young West Indian who had joined Essex, Keith Boyce. He was a brilliant all-rounder. He could score a blistering 60 or 70 full of sixes and fours but based all the time on a decent defence and a straight bat; his new-ball bowling was genuinely fast and he was a spectacular athlete. This gave him a smooth run-up and action and also made him the most exciting outfielder in the whole first-class game. His picking up and throwing on the sprint was superb. As the ball lodged in his right palm he would leap high in the air, both feet off the ground, twist his body to the right direction and throw. The speed of the throw was unbelievable until you had been run out by him. The trajectory was flat and it arrived like a rocket in the wicket-keepers gloves.

Not quite so skilful was Keith's command of the English language in those early days. He spoke so quickly and with such excitement that I can honestly say that I understood nothing during our 15 hours together, except that he thought oranges were good for his sexual strength. An awful lot was sign language.

On the final day of our first, four-day unofficial Test in Multan, our tour captain made his late arrival from Australia. He walked tall and upright through a sea of black faces towards our team chamiana at the ground.

191

He was meticulously attired in a cream light-weight suiting with matching tie. He carried a slender briefcase. It was impossible for Richie Benaud to idle away a day in Multan without doing a spot of work.

I was the stand-in leader for the match. 'It's like this captain,' I explained. 'We have been set a reasonable run-chase but we've only been here a few days and the batters don't feel in very good nick. The senior pros, David Allen, John Murray and Don Shepherd, think we should block it out this time and wait for the next two matches when we'll be in better form.' Captain Benaud chewed, the famous lower lip jutted out, then anounced. 'I'd go for them.'

We did. We lost. I received from the captain a commiseration.

'You aren't the first to get it wrong in these parts.'

'Oh, really!' I said. 'I thought we were the first to play a full Pakistan side here.' Benaud chewed again and looked up from his seat outside the chamiana. 'They say they gave Charlemagne the run around in these parts . . . back a bit.'

Most of our accommodation was in rest houses, simple but clean. At one stop I shared a room with David Allen, John Murray and Roger Prideaux. We slept on char-poys, those wooden frames with taut hemp crossweave, which overnight turned our backs into perfect surfaces for games of noughts and crosses. Each morning John Murray would painfully arch the vertebrae into a half-sitting position and yell, 'Bearer. Bed-tea.' The bearer would scurry in 'Bed-tea coming, Sahib.' He would bow and leave.

'And don't forget George, gurum chi (hot tea) . . . and tea strainer. Good boy George. Gelde, gelde.' Quickly, quickly.

JT, an old campaigner, had long since given up trying to remember the names of subcontinental bearers. They bore his universal nameplate, George. They appeared to understand.

The poor bearer had to deliver shattering news to us

on our first morning. 'Water not running, Sahib. There is blockage somewhere outside rest house. But I will bring water for washing.' He returned with one bucket of luke warm water and placed it in the centre of the room. We gathered around it as if it was a camp fire. This was for everything! It was immediately agreed that we started our washing with the teeth and wandered to other parts afterwards. When we were all done, one lucky man stripped off and had the bucket full swilled over him: his day for the shower.

Curry for breakfast was a challenge we were not prepared to take on. JT, off to the kitchen, was at the cook. 'Now look 'ere George. These are the eggs, this is how you fry 'em. These are the potatoes, this is how you make chips. So every meal, George, egg and chips. Goddit George? Good boy.'

Only John Hampshire was not inclined to follow the old pro's advice. He referred to his familiarity with the curry houses of Rotherham and set about the local cuisine. That day, when we fielded at Sarghoda, John bent swiftly for a ball in the gully. He never straightened up again. He just kept on running for the pavilion, returning ten days later, two stone lighter.

I learned a great deal about captaincy simply by watching Richie Benaud in action for six weeks. He never fussed over players; either they did well or they did not. He would advise but never waste words. It was as if he saw long debate as a waste of inner strength, words going out, random thinking, aimless judgements, all energy leaving the body instead of being stored inside. He was not locked into set patterns of field placing. Once, to a durable and almost strokeless batsman called Aftab Gul, later to play in Tests, he placed a semi-circle of nine fielders on the on side all fifteen yards from the bat. Mr Gul was rendered runless.

Richie helped our two fast bowlers, Keith Boyce and Ken Shuttleworth, to the form which soon got them Test caps. Both no-balled two or three times an over. He went out with them early in the mornings on rest days, making them think about their stride, hitting targets along the runway into the delivery. By the end of the tour they were almost foot perfect. Having studied Benaud at close quarters, much later, in commentary boxes, I know how prepared his public performance is, whether as a cricket captain or a television commentator. In the first place, he believes that planning, effort, and work are the requirements for success. I read in books how he practised his leg-spin endlessly in the nets: I know how hard he works at his writing and broadcasting life. He is meticulous in preparation as a commentator, on the ground early to study unknown players through his small binoculars, which fit precisely into his compact case. He plans his itinerary around Britain in the summer in tiny detail, even knowing exactly where and at what time a refreshing glass of white wine might come up along the way.

Also, on one occasion on that 1968 trip to Pakistan, I saw how he could write a large slice of cool theatre into his life. We were travelling by bus across the Thal desert along a narrow ribbon of road, burned-out terrain. Our bus had been described to us as first class and air-conditioned, which turned out to mean that it had a luggage rack and the door was missing. Mechanically the poor bus was infirm. The gear lever had the shakes. The driver rammed it easily enough from first to second to third, but when it got to fourth, it shook violently as if it had St Vitus's Dance. It did not want to stay there and would certainly have hopped back into third if the driver had not placed a young assistant in the seat behind him, to hang on to the gear stick with both hands and to hold it jerking violently for hours across the desert. In the distance, a speck appeared. Five minutes later its outline was clear. It was a trans-state carrier. The driver of this vast wagon and the bus driver then began playing the 'chicken' game. There was room on the road for only one of the vehicles; one of them had to give way, but neither would. With only 50 yards to go we were lined up for a head-on crash.

You will appreciate that it was much too complicated

an affair for our driver to snatch the gear lever from the iron clutch of the lad behind and slip down into second. We hurtled at the lorry and swerved at the last moment. The giant wagon, so affronted by the assault of a lesser machine in the pecking order of the Pakistan roads, kept straight on. There was a scraping sound and a smashing of glass as lorry and bus jostled for position. We lost. The bus stopped and everyone leapt out to inspect the damage to our off side. I noticed that Richie Benaud was still on the bus, alone. He was still chewing and reading in his seat, three-quarters of the way back on the outside, next to broken window panes and the scraped side. Not a glance up from his book.

We all gossiped back to out seats. The bus restarted, got back on the road again and the driver committed it to the agonizing fourth gear again. Our captain suddenly stood up, still reading. He groped and unhooked his portable suit holder from the luggage rail above and, without taking an eye off the text of his book, crossed to the other side of the bus. He hung up his suits, took a fresh seat and probably cursed himself for failing in the department where he loved to succeed most, forward planning. What the hell had persuaded him to sit on the dangerous side of the bus?

It was a rewarding experience to play under his captaincy. No detail was too small for his attention, but all preparation, all adjustment was for the purpose of attack, not defence. Domination by preparation might well be the Benaud household motto.

1970. You could see the heat shimmer on the tarmac as we droned into Subang airport. MCC on missionary business again. We would stay for an hour in Kuala Lumpur before being driven off for a match in Seremban and on to Ipoh, Singapore, Bangkok and Hong Kong. I was the captain; my manager was my old tour leader, Alan Smith.

It was sweltering in the airport. AC and I agreed that there was no need for the boys to wear blazers although

195

we might expect a formal reception because this was our first touch-down in Malaysia. I was not looking forward to a press conference. These were troubled days for cricket. The cricket world had just split over South Africa, the D'Oliveira affair had separated friend from friend. The evidence was our blazer badge. Under the white monogram MCC was a scroll reading 'East Africa and the Far East 1970'. However, at the eleventh hour, the East Africans had turned us away. MCC were no longer welcome in Zambia, Tanzania or Uganda because we had agreed to South Africa's tour of England in the coming summer. We had been warned officially at Lord's by a civil servant who knew about such things that Malaysia too was certain to be unfriendly, so Alan and I had digested the party line before we met the press. By the time of this stop in Kuala Lumpur I could recite it like a creed.

This was February. January had been explosive when the Test and County Cricket Board had confirmed its plans to welcome South Africa. It had become the subject of serious parliamentary concern. Of British professional cricketers, 81 per cent had said that they were in favour of playing against the South Africans. Mr Hassan Howa, president-designate of the non-white South African Cricket Board of Control, immediately announced that the East Africans were not at all interested in playing anyone who played games with South Africa. Malaysia were certain to sysmpathize with black Africa.

Flight AE 116 landed. Very quickly AC and I were shaking the hand of Mr P. Alegendra, a uniformed chief-of-police, also a vice-president of the Malaysian Cricket Association. He announced that the press were waiting for us. We followed this smartly tunicked figure through the crowds which hurriedly paced back to give him room to pass. He led us to a small crowded room, hot, and high with body odour.

'Will you let Geoff Boycott open the batting in all the matches?'

'Most of the time,' I replied. 'I know you all want to see him bat.'

'You must give us Boycott all the time. We don't want second best. You must not insult us. He must always open batting.'

'But there are lots of good strokes to be seen from Hampshire, Fletcher, Gilliat, Roope, Alan Jones and, who knows, Lewis too.'

'No. No. Boycott is the one we want to see.' End of conversation.

Next question. 'Will Geoff Arnold be told to slow down if he is hitting our men with bumpers?'

I tried the jokey response. 'If it's as hot as today, Geoff will be happy if he arrives at the wicket to bowl at all.'

'Who spins the ball most, Pocock or Wilson? Is Don Shepherd slow or fast?' The answer was 'don't know' to all, and I spread confusion when I said that Don Shepherd was definitely a finger spinner, but wicket-keepers often stood back to him.

The pleasantries were over. 'What are your feelings about the forthcoming tour of England by South Africa?'

AC set off on his lines. 'The decision to allow the Springboks to play in England this summer was made by the Cricket Council. Our loyalty lies with them. We are not for apartheid, mind you, but we will not refuse to play them either.'

Pencils scratched impatiently on pads. They had not heard what they wanted. 'What was your reaction to the anti-apartheid action which damaged all those county grounds around your country, all in one night, last month?'

My turn. 'Well, we despise the anti-apartheid group for using violent methods. They are not cricket-lovers or else they would not have damaged the 12 grounds. They are political trouble-makers. They have a perfect right in Britain to demonstrate peacefully. They should do it.'

Dull eyes turned slowly. 'What do you think your Mr Callaghan said to the men from MCC, the ones he called to the Home Office, we saw in the papers last week?'

197

'I don't know,' I said, treading water and looking back at the disappearing shallow end.

'Does Mr Smith think that the anti-apartheid demonstrators can stop the tour?'

'Probably. Disrupting cricket should be easy enough if there are people of a mind to do that. Administrators, I know, are aware of the dangers. That's why a shortened South African tour, say of 12 matches, may be played on what they call "fairly defensible grounds".'

'Why did Uganda and other East African countries turn you away?'

'Because Britain wants to have sporting contacts with South Africa.'

'Do you, Mr Lewis, want sporting contacts with South Africa?'

I wanted to say honestly that I did not know; that I had never been to South Africa but that I had really good cricketing pals there. I wanted to explain how my opinion changed with every next argument for or against a sporting boycott. I was against apartheid, but I thought I was against boycotts too.

Mr Alegendra was looking unsympathetic; a straight face under a police cap covered with scrambled egg. I began again.

'I'm just a cricketer and my loyalty is to MCC and the British Cricket Council.' Back to the parrot tactics. 'We are not for apartheid but we will not refuse to play a game of cricket against them.' It was a wobbly bat.

Tempers rose. The press had received none of the answers they had wanted. Suddenly, getting smartly to his feet was the hitherto silent Mr Alegendra. He rapped his stick on the table; the babbling hacks were instantly silent. 'And if,' he spoke slowly, 'if I read one line about politics instead of cricket in your papers in the morning then I will have something very special to say to the writer. The cricketers of Malaysia have longed for this moment. Remember that.' The next morning's headline in the *Straits Times*, 26 February 1970, was startlingly irrelevant 'MCC: Our aim to foster game.'

It was on this tour that I first got to know much more about Geoffrey Boycott. There was a lot to admire. At Lord's before we left, the travel agents asked us to leave some of our cricket kit behind to cut down on weight. Everyone discussed the sharing of pads and bats and working out if rubber boots as well as spikes would be needed. Not Geoffrey. He was a professional batsman and there was no way that he would leave the tools of his trade behind. I admired that.

On tour, no game was too small a challenge for him. I envied that. As my mind wandered around the exotica, Geoffrey Boycott fastened on his blinkers and was only interested in the 22 yards in front of him. Yet there was an avarice about his performance too, on and off the field. Even so, the job of a captain is to make all talents work for the side, and mostly, on a missionary tour, Geoff's did.

However, there was an incident which was a clue to much that was to follow in Yorkshire in later years. It was at Kowloon Cricket Club, 15 March 1970, Hong Kong versus MCC. In the damp mists drifting in from the South China Sea, Geoff and Alan Jones built an unusual partnership. In his civilized style, Alan collected runs regularly. Geoff spent most of his innings padding up to balls wide of the off-stump, and therefore scarcely scored at all. A crowd of keen expatriots and Chinese were confused. It was a rare chance to see first-class cricket in the East and they could not understand the great Boycott's performance.

The man who kept bowling wide at him did a lot of chatting. Geoffrey, pushing out his left pad and removing his bat high in the air, let him have a word or two in exchange. All this was plain from the pavilion. Jones cut loose, but the Boycott impasse continued. As captain, I was not too concerned because I was certain that Boycott, as ever, would win his war and get his hundred. The clouds were dark grey; the light was never good. It so happened that Syd Buller, our umpire, thought he would instruct the local umpire in the current first-class

199

procedure for ruling on 'bad light', safe in the knowledge that the batsmen, who had put on over a hundred for the first wicket, would not choose to go off. The umpires went to the senior batsman, Geoff Boycott, whom Syd, loudly going through his tutorial, informed that the light was poor and asked if he wished to bat on, or go off.

'We'll go off,' said Boycott smartly. Poor Syd could not believe it.

I went quickly to the dressing room attacking Boycott with the obvious, 'We've come 8,000 miles to show them first-class cricket for one day only, and you bring us off.'

Boycott looked pained and responded. 'You won't understand what it's like being a great player.'

'True,' I said, 'but what has that got to do with it?'

'Well, he won't bowl straight and Test batsmen don't play at balls out there.' Not a thought of the occasion, the expatriots, umpire Syd Buller or anyone else.

I managed to transform that break into an early lunch interval. Afterwards the innings continued to 190 for 0 declared, A. Jones 104 not out, G. Boycott 79 not out.

That incident always reminds me of Geoff Boycott's infuriating misdirection within a team context. It was to become his life-long hallmark. Yet having considered many times his self-styling as a great player, I see him as someone who truly believed what he said; someone who was absolutely genuine but hopelessly misguided. It was this pursuit of professionalism for its own sake which isolated him later. It meant telling himself day by day that he was a great player, acting the great player who should practise every living hour. Preparing his body with mineral waters, having his kit in perfect order. A great player must never get out. The team may require certain efforts but Boycott's great player grafts on. Others can take chances; a great player is involved in a single, personal pursuit. The Boycott plan required many postures. How does a great player dress? What car does he drive? What house does he buy? As Geoffrey Boycott's career continued the more the loss of the amateur was emphasized. Boycott was the antithesis of the cricketer who did not owe his life and soul to cricket, of the independent spirit who could make his every unselfish effort for the team.

Whatever happens to Geoffrey Boycott, I want to remember him as the young man in glasses striking Wes Hall for a blistering straight four, or cutting with ferocity to third man, all shots along the ground. He was a formidable opponent, solid and punishing. I thought his stroke play would widen as he matured, but, in fact, it became more frugal and he himself became more defensive, acquisitive and more remote, as the false gods of runs and reputation beckoned.

However, on this 1970 visit to Ceylon, Malaysia and the Far East, Geoff's thirst for runs greatly delighted the opposition, who enjoyed the tilt at him and appreciated his many centuries. The grounds were quite superb, the Selangor Club Padang in Kuala Lumpur, Singapore and Chater Road in Hong Kong, all rubbing boundaries with busy roadways. It was hot everywhere and MCC's usual issue of blazers of army greatcoat thickness had the sweat racing down the middle of the back, gushing like a waterfall between the buttocks and down into the sticky socks. The manager, Alan Smith, proved his devotion to formality when he had the tour party lined up at the Negri Sembilan Club Padang for pre-match inspection by his Royal Higness the Yang di Pertuan Besar. The sunshine scorched us in front of the clubhouse where we stood blazered and purple and waiting. H.R.H. was 15 minutes late and we swayed on our feet. At last the motorcycle outriders could be heard and the royal cavalcade turned into the ground. The royal car swished to a halt in front of us.

The rear door was opened by a dutiful attendant and out stepped a distinguished looking man in a dark grey suit. AC stepped forward in his best National Service style, clapped his heels together and announced, 'MCC ready for inspection your Royal Highness.'

'I am bodyguard,' the man snarled abruptly. 'Highness getting out that side.'

I led two MCC sides to Ceylon, one a minor tour, part of the same Far East trip of 1970, and the other sandwiched between two Test series, India and Pakistan in 1972–73. Ceylon were desperately anxious to prove themselves worthy of Test match status. The games were keenly played; they had obvious talent based on sound coaching in the colleges and I had no doubt that they would grow into a Test-playing country given the experience. Whether they could sustain a visiting Test tour was another matter. They would have to improve grounds and take the game to commercial sponsors, which would be more likely to come if Ceylon had television. As for fun, these were unforgettable visits among courteous and generous people.

I have returned to Ceylon, now Sri Lanka, many times since, either to watch the cricket or, at the invitation of the Bostock family, to take a holiday. A succession of MCC cricketers have enjoyed the entertainment of Mark Bostock, ex-patriot, old Marlburian, Chairman of John Keells and latterly of Walker Tours. I have seen him towing Barry Wood, a determined but unskilled water-skier, semi-submerged through the still waters of Ben Tote. He and his wife, Lif, and daughters Gillian and Clare are the ones who have shown my family the delights of Sri Lanka. Seeing the New Year in up on the tea estate at Aislaby, walking the gum tree forests, playing golf near to heaven at Nuwera-Eliya, I ask myself yet again 'What am I doing here?' The answer is always the same: everything began with cricket.

It was from the old planters' club, the Hill Club at Nuwera-Eliya, that I wrote back to the *Sunday Telegraph* a piece to hail the arrival of Sri Lanka into Test cricket in 1982. They were about to play England. I felt proud to have been part of their preparation for Test match recognition.

'14 February 1982. *Sunday Telegraph*.

My surroundings invite imaginings of the old days. England have played out their match at Kandy and have gone down to Colombo, but I have moved even

202

deeper, and certainly higher, into the mountain heart of Sri Lanka.

After a gentle round of golf with friends at the Nuwera-Eliya Club, I am now poised over my typewriter in the old Hill Club, once the exclusive resort of gentlemen whose business was mainly coffee, chicona and tea.

The cheetah crest still stands firm and upright on the large teapots. The golf clubhouse light bulbs are so dim they might well be the originals. But hard as time is trying to drag me backwards, in the shadow of the island's highest peak, Mount Pedro, there is a symbol of the eighties poised on the mountain top – the country's main television transmitter. It was placed on its vantage point by choppers, spectacular stuff for the casual, friendly folk, many of whom have heard that national television arrived here two years go, but have yet to understand the presence of the very rare domestic TV roof aerial popping up above the coconut trees. This is Sri Lanka's beauty. Whisky soda is "in", television is "out".

However, it is television, this week, ball-by-ball from the first Test cricket match ever played by their own team, which will spread the historic news. From next Wednesday, Sri Lanka will become humanly and statistically, and highly emotionally, a Test match country. The hour is at hand.

Sri Lanka has always been the country where Test sides called on the way to somewhere else. Stories abound of friendships in the game, and of personal experiences. Maybe this week gives everyone licence to recall his own point of contact with Ceylon and its cricket.

The deep voice from a dark corner of the golf clubhouse told of terror as he faced up to the demon West Indian, Prior Jones, in 1950, and how Clyde Walcott caught him and then let the ball slip out on purpose, smiling and saying: "You gave us some party last night. Have a decent knock, enjoy yourself."

203

Members of the John Keells Company are renowned for the warmth of their welcome to MCC touring sides. By coincidence I flew out here with a former director, who had not been back for 25 years.

"Remember a cracking night with the England lads in the early thirties. It was Harry Elliott, of Derbyshire, who tumbled into his room one night and because he had not seen a mosquito net before, went to sleep underneath the bed.

"I stirred him in the morning with a prairie oyster – always worked y'know. Ole Harry swallowed it without opening his eyes and stayed asleep there on the floor for hours."

It is exactly a 100 years since Sri Lanka played against an English side. The Hon. Ivo Bligh's team was on the way to Australia. Reports are conflicting, but I will go for the one which says England beat 18 of Ceylon in a two-day match and then set sail on the *Peshawar*.

Unfortunately the *Peshawar* was not far out of harbour before she collided with *Glenroy*. So back to Colombo went the England party and they were persuaded to play a one-day match against the Dublin Fusiliers. In fact the match was not completed. The ship repairs were finished sooner than expected and so the teams shook hands and went their separate ways in mid-afternoon.

In many ways, this was always Ceylon's trouble; how to be taken seriously. They were so obviously excellent cricketers, but they were always facing up to Test teams who were building up to a major Test series or cooling down from one. Colombo is on the direct line sea-route from England to Australia.

In many ways Ceylon cricket was done an injustice. Their fight for Test match recognition has been long and painful, full of toil and tears. They invited investigation, always stood up to the inquisition on field, but never satisfied the International Cricket Conference off it.

204

It is up in Nuwera-Eliya that I have learned of coffee planters of the mid-nineteenth century travelling 50 miles on horseback for a cricket match, beating a dangerous way through wild country.

The oldest Sri Lankan club was founded in 1863 in Colombo. By the 1880s there were 12 clubs in the country, now there are many hundreds. To find the spirit of Sri Lankan cricket you must look to the colleges, the most famous of which are Royal, St Thomas's and Trinity, Kandy. The Royal–Thomian annual dust-up, called the Battle of the Blues, is over 100 years old. Like so many other MCC cricketers before me, and after, I can recall attending school morning assemblies in Colombo and talking cricket to the whole school before going with other touring players to coach the First Eleven.

So, you might guess, that Sri Lankan cricket is based on discipline. Players are always perfectly turned out, shoes whitened, flannels pressed. Their sportsmanship is firmly rooted in the best of the Old Boy morality.

If I have a worry about this aspect of their Test Match presence it is that they may have to be corrupted by the stage-work of many of the England players, some of whom enjoy pointing a dismissed batsman towards the pavilion, or kicking up dust at an appeal turned down.

I hope that England will understand how the whole Sri Lankan cricket community looks to them for skill and honesty. The English County Championship scores are digested daily out here. Every morning, bets are laid on horses racing at Chepstow, or Newmarket, Ayr or Newton Abbot. The man known as the founder of Ceylon cricket, Ashley Walker, Royal College master of the 1880s, was English. Let Keith Fletcher and his men be up to this mighty ocasion in the little island, now in 1982.

Sri Lanka is 270 miles long, north to south, and 140 miles across at its widest. There are 14 million

inhabitants, mostly Sinhalese, who compete aggress-
ively with the couple of million Tamils in all matters
except cricket. It is a tea island, and rubber. You can
drive through rice fields and still hunt leopard.
Beaches are delightful, but filling up, because the
tourist industry has grown quickly. Sri Lanka is green,
almost smothered by tea estates and palm tress, and,
astonishingly, it proudly boasts a 90 per cent literacy
figure – almost all Sri Lankans have 'O' levels.

My own cricket in Sri Lanka was played against
such excellent players as Michael Tissera, Neil Chan-
mugan and Anura Tennakoon. Stanley Jayasinghe
was the most charming and talented emissary to
British cricket with Leicestershire in the Sixties. Clive
Inman, too, came from Sri Lanka to make his mark
with the same county.

I shall not forget the roar at the Colombo Oval, now
known as the P. Sara Stadium, when Geoff Boycott
had his stumps shattered with the second ball of the
innings in 1970: G. Boycott b. Kehelagamuwa 0. They
reckoned that the noise of the crowd was so loud and
prolonged that coconuts fell off the trees up in Kandy,
and, who knows, the light bulbs might have peaked in
the golf clubhouse up in Nuwera-Eliya.

There was another roar in 1973, just as loud if not
louder. "What was it for?" I asked the umpire.

"Ceylon take first ever first innings lead over
MCC." He grinned at me. Thanks to Don Wilson's 8
for 36 in the second innings, our dignity was rescued,
with a win.

So, back to the great day on Wednesday, and that
television aerial. The ICC were always concerned that
Sri Lanka could not sustain a Test match programme.
Where else could they stage a match other than at
Colombo? They have provided startling proof. Once
ICC agreed to their inclusion, money has spilled into
the reshaping of the ground at Kandy, called the
Asgiriya Stadium. They literally moved a mountain.

Around the ground there, and at Colombo, are

advertising hoardings, every bit as numerous as at Lord's or Melbourne. The key to the incoming funds? Television. The Old Boy brigade have learned quickly, and if admitting Sri Lanka makes more sense now than it did ten years ago, it is because television has arrived.

Through TV screens also, the administrators of the game – who have a cricket foundation which is starting to tend to the youngsters – want to disseminate the game's fun and skills. They want television coverage of matches to spread the gospel and encourage the formation of district competitions. Sponsors will be easy to find.

So all looks well. Sri Lanka's hour has indeed come. On Wednesday morning, Mriamma, the long-serving groundswoman, will tug her roller by rope as ever, and set up the stumps for a new history.

New Zealand was the last country to gain Test match status; that was in 1929–30. Some cruel statistician pointed out that over their first 50 years, in 136 Tests, they have won only ten times.

Tolerance and understanding will be required in the case of Sri Lanka. They are desperately keen to prove themselves worthy. I think they will be glad when the fanfares are over, the birds have been released and the balloons floated away. Once the first dot has gone into the scorebook, they are official for the first time.'

In 1974, after operations to my knee and achilles tendon which had effectively ended all hope of prolonging a brief Test career, I went to Barbados with the wandering club founded by E.W. Swanton, called the Arabs. I wriggled my toes in the white sand of Settler's Beach, sucked in a strawful of iced daiquiri, closed my eyes to the hot sun and fell back into the arms of a long-lost friend, amateur cricket.

I let the sea roll up over the surgeon's scars and forgot about ever playing for England again. I was 36 years old. With me was E.W. Swanton, OBE, in posture imperial, weighty and meticulous in prose, serious in judgement. How far apart we were in one sense. He was drawn to the gravitas of cricket, which had been the platform of his life's work, drawn to the established order and to the important people. I treated cricket less seriously, though with affection, and later could not hide the traditional strain of liberalism in my bones when Kerry Packer and his star players tilted at the very world for which Jim stood. Given our contrary views on some matters, we have agreed on most and the Arab connection has been one of the happiest in my playing days. This is because the Founder has drawn together players who believe that cricket is worthwhile only if played seriously and by sportsmen. A wandering club would not have celebrated its jubilee, as the Arabs did in 1985, if it did not have lasting merits.

I had toured West Indies with Glamorgan in 1970, playing in Bermuda *en route* to Dominica, St Kitts, Granada and Trinidad. I understood the West Indian mentality well, which wants to lash the ball like lightning to the boundary and bowl quicker than the wind. To my mind, the finest West Indian batsman I played against, omitting Gary Sobers, was Rohan Kanhai. Rohan could turn his fiery temperament to an innings of quite savage strokeplay, and yet it was controlled; it had an aesthetic quality at the same time. Somewhere in him, the West Indian flamboyance merged with an instinct for accumulating runs by delicate deflection. He was short, neat in his dress and movements, and the position to be avoided if you were in the field was deep point. He played the square drive off the front foot with such an electric impulse that the ball could be over the boundary before you had raised a trot.

The Arabs in Barbados found the going tough. Quite a number of them worked in the City and at first their minds were on the appalling and sudden decline in the British economy. It was January 1974 and the country was undergoing the dreadful cut-back known as Phase Three. One lunchtime in the dressing room I discovered

208

the boys listening urgently to the radio.

'One twenty seven,' someone exclaimed. 'Amazing.'

'Who has scored that?' I inquired.

No one looked up, but someone muttered, 'Not runs old boy, gold. 127 – that's the highest it's been. It's a record.'

In the main on this tour, our bowlers were hit hard around the island and the batsmen failed to get going. Jim, fortified in his island home, Coralita, grew deeper frowns daily. Nor was the fast bowling problem improved by the delayed arrival of the Earl of Cottenham, though he was received with great expectations. At a Coralita dinner one night, Jim announced to Rita his cook, 'The Lord's supper, Rita, he is due any minute.' Reincarnation flashed through her eyes. She was happier later in the evening, after Charlie Cottenham had been brought from the airport by Gibbons, Jim's Bajan driver with the slouch hat and few teeth. 'Gibbons,' ordered Jim. 'Bring in the Lord's luggage will you.' Loaves and fishes, thought Rita!

Frustrated by the erratic bowling of his side, Jim, as is his custom in Arab matters, tried to right things from the sidelines. Gibbons one day presented me with an envelope from the Founder. Inside was a long length of string. The note read as follows:

Tony, here is a 26-yard length of cord which you may think a help in guiding bowlers' line.

If you mark out a narrow rectangle outside the off-stump I'll answer Hutton's snorts by betting him five dollars he can't land in it six out of six. If you just stretch it wicket to wicket it would at least indicate where they must pitch a good length ball to hit off stump. Only a tentative suggestion – but I'd like the cord back. J.

I put the wayward bowling down to the fact that one of our leading practitioners had new boots and therefore bleeding feet, and Richard Hutton of Yorkshire and Tom Mottram of Hampshire were not exactly in control of their fitness and run-ups let alone their direction. The whole side had come out of the deep mid-winter and the Barbados side were very, very good. Of course, Jim's understanding of West Indian batting habits was perfect. They tend to hit every ball wide of off-stump through the covers and every straight ball to mid-on and mid-wicket, therefore, as a faster bowler, you have to bowl a line just outside off stump, on a good length, and hitting it.

At a cocktail party a day later, the Founder asked about the success of the rope theory. 'Marvellous, Jim,' I enthused. 'Do you know that Ian and Emma Balding have been sleeping in twin beds from the start of the holiday but now, with that cord, we've lashed their beds together and they're perfectly happy.'

The Founder snorted and left. I should have been more tolerant. In fact I was to blame for our heavy defeat in the three-day match against Barbados because I chose to bat first when I won the toss. Even as I walked off with the opposing captain David Holford, his big cousin, Sir Garfield, chuckled and told me what a big mistake I had made. It had rained in the early morning. Gary said the ball would fly. It certainly did. At lunch we were 30 for 6, under siege, muted by the hell of batting on a rock-hard pitch which had been moistened by rain. John Barclay, my not-out partner at the crease, announced, with youth on his side and the stiff upper lip of Eton, that facing Gregory Armstrong and partner was 'a most interesting challenge'. More realism came from Richard Hutton who had opened. He sat in the corner smoking but not smiling. 'Gregory was a fine bowler; Armstrong was a good bowler too. It's a good job this bugger can't bowl at both ends.'

Richard was reading the mid-day newspaper which carried a photograph of Mike Denness's MCC touring party, just arriving in West Indies for their major tour. 'Thank goodness the cavalry has arrived,' said Hutton.

Our match was lost early on the third day but the team generously did not discuss how the pitch had eased out under the sunshine. John Barclay had been brave, evidence of the resolve which would make him Sussex's

210

captain one day, and he was last seen that afternoon stretched out on the beach in bathing costume explaining to Charlie Fry's nanny what a clinking good game cricket was.

I imagined that the Arab tour would be my last visit to the crease in West Indies, but it was not. I so enjoyed my stay at the Coral Reef Hotel with proprietors Budge and O'Hara that I decided to stay on after a Test match there in 1981. I think a letter I wrote to my younger daughter's godfather, Cardiff solicitor Jeffrey Cohen, best catches the fun and the perils of taking on Bajans at cricket.

> Coral Reef Club,
> St James, Barbados
> 5 April 1981

My dear Jeffrey,
It is almost a month since we tucked away a couple of snorts in the attractive basement of the Park Hotel in Cardiff.

A month in Barbados! The England team has come and gone, currently continuing the unequal struggle against West Indies in Antigua. Holiday-makers come and go, but ARL and wife are still at the rum punch.

As well as writing to say hello, I want to tell you about my cricket match. The general manager of the Coral Reef insisted, late at night, that I ought to turn out for the ral Reef Waiters XI against the Colony Club staff from the hotel up the road.

'I am forty-two and knackered,' I cried. 'I have not played cricket for years. Besides I have no kit.' I was duly selected.

There were three days to the match. I launched myself on a Muhammad Ali slimming course ... you know ... the one which takes off stones in days and leaves you even more knackered.

Surprisingly for someone of my normal sangfroid, I became the victim of nightmares, memory sharpening memory. This was not my first rub with the Coral Reef Waiters. I remembered being here before with the Arabs, E.W. Swanton's wandering club. On that occasion, 1974, I was making a very cautious comeback after knee surgery and in order not to let down the Swanton corps, which I was leading, I asked a waiter if he could line up some bowlers for a net across the road on the Trents Ground.

He did. We strung up a back netting. I took guard and they,

three of them, measured out their runs. They almost disappeared from sight. In from 30 yards or so came the first. At the
split second before delivery he opened up the body into a
javelin thrower's posture, bent the arm and threw one of the
fastest bouncers it has ever been my great luck to avoid.

The ball hissed over my shoulders. However, by the time I
had raised from the crouch and was standing up again, the ball
was on its way back, catapulting out of the taut net and
whacking me between the shoulder blades. The waiter
beamed.

The second guy hurtled in and javelined another lightning
bouncer. Down I went, and stayed down. Back sprang the ball
again which he caught, first bounce at the end of the follow
through. I straightened up to meet the third.

This fella was not one for disguise. From the start of his long
run his elbow was bent and he kept it that way as he
crescendoed into the release. He wore a white headband. A
spear would have suited.

I was in the ducking position long before he got to the crease
and this was just as well because he actually despatched a
lethal beamer. I was angry now and stood up, but as I did, I
met the ball catapulting off the back netting. It struck me
between the shoulder blades. I vowed never again to tangle
with Coral Reef waiters.

So you understand, maestro, my diffidence. But there was a
point which even in the heart of the night had cogency – I
would now be on their side.

My selection by the hotel management aroused lively
interest among the waiters, all young and fit. They grouped in
corners of the restaurant, whispered and pointed. I detected a
flash of disbelief in their eyes.

Panicking at my thirteen and a half stone, I took to early
morning jogging. After the first time, I staggered back into the
apartment and slumped at the breakfast table, the sweat
pouring out of my forehead. I soaked my bowl of cereal and
made the cornflakes soggy without even pouring milk over
them.

The breakfast waiter lurked and looked; he could not hold
back his astonishment: 'Are you the Mr Lewis who is playing
cricket for us on Saturday?'

I could not speak. Joan answered yes.

'Oh!' he said. 'I don't think you'll make any good. That
Hartley Alleyne and his boys – fast, man.' He played a hurried

defensive stroke with a napkin, closed his eyes and made a whistling sound as the imaginary ball went past his head. Then laughed.

Well, Jeffrey, I don't know whether you have seen Mr Hartley Alleyne bowl for Worcestershire, but he is quicker than your average waiter. He is like greased you-know-what.

More research revealed that not only is Hartley Alleyne a dishwasher at the Colony Club, but four of the Barbados side are employed there. Apparently, one giant of an all-rounder called Hartley Harrison, fast bowler and batsman, a magnificent specimen of the male form, happens to be a bell boy! Send not to know for whom...?

More slimming, more jogging and an investment in Dunlop Green Flash tennis shoes. Came the day, 1 p.m. for 1.45 at Trents, 35 overs each.

We won the toss and batted. I was billed as number six and I sat with the only other holiday-maker who had fallen to the influence of rum punch, Jim Yates, 46 years old and a practitioner of village cricket.

The umpires, by the way, were an informal couple, one dressed in peaked cap (grey), shirt (yellow) and trousers (blue). He had a transistor radio to his ear throughout the game so that he could take in the ball-by-ball commentary on the Test in Antigua. The other umpire was out of his mind on rum. He wore yellow ankle socks, jogging shoes, shorts and tee-shirt. He sang throughout the whole game.

My panic returned when I saw goats cleared off the outfield to make way for Hartley Alleyne's long run. The first ball, a bouncer, went over the heads of the batsman and the keeper. Jim Yates and I shuffled uncomfortably on the wooden bench. Four byes. The second ball hit the batsman on the point of his shoulder. Every other ball in the over went through neck high at about 90 m.p.h.

The bowler at the other end was every bit as quick and nasty. In the third over, our opener was hit on the head. No helmets worn here. Jim Yates turned to the skipper offering not to bat at all. I too said what a pity it was for me to take up the position of a waiter who could only get off once a week. Jim and I would willingly do numbers ten and eleven. The skipper then pointed out that we only had nine men and that we were in the bottom four anyway.

Alleyne hit a second man on the head, whereupon Jim Yates performed instant maths to work out that it was costing him

£960 for the privilege of sitting in death row with his pads on.

The tale ends as a success story, though modestly told, I hope ... that A.R. Lewis followed to the crease a young man who was retiring with injury, a split finger.

Not for the first time in his life Lewis took guard in the pool of blood unreasonably left by the batsman before him. However, he made 30 not out, by reason of his long experience and natural cowardice. He saw the first slow bowler arrive, leapt down the pitch and belted him over the top for six, then four, the four careful blocks so that he would not be taken off.

Indeed, Lewis was never quite able to take the strike at the other end, and if the truth be known outside the basement bar of the Park Hotel, he actually ran out the skipper in a desperate effort to make a second run back to the safe end.

When the fast men were brought back, Lewis then demonstrated the retreating square slash and the innings ended where it started with bouncers and batterings.

There was one sadness. Poor Jim Yates did not get in. It was worse in its way than his batting. We took tea between innings, but he sat there with his pads on right through the interval, grey hair darkened by sweat, like a prisoner the brutal interrogators had refused to put out of his misery. If only he could have gone out there and have been hit on the head first ball, at least the inner turmoil could have ended. He craved for his own execution. He would prefer to be lying in a dark, air-conditioned room in the Holetown Hospital. Now he would never know. So Jeffrey, baby, as the good Mrs Lewis is greasing up for another day on the Sandy Lane golf course and my good friend Robert Sangster is sharpening up his irons ready to gouge a few more dollars from me over eighteen holes just to prop up Vernons Pools for the day, I suggest you give me a call if ever you want to play cricket in Barbados. I can offer white sands, a lively sea, beneath palm trees and manchineel – oh! and life assurance.

Love to the pretty girl who served us the whiskies on the frozen day in Cardiff.
Tony

19

Little Joy in Pakistan

Playing for England in Pakistan in 1973, unexpectedly, was not the fun it had been with the Commonwealth side five years earlier. Pakistan had just lost a war against India. Relationships with Britain were strained. On the day before we arrived a young Pakistani brandishing a toy gun had been shot by the police in London. At Karachi airport, there were no garlands, no handshakes, the photographers were gone. I soon discovered that the whole country lacked enthusiasm. The British in Peshawar, where we first played, were depressed. Their community had reduced considerably.

However, one of them took me to the wedding of their household bearer. It was shocking. A bullock was fettered to a post in the garden. It's throat was cut, it bled to death and then it was carved and cooked in huge cauldrons. It was raining which rather dampened the noise of jubilation, the continuous music, the pistol shots and the explosion of small dynamite parcels. The women were separated from the men. I was taken on a visit to find them huddled in a wide alcove, packed together, covering their faces when they saw me with the hoisted bodies of the baby girls which they tended. On the next day I went to holy communion at the Old Garrison Church of St Johns with John Woodcock, Bernard Thomas and a Mr Roberts, whom I recall as a retired British surgeon who was in Peshawar so that he could follow a yearning to do some missionary work. There were only two others there to hear the service taken by a Pakistani vicar. The large church could scarcely be maintained any longer, though seeing it next to the former British Army lines and the Peshawar Club, and observing the grooves in the pews where rifles used to be rested, it was easy to reel back the imagination to the imperial days. What am I doing here? Cricket again.

The England team was tired after an exhausting series in India and a fortnight in Ceylon. After training at the Lahore Gymkhana one day Jack Birkenshaw addressed the Pakistan press with a dazzling one-liner. 'After four months of this I'm as fit as a fiddler's bitch, but I can't bowl an 'oop down th 'ill.' Their mouths dropped open, their pens were poised, but they wrote nothing.

It was a moment of Glamorgan history when I went out to toss in the first Test with my county friend Majid Khan. Majid had been selected captain of Pakistan for the first time. It was Jon, the *Daily Mail* cartoonist, who was quick to spot this – not surprising for a Caerphilly boy – and came up with imagined conversation as we tossed, 'Maj. Has Wilf Wooller sent you his instructions yet?' On the rest day of the Test I went to Majid's home for lunch. The house was large and handsome with pillared porch, stout and spacious, for drivers to drop their passengers out of sunshine or rain.

Quite a few of Majid's relatives live in houses within a couple of acres. In front of the house was a neat lawn where family cricket was played. The wickets were always pitched in front of a thin tree so that the trees to either side of it, each about six yards apart, could be the slips. Two snicks hitting trees meant another Khan back in the pavilion. Human fielders usually lined up to right and left, off and on, so the run-getting area was straight, either side of the bowler. It was chancy to hit the ball in the air because there were lots of catchers and it was out over the wall or over the hedge in front of the house.

Majid's father, the hero of the Cambridge University groundsman, Cyril Coote, talked about the old times, deliberate but alert in speech: a tall man, hollow cheeked and with piercing eyes. I particularly enjoyed the stories of the classical music master who taught cricket at the famous Aichison College where Majid and cousin Imran were taught, in Lahore. The perpetual cry of Mr Aftab was 'Point your left elbow to the direction of the line of the ball, boy.'

There were photographs on the wall of Jehangir Khan in the first Indian side at Lord's in 1932. Also a replica of the Lord's museum piece of the sparrow he accidently killed while bowling at Lord's on 3 July 1936. It was fascinating to learn how Jehangir had stayed in England after the '32 Test. In 1933 he went to an athletics meeting with a friend who was a 220 and 440 runner. Jehangir saw the javelin for the first time and asked if he could join in and have a throw. Not only did he win it, he broke the Indian record with his first throw. He won the shot too. Later that year he represented India in the Empire Games at the javelin.

All three of our Test matches were drawn, but I was happy with the way England played, especially as our worst fears about the mood of the country were correct. In Rawalpindi, after we had beaten a strong Pakistan President's team on the Pindi Club ground, over a thousand youths rioted. They smashed the windshields of 17 buses and rammed a double decker into a wall. They manhandled drivers and conductors and pelted stones, injuring six people including a girl who was hit on the head. Police eventually stopped them while they were trying to set fire to the bus station petrol pump.

The best time of the day for England cricketers in Pakistan is early evening. The din of 30,000 screaming spectators is gone; where you had been on display all day, you are now in isolation: doors are closed and no one can touch you, pull a shirt sleeve, pat your back, leer or cheer. The Pakistan evenings are peaceful. It is a country of half light just after business hours. Streets are meagrely lit and the dark shadows you see are the ox cart late home or the overloaded donkey. For England cricketers it is a time to shower after a day in the dust-bowl stadium; time to sip a long whisky soda and think of home, perhaps sit in the open air in the rest house garden or on the hotel balcony and feel unashamed pride that you represent your country. As the muezzin wailed from the mosque, calling the faithful to prayer, as the rest house cook knelt on his mat in the darkest corner of the garden and the air was filled with the aroma of hibiscus and smouldering candlewood, I was drawn to see my role as MCC captain in heroic terms. Then it would pass, but my spirits would be renewed by the sense of mission. I would then go along to the team room for a drink with others or smarten up for some official function.

There is a day in my diary of 1973 which I entitled 'Pakistan – the longest day'. I have no reason to demote it, even 13 years later – 18 March. MCC were playing the first ever Test match in Hyderabad, which is in the middle of the Sind Desert. It was mid-March and ridiculously hot. The Hotel Sanjees made Fawlty Towers seem like the Dorchester. I had no water in my room, not a globule. Toast was not available at breakfast because the charcoal had gone out, and we waited almost an hour for any morsel of food to be hoisted from the kitchen which was on the floor below. Eventually a waiter scuttled our way to inform me, 'Sahib. I have to apologize for absence of head-waiter. It is our regret he has been stabbed by chef with knife.'

Good start to the day: not a particularly good start for the chef either. Alas he was dead by lunchtime. At the ground it was ragingly hot, even at ten o'clock in the morning. The dressing room was smaller than any at home. It smelled sickeningly of new paint and when the food was laid out in it at lunchtime, an army of insects flew escort.

There were 40,000 spectators in the ground every day. The home administrators were very proud of their field and, to be fair to them, it was almost a magic process which produced a few acres of green grass in the heart of the desert. The pitch itself was white, rolled mud, cracked all over and shiny from days of watering and heavy rolling. The rest was lush, tropical green.

218

Sadiq square-cut a ball from Geoff Arnold to the third man boundary. About 3,000 spectators ran onto the field to congratulate Sadiq. When they went back to their side of the fence there was no grass left at all on their route. Truth was – every square yard of the field, outside the 22 yards of playing surface, was becoming bald and sandy by the minute. The crowds persisted in running on to celebrate boundaries all day and by lunchtime we were fielding in soft sand. The sun roasted the skin even through shirts. There was no saliva, no air, just a thick coating of dust inside the mouth and on the lips which we tried to protect with white ointment. Alan Knott and Keith Fletcher, wicket-keeper and first slip, came to me with a problem none of us had faced before. They said that the shiny pitch was acting as a mirror and the sun rays were leaping up off the surface right into their eyes. They had tried pulling down the brims of their white sunhats but it was no use. Now in the mid-day, they were being blinded. Their eyelids were swollen and half closed. The only answer we could come up with was that they should expose their eyes as little as possible to the pitch. So, as the bowler walked back to prepare to bowl they looked the other way, fixing their eyes on grass. Also, between overs, instead of walking together up the pitch, heads down to the other end, still picking up the glare, they should take a longer walk, round through the covers.

We got Sadiq out and Talat Ali and Majid and Zaheer, but Mushtaq and Asif Iqbal played easily on the perfect batting strip. At teatime everyone confessed that at some stage of the day he had wanted to leave the field. Mike Denness struggled with gout, Norman Gifford bowled 30 overs, his face a shocking mauve, his lips white and frothing with protective ointment; his feet hurt, and on this rock-like surface he had jarred a calf muscle. Tony Greig was hit a painful blow on the foot by Zaheer when he was fielding close. He limped through the day too and even struggled through a few overs before the end. Astonishingly, one or two, running around in soft sand, had sprung under-the-skin blisters on the balls of their feet. At close of play Mushtaq was 90 not out and Asif 70.

There was still no water back in the hotel except in the rooms of Donald Carr, the manager, and Bernard Thomas, our medico. I lay on the bed for a while, ordered a sandwich which never came, opened my laundry, which had been returned wet, and in a move of desperation to get some sort of achievement in the day, shaved in hot tea. I went to Donald Carr's room for a shower.

'Thought you might have taken the new ball earlier,' he said.

'Et tu, Manager!' I cried. 'Or in the language of Lord's, bollocks!'

Our third Test was abandoned because of rioting and dust storms in Karachi where the sun blistered down again for five days. The riot squad were with us from the first day because crowds spilled on to the field and carried on their own gang warfare. They charged each other, flailing studded leather belts; the police waded in whacking everyone with their lathi and then the blue-helmeted riot squad lambasted everyone with sticks. This incensed the crowd who broke up chairs, pulled down the chamiana poles and started fires around the ground. The crowd stoned the police; the police stoned the crowd. The temperature was over 110 degrees. We sheltered in our dressing room watching the television transmission. Outside there was holy war but the cameras avoided it. All that went on TV to the nation was a long tedious chat between commentators on the merits of having two slips to the new ball in the morning's play.

On the day off, Mr Abdul Hafeez Kardar, former Oxford University and Warwickshire player, once captain of Pakistan in the fifties, Minister for Food in the State of Punjab and President of the Pakistan Cricket Board, made a speech at the official dinner in which he claimed that Pakistan should be the centre of world cricket. 'Geographically it would be easier,' he said. 'Pakistan is now a major cricketing country. It would be a fitting centre of cricket administration.' It was only then that I was certain of what I had long suspected – he was mad. I was straining to get up and speak, but Donald Carr did and turned the other cheek, probably with much more sense, beginning his reply 'My dear old friend Hafeez'.

I took it as a snub against MCC and I looked hard for Mr Kardar in the third Test to ask about riots, the chaos at the sightscreens, the absence of details like bowler's markers – we were given bottle tops at Hyderabad, where incidentally, there was no mower at all on the ground – and what about the umpire in Karachi who took the field with no new ball? All these petty points proved that the manager's approach had been the right one. He did superbly to pat Kardar on the head, as if to say, 'My dear little boy, there you are, that's long enough playing with your nasty little toys tonight, up the wooden hill you go and off to bed.'

And so it was farewell to Pakistan with a brick through the window of our bus which just missed Pat Pocock. I felt sorry for their highly talented cricketers. They and their friends were proud and courteous. Their Test team were impeccably honest and fair in competition. They deserved to have their game disentangled from politicians who were constantly manipulating every cricket occasion to boost their own end. It was obvious that a strong, straight cricket administration was needed which could take on the government if possible and create a game of opportunity for a talented nation.

20

Amateur Aftermath

Any old first-class cricketer will tell you that turning part-time amateur is difficult. It is first of all difficult to leave the county game, and then almost impossible to concentrate in friendly matches. There was a whole range of cricket for me to play after Glamorgan. I loved the company, the venues were fun, but could never again truly concentrate. The weakness, I accept, was in me and not in the standard of play which was frequently excellent.

Indeed I once took a week-end off from cricket-writing for the *Sunday Telegraph*: three days of my annual leave. Thankfully Trevor Bond, my sports editor then, and David Grice now, did not mind me being away from the County Championship on the odd occasion because they understood that if I was at a sporting event of any sorts, snooker to snorkelling, an anecdote or two would appear in some future piece for them.

The match was for my favourite wanderers, the South Wales Hunts; the opposition was I Zingari. I was using Lord Cobham's dispensation allowing a member of I Zingari to turn out against the Club. It was a two-day match played at the picturesque ground of the Royal Regiment of Wales at Cwrt-y-Gollen, near Crickhowell in Powys. In the first innings I found myself at the crease with my close friend and neighbour, Mathew Prichard. Mathew was a good cricketer, a powerful straight-batting Old Etonian. He is also the grandson of Dame Agatha Christie. I had not played with the Hunts since I led them against racing trainer Ian Balding's side at

Kingsclere earlier in the season. Mathew had alarmed the Hunts side even then by taking a superb outfield catch while fielding substitute for a Balding man, so winning the game for them and killing us off. Another of the Hunts, Gruffy Phillips, expressed our disgust. 'Oh God! What has Mathew done! You'd think with a famous detective writer as grandmother he'd have thought up some escape from the time he saw the ball leave the bat at 6.03 precisely and arrive in his hands, seven seconds later.'

Against I Zingari he had another surprise for me. 'Yes. Come on ... no ... sorry.' Lewis run out 0.

On the second day of my holiday, in the second innings, I took easy guard, looked around the field, pushed forward to a ball from Henry Wyndham, which popped, took the shoulder of the bat and was caught by a one-eyed friend in the gully called Anthony S. de R. Winlaw. What a way to spend a holiday! A 'pair' for the Hunts!

I played for I Zingari, the Arabs, the Quidnuncs, the Heartaches, the Lord's Taverners and in benefit matches for county players. I also played many times in MCC matches against clubs and schools. As a former first-class cricketer you are expected to succeed. However, it is jolly difficult to find meaningful conversation when you have been bowled out for nought by a Dulwich College seamer. At the end of such games there was always the farewell on the pavilion steps. The chairman of the home club had come to see you off after the match. He would shake your hand quite savagely, breathe beer all over you and say, 'Sorry we didn't see you at your best, Lewis, but you've no idea how much you made the day of the young lad who got you out for three ... or was it two?'

'No. I enjoyed it,' you lie. 'Such a lovely change from being l.b.w. to Shackleton at Southampton or bowled by Brian Statham.' You fix a smile. Excuses are no decent currency for a good sport at that moment. You just bow again to the great game, a willing victim of the truth that any man or dog with a ball in his hand has a chance of rolling you over. Amateurs knocking over the stumps of erstwhile professionals is one of the world's most delicious pastimes. And why not?

I remember being drawn to this subject by Tom Graveney in the mid-seventies. He had represented the pub which he ran in a national pub knock-out competition. He was the main hope of the Royal Oak at Prestbury in Gloucestershire. In the match against the Three Pigeons he stroked 51 runs not out in the 12 overs left to him. The Pigeons were not impressed and smashed off the runs with four overs to spare. Yet, d'you see, the Pigeons lost their next tie to the Air Balloon and they went off to meet The Lamb and Flag at Witney. When the Lamb and Flag won, they were then advertised as the side which beat the side, which beat the side which beat Tom Graveney's pub. As long as he kept playing Tom could only lose.

Of course, the clock never goes back perfectly and you need some luck. Colin Cowdrey and I once played together for the *Sunday Telegraph* at Brockham Green in Surrey. It was a 20-over match and Colin went in at number four. He timed a few nice strokes: his status was intact. However, the sports editor, automatically captain, had carefully noted in Colin's autobiography a reference to his youthful skills as a leg-spin bowler. We had not been fielding a dozen overs when the call came, 'Next over Colin. A few leggies?'

Colin offered the innocent schoolboy look – what, me? His long career with Kent had left him a shade underbowled! Next over the familiar Womble-like frame was turning slowly and the ball was carving reluctant arcs ever so high in the air. It did not look at all promising for him though he had been accepted by the side as a stock bowler simply because he had been a professional batsman. His bowling was played easily, but then pride took over and, scraping the depths of his bowling talent, hurling the clock back to his schooldays when he tweaked a cunning bosie at Tonbridge, he attempted the googly. Practitioners of the googly will know that to produce the legerdemain at the finger-tips, and the back of hand towards the batsman, the shoulder has to twist that extra bit further through its socket without betraying the intention. I can only describe the Cowdrey shoulder as short of axle grease.

As the brave arm went up to produce the sharp twist from the back of the hand, so the left shoulder sunk downwards until it grazed the popping crease. Then, as if his cover was not already blown, the great man let out the groan of a veteran entertainer and came out of this painful routine wearing the set smile of Archie Rice. This particular ball was a long time in flight but miraculously fortune lurked. The batsman was so confused by the sight of a household name upside-down that he played and missed. The ball bounced two inches in front of the stumps and he was bowled. 'Got him with the wrong'un Colin,' the keeper quickly offered. Colin smiled at me: no need for words. We knew that his reputation was saved for another day, but soon he would be cornered by the committeemen who would say, 'You know, Colin, you've no idea how it's made that man's day to have hit you for those five sixes in the over.'

I shall avoid unhappy endings and tell you of the time I turned out for the Cambridge Travel Agency, Beach Villas, at Hilton, near Huntingdon. I was enveigled into this appearance by old friends after many pints of beer at Fenners while watching the University. It seemed a good idea to be smuggled into the local six-a-side competition that evening. I accepted that I was not to conceal my identity from the opposition – bad show tó conscript an England player, however long retired, and indeed I changed from the boot of a car, away from the pavilion. The skipper gave a pep talk. He badly wanted to win.

We fielded first. He issued brusque orders. 'Down to fine leg,' he instructed and so I stood right back, close to the road which runs across the common. 'No,' shouted the skipper, 'Right back you go, old boy. Over the road. It's all in play over there.'

This was a new fielding experience. I have never had a

road, along which cars passed from time to time, between me and the cricket. I had been surrounded by cars as in the old ground at Chater Road in Hong Kong. Cars had skirted the grounds at Singapore, and at Kuala Lumpur too where the cricketers are not far from the passing traffic. But no. I could not recall fielding on the other side of the road. Unfortunately, long years of professional habit had me walking in with the bowler's run-up and I ended up each time perilously parked with the crunch of spikes on tarmacadam on double yellow lines.

When the time came to bowl, my two compulsory overs were smashed around to all parts of East Anglia and I suffered the humiliation of having to switch from leg-spin to seamers and back to leg-spin again ... all within 12 deliveries. However, the batting went well enough. We won.

As I walked off towards the pavilion I took off my gloves, smoothed my hair back, prepared to amble modestly into the applause. Habit again. However I was greeted some 30 yards from the pavilion by the skipper who quickly turned my shoulder and redirected me to the car, which was already revving up. 'Don't bother to change, old boy. We are having a party to celebrate. Have a shower at home. I'd prefer they didn't see you.'

How do you change from a professional, who has toiled for his applause and lives for the acclaim of members up on their feet in the pavilion, to a faceless extra? How do you settle for the unknown warrior bit-part?

Occasionally, in retirement, there is satisfaction in demonstrating to the young how age has left your silken skills untarnished. But who can select you? Club teams will not have you because you cannot practise or play regularly mid-week; your travelling job keeps you out of the nets and your untravelled wife keeps you in the garden at the week-end. Also, if I told the truth, driving the car up and down the M4, foot fixed on the throttle, has cemented the right knee joint. So what now? It is time you played what is called casual cricket for private teams. You must dig into school magazines to see if they still run an Old Boys outfit, or ring up the British Legion or the Working Mens' Club to see if there is even a 20-over bash some time.

If no one picks you to play, then form your own club. This was done with success by Tim Rice, long, left-handed lyricist. For several years he had three shows on in the West End, *Jesus Christ Superstar*, *Evita* and *Joseph's Amazing Technicolour Dreamcoat* as well as a cricket team on the road, necessarily vagrant, because it owned no ground. It is run from the Rice household in Great Milton near Oxford. So Tim started the Heartaches Cricket Club, the Clava Recta, on 8 July 1973. I played occasionally and was delighted to be called upon to turn out in a special event to celebrate the 100th Heartaches match.

His shy colours are red, pink and green. His men are a sock-it-to-me lot who attend their games in crinkled kit expecting to lose. There is a nobility in this. It is a self-imposed guilty-until-proved-innocent streak which marks them out from all others. To celebrate the 100 Heartache matches, which had begun 2,097 days earlier, Tim Rice's XI was matched against his brother Jo's XI. Only previous Hearts could apply and the instructions were roughly as follows.

'Lord Porchester has kindly lent us his pitch on the Caernarvon estate, Highclere, Hants. It is one of the finest pitches in the country in one of the most beautiful settings. The pavilion and other facilities are first-rate. Four showers! 11.30 – choosing of teams. 12.30 – prompt start. T. Rice. Skipper.'

I arrived at 10.45. The sun shone, brids sang and all that, and we all prepared to be part of history itself. Then the skipper announced 'No play until the van comes.' 11.20 – the van cometh bearing the crest of Laytons Wines. In no time a Champagne Deutz cork had hit the air and the bubbly overture was underway. It did not turn out to be the quick toast I expected. There was jovial reminiscence, oaths, banter, lots of photography, more quaffs of bubbly and a vague separation of players into sides of equal talents.

At 1.25 Jo Rice's team took the field. Two overs later they came back in. A lunch of many courses was slowly devoured. Because I was 2 not out, I decided to give the vin rouge a miss. Bacchanalians tumbled, the skipper perused the banquet with the glazed beam of a megastar. He was confident: he knew this was one match the Hearts would not be losing.

I should have known better. My temperance had the reverse effect. The unwisdom of professional approach was made plain when I chipped a catch to mid-on where Andy Rossdale made a clever catch off Jo Rice's bowling. I departed for nine runs.

Everything went predictably. Tim Graveney, son of you-know-who, got a century for us and Graham Chidgey, the Laytons vintner, got one for them. Radio One's Mike Read, blazered and helmeted I thought, but a bit later found to be operating under a matted, busby hair-do, bowled steadily for them and Tim Rice ploughed stoically through his eight overs for us. All this, as I say, was predictable.

Wholly expected too was the compulsory injury, though sadly it was a bloody affair which removed the front teeth of wicket-keeper Chris Pryke. He left for Basingstoke General Hospital, but then someone usually does. The official match report from the Skipper's log reads as follows:

'Pryke was now ex-wicket-keeper (and possibly ex-friend) and had to be replaced. Two figures leapt into the breach immediately. William Heath and Soames, both of whom adopted an alert crouching position where Pryke had so nobly fallen. Soame's offer was eventually refused with reluctance by J. Rice on two grounds (a) he had not played for the Hearts before and (b) he was a dog.

The Hearts said farewell to Highclere, the vice-captain's team winning by five wickets. The full cast left for another venue, north of the M4, where the night was twisted away to the strains of the Searchers, a live show by the old favourites on the lawns of Romeyns Court, the dashing skipper's home.

Pryke was back smiling emptily and swinging a mean shoe, sausages sizzled and all was red, pink and green in the Heartaches world ... that is, until the tall golden-haired, balding but exceedingly pale skipper slowly emerged from one of his many studies to announce grievously that he had done a recount and that this was indeed a more sensational event than that previously planned. It was not in fact the hundredth game: it was the 99th, and as the Skipper put it, 'Not many clubs celebrate their 99th game with such a p-up.'

In August 1981. Out came the faded Test match sweaters. You could not take a step in the small, friendly dressing room of Smethwick Cricket Club without stumbling over crowns and lions. The Courage Old England team were on the road for the very first time.

With apologies to T.S. Eliot, time past was just about to be contained in time present, with not a chance of it having any relevance at all to time future. We were old internationals on our last legs. But not so our philosopher captain F.S. Trueman, who viewed it thus: 'Couple o' weeks in t'soonshine an' we'd stuff those Aussies art 'o sight.' A reference to the current tourists. The parade to lunch brought oohs and aahs of adulation from club members who generously remembered the best of us. Marvellous game cricket. When you retire the bad old days go: the careless snicks, the long hops. Only the best remains.

But then it was time to change into whites: time to search for the old skills again. The dressing room chatter got heady and, would you believe, quite nervous. The veterans knew that cricket is only a generous lady when you have laid down the bat and ball forever. Toy with her, make a comeback, yes, play for Old England, and she becomes the mischievous, elusive mistress again.

The England sweaters looked like shining impregnable armour, but underneath, we all knew, were sagging bodies, rolls of fat and varicose veins, the legacy of a million fielding sessions. 'Who has got a bat I can use?' pleaded Tom Graveney. 'I need socks. Spare socks anyone?' D'Oliveira was back in town.

'Good grief!' exclaimed Don Brennan. 'I've just realized. By taking a match fee today, I've turned pro for the very first time in my life.' True, Mr D.V. Brennan, as *Wisden* lists him, was about to become, at 61 years old, the oldest amateur in cricket ever to turn professional ... we think!

There were surprising nerves from Peter Richardson, cool Test opener of the fifties and sixties, who imagined that the opposition of current Midland League players might have Lillee and Thomson to open the bowling. I was to open the batting with him and this was his plan. 'We've got to look old,' he said. 'Then they won't ping the ball around our ears.'

'We *are* old,' I replied, even though I was the baby of the side at 43. The Richardson theory unfolded. 'Because you've still got all that dark hair, you look young, so cover it up with a cap, and because I have lost most of mine, and what's left is grey, I'll go hatless. They'll feel a bit charitable then to a couple of old-timers. Maybe.'

Brian Close girded up for number three, said he believed cricketers should never retire. 'Have bat, will travel.' Don Wilson agreed with him. Happily, throughout Old England's 40-over innings, egos stayed intact. Methods were sound – face of the bat, ball into the V. However, the first sign of strain came after an over in which Richardson and Lewis took three quick singles. They met, by long habit, in the middle of the pitch for the essential chat, but, although only a yard apart, both found speech impossible. They stood momentarily gulping, staring at each others knees, and returned to their own ends without a word exchanged.

Close hit massive sixes; Graveney needed only to lean

into one of his classic cover drives to tell the 5,000 crowd what a player he had been in his day. 220 runs in 40 overs. Not at all bad. We took the field and it was then that the mischievous mistress dangled us around her little finger.

Firstly, there was a scramble to field at the top end of the square, the one with the short boundary. It was won by D'Oliveira, Milton and Richardson. On the other side, the rest of us proved it possible to set off after a ball two yards behind it, and end up at the boundary four yards behind it. Hamstrings twanged like sitar strings. Richardson threw his arm out at his first pitch to the wicket-keeper; Titmus was struck in the ear by a ball which hopped up from a violent square cut. Blood ran down his neck.

The opposition was powerful. Three Test players – Ron Headley, John Jameson and Mushtaq Muhammad – with former County players Roy Virgin of Northants, Doug Slade and John Aldridge of Worcestershire. The spinners bowled beautifully, the old arts of Titmus and Don Wilson reviving.

The Midlands levelled the scores with one ball to go. No fixing. One of their lower-order batsmen came in to face our leader, Frederick Sewards Trueman. Fred announced that he would bowl a yorker on or outside leg stump. Don Brennan would be waiting there, standing up while, in case the ball should run away off the batsman's pads, Brian Close and Don Wilson would lurk a few yards away to initiate the inevitable run-out, if the yorker had not done its dreadful business. Either way we would win. Typical Yorkshire!

The rest of us just crowded around, ankles creaking and cracking in the starting blocks. I practised toe-touching; Dolly jogged on the spot, F.S. Trueman, the great warhorse with the floppy black mane, turned-in toes and the now ample 50-year-old figure, clattered in on the well-worn tracks of one of the games's finest bowling actions. It was still a superb sight. Alas, after the ball left the famous fingers it scarcely lost a foot in height down the 22 yards. It arrived firmly, a full toss, right in the meat of the bat and was next heard rattling among the wheels of the sightscreen behind him. Defeat for Old England at the first time of asking.

Afterwards in the dressing room, Closey reckoned he could have bowled it better ... of course; Don Wilson was glad he did not have to bowl it at all; and F.S.T.? The great man simply looked up and proclaimed, 'Twenty years ago, sunshine, an' that'ud 'ave bin a perfect yerker.'

None of us is ready for the next Test.

September 1984, leading an MCC tour for the last time, I arrived with my team on the kerbside outside John F. Kennedy airport in New York to no reception. People stared at us and as they fixed eyes on the white monogrammed MCC on the breast pocket of our blazers, they wheeled suitcases over our feet and ran trolleys into our big cricket bags. Eventually someone risked the comment, 'Gee! You guys a band or something?'

After a while the President of the United States Cricket Association arrived. He was a Pakistani, Naseeruddin Khan. 'President,' I enquired, 'are there any nets available for us tomorrow?'

He gave us the rocking head, side to side, the gleaming smile. 'Fishing nets only available.' His little joke, but I knew from that moment where we were in effect, Karachi! We would need to slip into sub-continental tempo; so, I sat down on a case. Other experienced voyagers to India and Pakistan, overhearing the overtures, had worked it out before me. They were already sitting down: Fred Titmus, Mushtaq Muhammad, John Jameson. They had worked out the sum: 14 large cricket bags and 14 suitcases into one Pakistan president's car ... don't go!

An hour and a half later, still on the kerbside, Titmus, veteran of tours, fashioner of wry observations, squeezed words from the side of his mouth; 'Captain, I always said you could do one tour too many.

The painful impression that we were in America on missionary work, to demonstrate the art of cricket to the Americans or to take on the expatriate British, had vanished. Americans do not wish to know about cricket.

Lying in wait for us, even as we sat on those cases, were immigrant West Indians, fit and ferocious; Indians and Pakistanis, wily men, brought up on the sort of matting pitches on which we would play; tenacious Sri Lankans; all these lusting for the old fun of their homelands where visiting MCC cricketers had stood for Empire and the white man was there to be knocked over.

MCC had never before done a complete tour of the States. Pioneers, we were set to take guard in New Jersey, Washington, Philadelphia, Chicago, Los Angeles and San Francisco.

The MCC team was a perfect mix of old and young, of blockers and sloggers, spinners and seamers, amateur and professional. There was the ageing Test quartet, Titmus, Mushtaq, Jameson and Lewis; the professionals, Nick Pocock, captain of Hampshire, Nick Cook of Leicestershire, Bill Merry of Middlesex, Nigel Ross formerly of the same, Simon Dennis of Yorkshire. Then the amateurs, Cambridge Blues all, Philip Hodson, Chris Goldie, the stumper, and Stephen Henderson. The player-manager was Freddie Millett, MCC committee-man and once a minor county player. Also in attendance was the United States Cricket Association's representative in England, Vic Lewis, erstwhile band leader and musical entrepreneur.

I am keen to make public the cast, because they were largely anonymous in a non-cricket-playing country. The nearest we got to recognition of our species was in our first hotel. Riding the lift one morning in full regalia, white flannels, sweaters and shirts and carrying pads and bats, an American gent offered: 'Don't tell me friends. I goddit, you're cricketeers.'

It was later, on a flight from Washington to Chicago, that a young air stewardess made a bold try at the definition of cricket.

233

'Tell me about this cricket. Now is this the game where you hit the ball with a piece of wood?'

'Yes, good.' I said.

'Through the iron hoops,' she enthused.

'Er . . . no, my love. That's croquet.'

'Then on horseback like Prince Charles.'

'No, dear. That's polo.'

'Gee! Isn't that Princess Di really something?'

'Yes, but not a close friend. Back to the cricket. Let me explain.' She tried hard to understand. She could see the analogy between the two sets of stumps and baseball bases. 'There are only two bases,' I heard myself saying. 'The pitcher runs in here, the striker waits there, and behind him the catcher.'

Ten minutes later she disrupted the whole flight. 'Hey. Wait, you fellas! You guys sending me up? You're saying that one game can last five days and that in the end no one wins? Come on! Crazy fellas! Is that what you're saying?' We continued the tuition but then she doubled up with uncontrollable laughter. 'Not true! Not true!' she kept shouting. 'Wait a minute . . . if the ball hit the striker on the leg and it was a good pitch he is put out?' She was out of control. I was a bit put out. I felt like Walter Raleigh calling London to say that he'd discovered tobacco. 'Don't tell me Wal, you roll it up . . . put it in your mouth and you what? Set fire to it Wal?'

So, unknown we were. First, a sunny day: breakfast of scrambled eggs, hash brown toast, jam and coffee. Overpeck Park, Leonia, New Jersey, venue of the first match, was a public park, a rough ridged ground, deep in grass cuttings, on which it was impossible to run quickly without breaking an ankle. 100 runs would be worth 200 here.

The mat was stretched and pegged. Our pavilion was the grass near two young trees. John Jameson took the first ball of the tour. The MCC flag was draped over a low branch. There was a disconcerting feature about playing at Overpeck Park. The pitch was dangerous. Mushtaq was hit on the head. From the boundary I saw blood. I ran on to assist. When I got there his eyes were closed, but he squawked.

'Captain. You never tell me that I come to States to finish off my career; hit on head by wild West Indian in non-cricket-playing country. What a death.'

A nervous MCC batsman was prompted by this accident to ask a jogger where the nearest public lavatory might be. 'The bethroom? Couple 'o miles down there, Sir.' The batsman set off.

Around the concrete surround, millions of joggers plodded – earnest ladies, bent, pendulous into the breeze; desperate men, eyes on eternal self-preservation. Another million or so whizzed around on bikes, half a million on skates. The whole of America was on the move. Whatever did they make of us, moving slowly in long whites to take gentle tea under the trees? Truth is, Americans do not understand the dimensions of a cricket field. Bill Merry fielding at point, suddenly heard a voice over the shoulder.

'Now what sort of game do you have here?'

'Cricket,' replied Bill.

'Cricket? Gee! Is that right.'

'Yes, and you are on the field of play.'

'Really? But aren't you the outmost base?'

Fred Titmus had a new cricketing experience. His first ball in America was no-balled by the umpire.

'But I never bowl no-balls,' Fred pointed out plaintively.

'You are no-balled according to the laws of cricket,' pronounced the umpire with a loud show of learning and authority. 'You failed to inform me that you were about to bowl right-arm over the wicket.'

The call was early: the ball was hit for six. Fred shrugged. 'Just where I came in ... Regents Park ... getting slogged all round a field like this 35 years ago.'

There was surprising support for MCC at this first match. Half-way through the afternoon, a shortish man, impeccably suited, walked across the park with his wife, Sir Anthony Tuke, the President of MCC himself. Fine performance! He sported the egg and tomato member's tie and made a note of our travelling and other disasters to date. Chaos would be ordered from now on.

Then, a little later, a great family friend, Rhodri Thomas with American wife Karen and two children, arrived. Rhod, once the London Welsh outside-half and Welsh trialist, Oxford Blue opening batsman, said that he had given up cricket in the face of American ignorance of the game. Indeed his father-in-law had taken possession of his cricket pads because they were perfect gardening gear – leg-wear for kneeling at the flower beds in the garden, protecting the trousers from nasty brambles, or padding up to the odd stone thrown back by the lawn mower.

Our first match was won. Nick Cook took 5 for 35, but early questions were being asked. Would our heroes survive 11 days more cricket against such skilled black opposition, without lavatories? Would transport ever arrive on time? Would the dollars last a week more in the expensive hotel bar? Could manager Millett ever be harnessed for action? Who would be hit on the head next?

I was a mere 45 years old on this trip but one day, as I went to toss with the opposing captain, an Indian, I began to feel seriously past it.

'I remember you playing for MCC at Ahmedabad,' said the Indian.

'Oh! Great! Were you playing in that match?'

'No, I was only 12,' he said.

But then I was rescued. Across that lovely parkland of Elizabeth, New Jersey, an Uncle Sam figure approached, serious, bearded, under a wide-brimmed Pilgrim Father's hat; maroon blazer, maroon and white striped trousers. Charles R. Olszewski is the only United States born cricketer in the New Jersey Cricket Association. He is the secretary, he loves the laws, he is forming an umpire's guild. He took up cricket six years ago when he was 35.

'Do you bat, Charles, or bowl?'

'I think I bowl, though my team are suggesting maybe

I try batting.'

He gave me my history lesson over a pizza lunch on the boundary. Cricket was probably the biggest team game in America. Lacrosse is the oldest. Only England of the major Test-playing countries has played cricket longer than America. The great days were in Boston, New York, New Jersey and the spiritual centre of the country's cricket, Philadelphia. Tales of lovely grounds. Merion, Long Branch, Haverford College, Staten Island and the Elysian Fields in Hobolton where George Parr's English team drew 24,000 fans in 1859. W.G. Grace toured the States in 1872. In 1896 the incredible scorecard read: Philadelphia 282, Australia 121 and 101.

Yet the history is ancient and virtually lifeless, all but unconnected to the present day. The expatriate British interest had died, except in the west. Furthermore, cricket has been resurrected at quite a different end of society by a new selection of coloured immigrants. I had no idea that I would be going to America for reggae music and raga?

Normally you can find an MCC member under every other stone in the world. Not in the States. Actually, apart from Sir Anthony Tuke I only caught sight of one other member and he was singing on television. Under the long hair and beard of Count Walter in the opera 'Louisa Miller' was Gwynne Howell of the delicious voice, my old friend from schooldays in Neath.

One morning in Maryland, Titmus, Jameson and I were breakfasting with out host Dr Keith Mitchell, formerly a political activist in Grenada, also their cricket captain, when he told us that the two bowlers we were about to ⸳ace in a couple of hours time were the fastest ever to le⸳ve the West Indian islands. Wonderful news for the digestion!

Our driver could not find the park for a long time, but eventually we located the Potomac Park West, just alongside the bridge into which an aircraft crashed a year before, spilling passengers to an icy death in the wide river below. Giant planes screamed over us,

237

beginning their ascent right over the middle of the mat. There was no point in calling for a single or sending anyone back. It was sign language only. All America was still jogging around us and, glory be, there was a 'bathroom' 200 yards down the road! There was a public telephone outside too. I inserted a dollar or two and phoned home, then Cloncurry Street in Fulham. Joan, my wife, was in fine form. There was a further bonus. The West Indian quickies had not been able to find their way to the ground either and arrived too late to play.

The main representative match, United States Association against MCC over two days at Philadelphia, was won mainly by Mushtaq Muhammad. He was my room-mate at the time. 'I will win it for you, captain,' he declared, before settling into his 100th cable TV movie. He did jeopardize his fitness by trying to stay awake all night for the double 'X' feature which began at 4.20 a.m. Silly really. Anyone of the younger members of the side could have given him an early morning call on their way in. On the field, Mushtaq lowered the trajectory of his leg-spinners, got them to loop, dip and bounce high off the mat, so from 39 for 1, the United States, albeit pursuing an easy target, were out for 77, Mushtaq 7 for 15.

British consulate hospitality was gratefully received along the way, although the Consul General got himself in a small knot in his whirlwind handshakes by introducing me to an Indian diplomat as 'MCC vaptain, Vic Lewis.'

'Hello Vic, are you on the way to Austraia?' came the diplomat's response.

The explanation would have taken too long so I nodded.

'Ah,' he went on. 'But where is Mushtaq Ali?'

'Will Mushtaq Muhammad do?'

'Yes, he'll do.'

I unleashed the manager Freddie Millet on the concrete pitch of Chicago's Washington Park. The crowd was hotted up by inter-island rivalries, rum and dominoes. 'Lash it, lash it, win or lose. Hit out, man.' That's what they gave the silver-haired, 54-year-old, former hero of Cheshire's minor county cricket. True Brit, the manager fought it out, but his fielding on a rough surface was understandably hesitant.

'Hit it to de fat man,' they shouted. 'Dere's runs to Benny Hill.'

The final matches were out west, first at the pretty Woodley Park in Los Angeles. An old man from Yorkshire regaled me with a story of Errol Flynn when he was playing in the glamorous Hollywood Cricket Club at Griffiths Park. 'That Errol Flynn could hit. He hit one right from the middle of pitch, over the trees, over the road, over the stables into the field.'

'Good player, Errol Flynn?' I asked.

'No,' said the man, who had left Barnsley 60 years ago but had lost none of the Yorkshireman's plain speech. 'But 'e could 'it.'

I went to the crease for what I intended to be the very last time in my life. It is no longer fun standing in the field on an arthritic, stiffening knee. Hills were behind me – the reclining Mont Tamalpais, known as the Sleeping Lady. The Corte Madeira creek, which runs down to San Quentin, lapped the deep-mid-wicket boundary.

The cricket supported my decision to retire. I play and miss. Up goes the appeal: up goes the umpire's finger. The home skipper offers me a return to the crease. 'No one thinks you hit it,' he sportingly said. But I had to go. Obey the umpire, that had always been my duty. I was a 'walker'. It was not my practice to stay knowing that I was out, because it meant that I would have been acting an untruth. That is as near to lying as you can get in my book. I had scored 13. Even that seemed inevitable. No pavilion: just back to the lads sitting on the grass alongside the MCC flag which was draped over a 3-foot Monterey pine. Titmus was not short of a word: 'Come in number four your time is up.'

A very sad umpire came to me lunchtime. 'I can never

go home again,' he said. 'I made a terrible decision.'

'Don't worry. Where are you from?' I asked.

'Swansea,' he said.

'That's my birthplace too.'

'I know, I know,' he bleated. 'That's why I can't go back.'

It must have been the sign. Alpha and omega: the beginning and the end. Thus did I officially retire from cricket, for the first time. I left my kit in San Francisco.

21

Shanghai in Bombay

I was going out to lunch in Bombay. Saturday 18 February 1984. For the extra interest of my travelling companion, Roger Michaelson, former Cambridge University rugby captain and Welsh international, I suggested we spend an hour at the cricket. India and Pakistan, past and present, were combining to play a Rest of the World side at the Wankhede Stadium in a benefit match for Farooq Engineer. Our wives were in the safe care of our hosts the Hamieds, Yuku and Farida. We would meet up at the Oberoi Hotel buffet, the scrumptious Outrigger.

Roger was astonished to see a crowd of 15,000 to 20,000 building up, just for a benefit game. Cricket in India is watched with passion by millions; they love their stars. India and Pakistan were fielding.

'I'll just pop into the World dressing room to say good morning, Roger.' I walked in to be met with a bear hug by the West Indian Wes Hall, manager of the World side. He got very exciteable. 'Jasus, Sobey, look what's come in, man. We got another player.' Gary Sobers smiled his widest smile.

'Tony, man. Great to see you. You're playing.'

I protested. 'Look lads. I only came to say good morning. I haven't played for ages. I am a stone overweight and, anyway, I'm meeting my wife and friends for lunch.'

It was then that big Wes towered over me and put a fatherly hand on my shoulder. 'You not only playin' man; you in, next but one.'

I looked around the dressing room. There was Joel Garner locked in incomprehensible gossip with Michael Holding. Across the way was Dennis Lillee looking sharp and slender. Great fast bowlers to the left and right. That clinched it. I was on. I had never been in a dressing room with such ammunition before.

Flannels with an elasticated waist band solved the sartorial problem. Dennis Lillee fitted me up with rubber soled shoes half a size too big but expanded my feet with two pairs of socks. The match sponsors provided shirts and so, give or take a jock strap, box and bat, I was ready. There were roars outside. We lost Gabriel, the West Indian, and then just as I was selecting a bat, Moshin Khan, our borrowed Pakistani, got out. Bats had changed since my first-class days. The handles were fat, overlayed with several rubber grips. There was not one under 3 lb. in weight, all like railway sleepers. I used to play with something nearer 2 lb. 3 ozs. Thankfully, Bruce Yardley came up with a lighter weapon, a Gray-Nichols as I always used, and out I set, into the dazzling sunshine for the amusement of 25,000 Indians.

What was I doing playing here, making a debut at the Wankhede Stadium at the age of 45? My salad days had been at the Brabourne Stadium up the road. As I walked to the middle, memories of past Indian Tests came back to me, of chanting crowds, crouching close fielders, of Chandra, Bedi and Prasanna. I decided that there was nothing more certain to ruin the humour of a benefit crowd than an ageing blocker. To turn myself into an ageing stroke-maker was the only acceptable plan.

After a couple of sighters I went down the pitch to Ravi Shastri and performed a passable and effective cover drive. I settled and hit the ball well. I scored 43 and put on over 80 with my partner, but his performance was the real weight of the whole experience both for me at the other end and for the whole crowd. Gary Sobers could walk only with difficulty because of arthritic knees. He scarcely ran at all. But, I can tell you, he had not forgotten how to bat. What struck me first was his

242

absolute concentration, as if it was second nature. He laughed and joked between balls but never once toyed with the great game itself. He had too much respect for it. In one stroke he produced a thunderclap of a reminder of how superb he was. He flicked a ball from Shastri, with the spin, off middle-and-leg through mid-wicket for four. His bat scarcely made a sound: it was all eye and timing. Was it really happening again? Sobers in full flow? That shot had a ghostly perfection to it. He scored 41 and was given a tumultuous standing ovation. I did not miss one drop of the old Sobers mix of ferocity and grace.

I retreated from my own contribution puffing and perspiring. When I got back through the door of the dressing room I was met with a drink and a gleaming smile, a handshake and a hug from Govind, my old bearer of 1973. 'Sahib looking stronger,' he beamed, 'very strong man now sahib.' He was patting my tummy.

Yes, strong but slow as it turned out. The fielding was hard. The out-field was short of grass and I was forced to reflect on the hopelessness of fielding at cover when Zaheer Abbas is in form. I was last seen turning and chasing from point deft cuts to the deep-third-man boundary, or frantically regathering balls which had richocheted violently off my knee. So what had changed?

Gulping down 7-Up in a Bombay dressing room – was this at last the final exit? Would cricket now leave me in peace? Was the ultimate mark on the scoreboard writ – A.R. Lewis b. Gavaskar 43?

INDEX